"We need government to be more innovative and inventive, and in *We the Possibility*, Mitchell Weiss shows that achieving it isn't a pipe dream. It's within our reach."

—**MICHAEL R. BLOOMBERG,** 108th Mayor of New York City; founder, Bloomberg LP and Bloomberg Philanthropies

"As an optimist and businessperson who started several companies before I served in government, I felt that *We the Possibility* struck a chord with me. At the Department of Commerce we hung a sign in our office that read, "Trust your crazy ideas." That sign continually encouraged us to unleash innovative thinking, experimentation, and an entrepreneurial spirit for the benefit of America's businesses and workers. Mitchell Weiss captures this mantra well by offering a myriad of examples that show how to make our government operate better at a time when we most need it to solve tectonically significant challenges and create more-inclusive opportunity for all Americans. This compelling book is well worth a read."

—**PENNY PRITZKER,** entrepreneur; former US Secretary of Commerce

"In a sector crying out for innovation but where politics punishes failure, Mitch Weiss shows us how and why thoughtful risk-taking in public policy and government is the path to a hopeful future."

—**DEVAL PATRICK**, former Governor of Massachusetts

"America's social contract is in tatters, and the moment to rewrite it is now. To do so requires new voices with new ideas that will re-animate our democracy. Mitchell Weiss is one such voice, and *We the Possibility* provides exactly the kind of framework we need to make our new ideas a reality and help deliver a better democracy."

—**ALEC ROSS**, author, *New York Times* bestseller, *The Industries of the Future*; former Senior Adviser for Innovation to the US Secretary of State

"*We the Possibility* is an important book for public-sector leaders looking to build bridges between government and top innovators in science and technology. To bend the arc of progress toward public good, we must confront the dilemmas of emerging technology by shifting our mindset to public-sector entrepreneurship."

—**ASH CARTER**, Director, Belfer Center for Science and International Affairs, Harvard Kennedy School; former US Secretary of Defense

"Mitch Weiss is one of the world's best thinkers about government innovation—and I've been waiting years for him to write a book. I'm pleased to say it's been worth the wait. *We the Possibility* is chockfull of great ideas for transforming the public sector. Essential reading for anyone who wishes government was more capable and creative—this book shows how that dream can become a reality."

—**ROHAN SILVA**, former Senior Policy Adviser to British Prime Minister David Cameron

"This extraordinary book vanquishes the idea that government innovation is an oxymoron. The status quo, Weiss reminds us, can present the biggest risk of all. Through deft combinations of public-sector adventure stories and thoughtful analysis, Weiss leads readers out of the dead ends of binary thinking (government = bad; tech sector = good—or vice versa) and into a world in which government is as flexible, imaginative, and hopeful as the people it serves."

—**JENNIFER BRADLEY**, founding Director, Center for Urban Innovation, Aspen Institute

"Innovation is hard. Innovation in government is a lot harder. Mitch Weiss, one of the leading experts on civic innovation, has written an inspiring and practical guide to the art of the possible, of actually getting new things done in government."

—**DAN DOCTOROFF**, founder and CEO, Sidewalk Labs

"As the mayor of one of America's largest cities, I know that governments are too often tied to staid approaches to keep pace with a rapidly changing country. That was true even before we began trying to address a global pandemic, civil unrest, demands to address long-standing racial inequities, the threat of climate change, the impact of automation and globalization on our workforce, mass unemployment, and a lack of access to affordable housing and health care. Fortunately, this book provides a road map for local leaders who want to create a culture of public entrepreneurship that encourages the kind of fresh thinking that can lead us to the innovative solutions our times require."

—**ERIC JOHNSON**, Mayor of Dallas, TX

"Now more than ever, policy makers must ask what's possible rather than settling for what's probable. Mayors often feel as though we're supposed to stick with what we know. But to meet the demands of the largest problems of our day—Covid-19, climate change, racial justice—we must innovate and accept the risk that it might not all work. We need to build, measure, and learn. *We the Possibility* provides a guide and, importantly, the inspiration and insight we need to step into the unknown in pursuit of the best solutions to meet our communities' needs today and well into the future."

—**LAUREN MCLEAN**, Mayor of Boise, ID

"*We the Possibility* is full of stories I loved reading. They demonstrate how we can be more open to taking calculated risks. The distinction the book draws between probability and possibility government is illuminating, and something I would like to remind myself as I govern."

—**NAN WHALEY**, Mayor of Dayton, OH

"At a time when our problems seem to be getting bigger and bigger and our minds and hearts seem to be getting smaller and smaller, governments need to be able to try more, fail more, and succeed more. Mitch Weiss offers us a way forward through Possibility Government, presenting practical and thoughtful solutions for how we can generate new ideas, test them, and replicate good ones."

—**NAHEED NENSHI**, Mayor of Calgary, Alberta

"We see increasing public frustration with government's inability to find answers to the basic problems at the forefront of our everyday lives. As a mayor in today's evolving and escalating web of challenges, it's becoming increasingly difficult for government to deliver answers that will actually improve people's lives. Amid this paralysis, Professor Weiss brings critical lessons for leaders of governments in a time of unprecedented need. *We the Possibility* defines what's lacking in government problem solving and maps out a path forward for governments to actually innovate and meet the challenges of today."

—**TIM KELLER**, Mayor of Albuquerque, NM

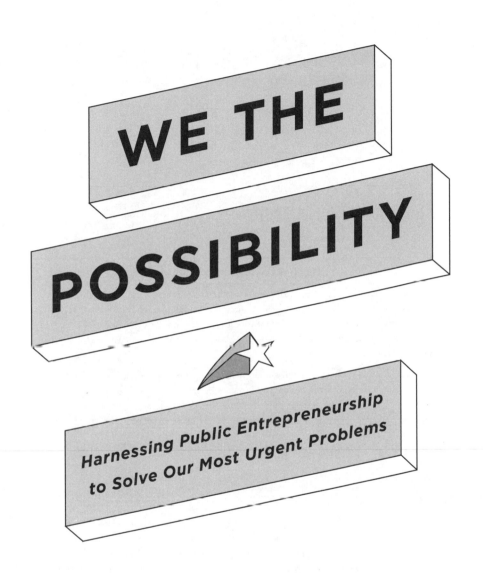

WE THE POSSIBILITY

Harnessing Public Entrepreneurship
to Solve Our Most Urgent Problems

MITCHELL WEISS

Harvard Business Review Press

Boston, Massachusetts

HBR Press Quantity Sales Discounts

Harvard Business Review Press titles are available at significant quantity discounts when purchased in bulk for client gifts, sales promotions, and premiums. Special editions, including books with corporate logos, customized covers, and letters from the company or CEO printed in the front matter, as well as excerpts of existing books, can also be created in large quantities for special needs.

For details and discount information for both print and ebook formats, contact booksales@harvardbusiness.org, tel. 800-988-0886, or www.hbr.org/bulksales.

The web addresses referenced in this book were live and correct at the time of the book's publication but may be subject to change.

Library of Congress Cataloguing-in-Publication is forthcoming

ISBN: 978-1-63369-919-9
eISBN: 978-1-63369-920-5

The paper used in this publication meets the requirements of the American National Standard for Permanence of Paper for Publications and Documents in Libraries and Archives Z39.48-1992.

For Mom and Dad

CONTENTS

Contents

PART FOUR

WE GET THE GOVERNMENT WE INVENT

Can We Solve Public Problems Anymore?

Their tears told me something my emergency notifications hadn't yet. People were streaming from the direction of Boylston Street as I stepped outside my apartment. I lived close to five hundred yards from the blasts, but hadn't heard them.

Stopped by police officers at first, I snaked my way toward—and then into—the medical tent. Everything seemed, strangely, organized. Except that I do remember a handwritten sign off to the left: "Morgue." In a few minutes I would myself be on Boylston Street, talking to the mayor on the phone. "You are my eyes and ears," he would say, but I already knew that when I looked in.

The makeshift morgue was empty, but three people had lost their lives along the race route. More than two hundred—we'd later learn—had been wounded by shrapnel from the pressure-cooker bombs that two terrorists had detonated at the finish line on Boston's best day of the year. Immediately following the blasts, the rush was on to save their lives, to track down the perpetrators, and to put a wrecked city back together.

I would have nothing to do with the first two tasks, but would play some role in the third, and doing so left me with the questions I've spent all the years since investigating: Can we solve public problems anymore? Can we do new things?

The new thing we intended to do in 2013 was stand up a new fund to channel money from generous people everywhere to the families of the victims and to the survivors. Traditional methods of dispersing donations in the wake of attacks like this were plodding. Eight months had passed since twenty children and six adults were killed at Sandy Hook Elementary School, and I'd heard that not a penny had made it to the families of those who died there nor those injured. Now, Boston's survivors would have life-changing decisions to make about limbs, homes, and jobs, and they couldn't wait for relief. If we started up a new organization, instead of going with a trusted and long-established institution in town, we had a fighting chance of getting relief to them quickly enough.

The head of Boston's century-old community foundation did not see things the same way. The morning after the bombs went off, as I stood inside Brigham and Women's Hospital, where the mayor would later visit survivors being treated there, the foundation chief was berating me over the phone. "You'll raise less money," he insisted. "You can't start something new."

We rejected those objections, started One Fund Boston with a PayPal account that night and a post office box the next morning, and raced to collect and distribute as much money as possible before July 4, Independence Day. A year after the marathon attacks, two survivors asked me to tell them how One Fund Boston had come to be, and then urged me to tell that story to others: "You have to show people that government can do new things."

Which is it, really, most of the time? Is it what the foundation head or the survivors had said? Can governments start new things? Need public officials be so afraid to try new solutions, or can we do something—all of us, the public and the people we put in office—to change that?

Turning toward Something Else

Five years after the marathon attacks—even though the question "Can we solve public problems anymore?" was on my mind for most of that time—I finally set out to write this book. I saw so many reasons why we needed new ideas about government doing new things. There was a long list of vexing problems: hunger, poverty, climate change, extreme inequality, crumbling infrastructure. There was the breakdown in faith between people and national governments that this pileup of problems had created; in 2015, less than half of the people in Organization for Economic Cooperation and Development (OECD) member countries were found to have trust in theirs.[1] There were threats from competitors or adversaries who might race ahead, and some threats were existential. Russia's Vladimir Putin, for instance, has said that whichever nation leads in artificial intelligence "will become the ruler of the world."[2] A talent crisis loomed in the public sector, as the retirement of baby boomers from such jobs was called a "silver tsunami."[3] Many younger adults (64 percent of American millennials and 70 percent of Generation Z) said they wanted government to do more to solve public problems.[4] But how? Several entrepreneurs were about to leap into the US presidential campaign.

The number of startups entering into public entrepreneurship was growing almost every day. The Facebook hearings in the spring of 2018, which I had come to see as a sort of Rorschach test, exposed a tech–government divide that needed to be bridged. Techies who had watched Senator Orrin Hatch question Mark Zuckerberg on how it was that Facebook made money if it didn't charge customers ("Senator, we run ads.") grumbled at government's ignorance of technology, but policy types who had watched Zuckerberg wondered how he could have set out to create a new civic square while knowing so little about government.

All these reasons—the pileup of problems, the public's lack of trust that its leaders can and will address them, the stepping in (and sometimes stepping in it) of the entrepreneurs and the techie types—would justify setting out to describe a new way forward, but they weren't my reasons. Nor did I decide to write the book when one mayor I was with said, "I feel like the weight of the world is now on our shoulders," even though that feeling was common to many of us. Ultimately, what motivated me to write the book was the sense that all over the world people were turning on each other, and that we should try to get them to turn together toward something else instead.[5]

Possibility Government

Can we solve public problems anymore? Yes. If.

We'll need to move on from what I've come to call Probability Government. That's the kind of government that does mostly what's pretty sure to work, but leads often to middling, mediocre outcomes. We'll need to move toward Possibility Government instead. That's the kind of government that pursues efforts that only *might* work, which means . . . they probably won't work. Possibility is the realm of the entrepreneur. More than 70 percent of new ventures fail, but a few that succeed transform our lives and our society, ideally for the good.[6]

Possibility Government is new and not new. Ever since we've had government, we've had people inventing it. Upon hearing of this book's subject, a friend of mine teased, "Wasn't it Socrates or Aristotle who did that?" Every type of government was invented at some point before or after the ancient Greeks. And every apparatus of government—money and central banks, post offices, patent offices—was too. Every policy has at one point been imagined and tried (likely at more than one point): policies to enhance workplace safety and to improve the quality of the water and the air; policies aimed at training people for new jobs or at taking them into space. Taxation of every sort has been tried and retried: regressive and progressive taxes; federal, state, and local taxes; stamp taxes and "sin" taxes. And so have all of those things taxes pay for: highways and their maintenance, public education, the social safety net, and every branch of the military and all of the equipment anyone serving in those branches has ever used.

Possibility has been a part of government as long as there's been government, but so has the pushback to it. This tug-of-war between the two has been enshrined in forms of government. The creation of a two-chamber US Congress was an exercise in balancing power among larger states and smaller ones, but it was also an exercise in balancing the future and the past, of what's been and what might be. The US Constitution made sure that the government of the young country would tend in both directions. Even the word *constitution* expresses this duality. It derives from the Latin *constitutio* meaning "act of settling, settled condition, order" and also *constituere* "to set up, establish, form something new."[7]

Over time, the new has been too snuffed out in favor of the settled. This has been a matter of political philosophy and politics; of dominant strains in public management practice and education. And it's been a matter of existence. The famed management guru Peter Drucker once wrote, "In the existing business, it is the existing that is the main obstacle to entrepreneurship. In the new venture, it is its absence."[8] The founders of our nations, our towns, our agencies, had to create something from nothing, which is difficult. We have to create something else from something, which is proving to be difficult too.

Elinor Ostrom was not the first person to suggest that the new giving way to the settled in government might only be temporary—and that with novel forms of action and leadership we might provide new public goods and services again—but she was the first, I believe, to coin the phrase *public entrepreneurship*. In her 1965 PhD dissertation about groundwater basin management in California, she wrote, "The existence of entrepreneurship in the private sector raises the question of whether there is a comparable function performed by those who undertake to provide public goods and services in the public sector, which might appropriately be characterized as public entrepreneurship."[9] Nearly forty-five years later Ostrom would win the Nobel Prize in economics, but not primarily for her work on public entrepreneurship. She mentions it just once in her prize lecture, and it never became a household phrase.[10]

It might have. In 1993, David Osborne and Ted Gaebler—a journalist and a former city manager, respectively—laid out a strong case for public entrepreneurship. In *Reinventing Government: How the Entrepreneurial Spirit Is Transforming the Public Sector*, they wrote, "Our governments are in deep trouble today . . . This book is for those who are disturbed by that reality . . . It is for the seekers. If ever there was a time for seekers, this is it."[11] The revolution they had hoped to prime never came to pass in full.

We the Possibility

Politics has long had a language of possibility, though the rhetoric has often exceeded the reality. When a former US president said, "While I take inspiration from the past, like most Americans, I live for the future . . . I hope you will let me talk about a country that is forever young," he was uttering sentiments that could have come from almost any president in the country's history.[12] It was Ronald Reagan, in 1992, but it could have been Barack Obama, in 2014: "We choose hope over fear. We see the future not as something out of our control, but as something we can shape for the better through concerted and collective effort."[13] It could have been Robert Kennedy or Franklin Roosevelt. It could have been Angela Merkel: "The question is not whether we are able to change but whether we are changing fast enough."[14] Or Jacinda Ardern: "This stardust won't settle, because none of us should settle."[15] It could have been the Mexico City mayor we'll meet in chapter 3, or any of hundreds of other mayors delivering a state-of-the-city address, or local committee chairs championing a new transportation plan, or school principals launching school turnarounds. Summoning the future is a time-honored endeavor. Occasioning it is tougher stuff. We talk about ushering in the future, but in practice we don't really know how.

Many people would deem public entrepreneurship, aka Possibility Government, crazy. One of my favorite books on entrepreneurship starts:

If you tell people that you want to become an entrepreneur, they'll tell you you are crazy. And the trouble is they might be right. They might be right! How would you know? How could you possibly tell the difference? Maybe you have spotted a huge business opportunity and have come up with a world-changing solution to it. Or maybe you are just another deluded dreamer who is about to make the biggest mistake of your life. How would you know? After all, if you are the deluded dreamer, you are the last person in the world you ought to listen to. Who and what should you believe, and why? It's all going to come down to how carefully and precisely you think about this.[16]

If we are not deluded dreamers, if *public entrepreneurship* is not the oxymoron everyone makes it out to be, we'll have to carefully and precisely think about and engage in its pursuit.

In particular, we'll need to achieve three things.

We'll need new ideas. So chapters 1 and 2 ("Problems as Opportunities" and "Reach Out to Reach Up") look at the challenge of building government that can imagine. We are swimming in policy proposals but are still short of fresh thinking, and the reason is that our creativity is too limited by the resources at hand (our funding, our people, our assets). These chapters cover how to be opportunity-driven rather than resource-driven and how to look outside of our organizations—to the "crowd" and especially to the people we serve—for new solutions. We'll meet a man in charge of equipping the US Special Forces and follow his effort to make sure the Navy SEALs, Army Rangers, and other special operators get access to the newest ideas, and that the newest ideas—including a hoverboard and the Frenchman flying on it—get access to them. We'll acquaint ourselves with a Cincinnati resident who returns to her hometown to help solve its opioid epidemic with a weekend-long hackathon, so that we can uncover how best to reach out to outsiders who might produce new ideas we can actually make use of. We'll meet a former Facebook product manager while he is waiting in line for food stamps. He left to start his own company that would help serve low-income Americans, and his experience can help us learn what lengths we need to go to with our users to see how they experience government, and to harness their insights for our new solutions.

If we can successfully come up with new ideas, we'll need ways to try them. We'll need to build governments that can take on riskier projects. Chapters 3 and 4 ("Experimenting in Public" and "Regulating the Future") look at techniques for building government that can try new things. The head of Mexico City's innovation office says, "A thousand things could have gone wrong," when she and her team set out to crowdsource a map of the city's thirty thousand buses, minibuses, and vans, and we'll watch her proceed anyway in a series of short experiments so that we can pick up the build-measure-learn techniques of lean startups and see how they can be applied in public and when they should be. The mayor of Pittsburgh reasons that he has to be both a pragmatist and a politician, and we'll observe him try to balance the two roles as he welcomes autonomous cars to his city's streets. We'll follow him through the aftermath of a fatality involving a self-driving car on the other side of the country so we can see how to persevere with build-measure-learn techniques even when the thing you are building might be dangerous. We'll meet the head of global partnerships for Airbnb and her innovation counterparts in Amsterdam's city government as new home-sharing options emerge in a famously permissive city to considerable pushback. We'll examine the partnership they craft for trying out this sort of thing so that we might use some of those tools for trying out whatever is coming next.

If we can imagine new ideas and if we can try them, we'll need to be able to scale the successful ones. It's essential to the logic of the entire possibility enterprise—that is, that a handful of huge successes will more than cover for the many failures. Chapters 5 and 6 ("Government as a Platform" and "Trisector Entrepreneurs") cover government that can scale. We find leaders at Waze in the middle of their effort to take a data-sharing partnership to every city in the world so that we can see how "platform thinking" is the tool kit behind that kind of ambition.[17] It allows us to imagine what we could achieve with government as a platform if we thought in a similar way. We'll see how the man once described as India's Bill Gates uses that kind of thinking to provide identity and enable opportunity at what he calls population scale, in a country where population scale means more than a billion people. We'll also see how Amazon is building platforms-as-government and where, in the interest of equity, privacy, and democracy, we should draw the limits. We'll see that entrepreneurial leaders who navigate winding careers in the public, private, and not-for-profit sectors will be essential for sustaining possibility over time. We'll meet some who've done that, so that you might pick up tips for crafting such a career, and also so that we might consider whether we should welcome a rush of private entrepreneurs into public office and by what criteria we might judge them.

While the first six chapters focus mostly on what Possibility Government is, chapter 7 ("Inventing Democracy") focuses on what it could be for. Of all the things to turn our "new"-found entrepreneurial skills and tactics to, protecting and enhancing democracy in the United States and around the world is urgently important. So we'll sit on pins and needles as Uber's former lobbyist, a cybersecurity specialist turned entrepreneur, and West Virginia's secretary of state pilot mobile voting, and we'll meet several other democracy entrepreneurs to evaluate how far we can go in deploying possibility's techniques and tools. About the mobile-voting experiment, one person tweeted afterward, "Bonkers, America." But which is more bonkers in light of a fraying democracy: to do something or to do nothing? What's more bonkers in light of fraying *everything*?

As the book comes to a close we consider the critiques of Possibility Government. Maybe this is all deluded dreaming? And we check in on one more episode of it—on Jason Bay and his team at GovTech Singapore and their eight-week pursuit amidst a global pandemic to deploy the first nationwide Bluetooth-enabled Covid-19-tracing app— so that we might test ourselves on whether we'd know the difference.

Possibility in Our Time

If ever there were a time for seekers, *this* is it.

I first purchased Osborne and Gaebler's book while I was in college, in the late 1990s, and the idea that you could combine entrepreneurial skills and government hit me like a lightning bolt. I had wanted to be in public service all my life. As a nine year old, I had sketched out campaign signs that read, "I will lead your nation like my mom leads me." I'd dressed up as a voting booth for Halloween. But I'd also always wanted to build stuff and start things. I'd dabbled in computer science in college, but majored in economics. When the two authors wrote that they hoped their road map would "empower *you* to reinvent *your* governments," I really believed they meant *me*.

And while I was alight with their suggestions, so were many others. The book's ideas had inspired President Clinton to announce a six-month review of the US federal government, to be led by Vice President Al Gore. Clinton and Gore, two sunny leaders, were photographed grinning ear to ear and cutting actual red tape on the sunny White House lawn. "The reinventing government movement now holds the attention of the nation," wrote one scholar in 1998.[18]

Clinton had also said in launching the effort that it was past time for the government to adjust to an economy that was increasingly "information based." By 1996, there would be ten million computers connected to the internet, when half a decade earlier that number had been less than half a million.[19] In 1993, Mosaic, the first graphical web browser, had been released, followed by Netscape Navigator the next year. Yahoo was founded to help people find things on the internet, and then Google arrived to make search even easier. Clinton and Gore launched the first official White House website in 1994. The nascent European Union was encouraging "e-government" at the supranational level, as were its member countries and so many other administrative entities.[20] If governments were going to become more entrepreneurial, that entrepreneurship, by dint of opportunity and timing, was going to be tied in with the speedy march of digital technology.

I took my first full-time job in government in 2004. For a year and a half, I sat just outside Boston Mayor Thomas Menino's office, serving as an adviser. My first assignment had me transporting leftover computers from the Democratic National Convention in the back of a truck we had borrowed from animal control. That was the convention, in Boston, at which an Illinois state senator named Barack Obama referenced his parents' "abiding faith in the possibilities of this nation."[21] The PCs eventually made their way to new computing centers in senior housing. Trailing the mayor out of one such center after a ribbon-cutting ceremony, I saw residents already using the computers to look for "adult" material. These were the same computers the mayor had just announced would enable grandparents to email their grandkids! It was not the last time I would see the unanticipated outcomes of government + new + technology.

I would soon be awakened to both the public's and the press's role in making us leery when it came to innovation, too. The first new idea that was really my own in government was an embarrassingly simple one: we should let people sign up for email notifications about snow emergencies in Boston to alert them to move their cars. When Mayor Menino announced it, *Boston Globe* columnist Brian McGrory called it perhaps "the most ridiculous idea to come out of a local agency in years."[22] It was lampooned in a political cartoon, which the mayor then framed and gave to me with a note of encouragement. So I was also alerted to the role that cover from the top could play in making innovation happen.

I helped on more successful and more effective efforts as well, which is presumably why the mayor asked me to come back to city hall after a four-year hiatus to be his chief of staff. I'd left to be a social entrepreneur at a not-for-profit conceived by a business school professor of mine. I'd geeked out there a bit on the idea of open innovation after getting to know Yochai Benkler and reading his account of NASA's Clickworkers experiment, which sought to determine "if public volunteers, each working for a few minutes here and there can do some routine science analysis that would normally be done by a scientist or graduate student working for months on end."[23] When the mayor asked if I'd rejoin his administration for his fifth term, I said yes in part because I had a crazy thought that if we could try open innovation in Boston, we could change the city; and if we could change the city, maybe we could change the world. With two amazing public servants, Chris Osgood and Nigel Jacob, we founded the Mayor's Office of New Urban Mechanics, which became one of the first big-city innovation offices in the country, one infused with the idea that the key to public entrepreneurship was citizen participation.

We had at our fingertips, as did public leaders all over the world, incredible new tools. Wikipedia had arrived in 2001, and if you could crowdsource an encyclopedia, it seemed at the moment like you could crowdsource almost anything. LinkedIn, Facebook, YouTube, and Twitter all arrived in quick succession, and so in 2006 it seemed to make perfect sense that *Time* magazine named "You" its person of the year, honoring all the individual content creators. The forefront of digital government those days was open government. Data.gov, the US government data website, was launched in May 2009, on the heels of President Obama's memorandum on transparency and open government. The memorandum had been issued on Obama's inauguration day, with recommendations for making the federal government more transparent, more participatory, and more collaborative.[24]

Both the iPhone and Android's releases in 2007 meant that participation had also gone mobile. Mayor Mike Bloomberg's administration launched New York's first NYC BigApps competition to ask the public to marry up the raw city data that was now available in city-specific applications and make it available for smartphones and the web.[25] Startups encouraged residents to use their phones to make their concerns known to their leaders. FixMyStreet was launched in the United Kingdom to allow residents to tell their local leaders about potholes, broken streetlights, and such. A community member in New Haven, Connecticut, frustrated with his government's lack of responsiveness, started a company called SeeClickFix in 2008 to allow residents to do the same. In 2015, a report of graffiti on the side of a public building became the *two millionth* issue that the company had collected and directed to a city agency.[26] I'd cold-emailed Apple's CEO Steve Jobs on a Thursday in November 2010 to tell him Boston's mayor was launching the second version of our own citizen-reporting app four days later, and that we were having trouble getting it approved for the company's App Store. By Monday, lo and behold, we were ready to go. Jen Pahlka wondered at TED whether government could "be run like the Internet, permissionless and open" and started Code for America to recruit a generation of talent into government that could make it so.[27]

In 2014, I returned to Harvard Business School to join the faculty. The school's dean had chatted with me after an event. He and I knew each other somewhat, and he asked if I was going to run to succeed my boss. Mayor Menino had announced in March 2013 that he would not run for a sixth term in office. I laughed at the prospect, and the dean asked what I was planning to do. Eventually, I sat in his office and told him this: "I've seen so much opportunity from entrepreneurship in government. But I've also seen how difficult it is. And I think one reason it is difficult is that we are training people wrong. At policy schools, we tell people who want to go work in government to be analysts and strategists, and not inventors and builders. And while government needs analysts and strategists, it needs inventors and builders, too. And at business schools, like Harvard's, we have people who want to be inventors and builders, but we don't teach them that they can invent and build in government or for government." He replied, "Come do that here." So I came back to the school and created a course on public entrepreneurship in 2015, I think the first of its kind at any business school in the country.

The course is built around the same question as this book, "Can we solve public problems anymore?" The question has taken me around the world to look for answers. I begged my way into a data center in Tbilisi, Georgia, where they were "mining" for bitcoins but also helping the government there try to protect property rights using the blockchain. I've listened in on gunfire detected on America's city streets by sensors that sorted the sound from fireworks using algorithms in the cloud. I interviewed the former health minister of Rwanda, Dr. Agnes Binagwaho, who told me "of course I'm a public entrepreneur," and who insisted there was nothing very adventurous about Rwanda's effort to use drones to deliver blood and antivenom. But I've also heard from dozens of people who told me that none of this—the course, the book, the very idea of Possibility Government—

would ever work. I went to Amsterdam, where an official told me, "Please don't take offense, but we don't trust US tech companies very much." I was in Beijing to understand the rise of one of China's bike-share behemoths. While there, I got to see SenseTime, the world's largest AI startup and one of the world's most controversial, for its surveillance capabilities. And no doubt while I was there, SenseTime got to see me.

Although I had landed back to teach where I had gone to school nearly three decades before, the world had changed utterly. There were now four times more connected devices on the planet than there were people, and some of them were artificially intelligent.[28] Booming startup cultures had spread way beyond Silicon Valley, although not equally across countries or within them, and those divides had helped fuel frustrations that were boiling over. The cloud had given millions the chance to start things on the cheap, and millions had. Floods of venture capital had given those millions billions, but now society was awakening to a fear that hypergrowth had concentrated power and risk. A wave of tech had swept over us, but then, after it exposed our privacy and made vulnerable our democracy and threatened our jobs, a distrust of big tech, the so-called techlash, ensued. Tech for Good was one response to the backlash, promising to turn technological advances toward things like cleaner water and more affordable housing and longer lives. But that too seemed vulnerable to a bubbling #techforgoodlash. Millennials (and not just millennials) weren't sure they wanted their companies getting in bed with their governments on some issues—or getting involved with them at all. When I was in college, 2020 seemed like a distant, science-fiction future. But now that we had arrived, I had to wonder: Was there any prudent way for government to collaborate with technologists and entrepreneurs that didn't make one or the other a villain? Could we, together, solve public problems anymore?

If I were going into government now, if I were working in a town hall or a federal building, on an army base or in a classroom, I'd want a book like this on my desk: one that told me what I knew deep down but that might have been worn out of me—that government *can* still help solve public problems. And I'd want a book that showed me how: how to try the things that I'd thought of and how to persevere with new stuff even in the face of risk. I'd also want to know how to think about the endless new technologies being offered to or sometimes foisted on government, and how to respond. If I thought about running for office, I'd want a book that made me braver, that gave me the tools to try what I had actually run for office meaning to do. I'd think about all that had changed over the last thirty years, and I'd want a book that helped me think about how to handle what was coming next.

Several years ago, I was invited to speak on public entrepreneurship at 10 Downing Street in London. I finished my talk by noting that of all the new government services we could invent with startup methods, perhaps the most important thing we could do was show a new generation who had grown up on those techniques that they could go into government and make a difference with them. If I were young again, I'd definitely want a book that showed me that.

And since I'm none of those things, not young and not running for office and not working for those who are, I'd want a book that told me how to regard those who were. I'd want to know how to vote in an age of uncertainty. I'd want to know how much experimentation I should tolerate by our public leaders and how much I should encourage. I'd want skills for sniffing out leaders who would truly solve problems, as opposed to those who would merely talk of doing so. I'd want to learn how I could participate in an entrepreneurial movement and how I could make sure others could, too. This is the book I've tried to write.

Mater Artium Necessitas?

"Necessity is the mother of invention," we've been told.[29] If this is true, it never appeared more so than when Covid-19 ravaged the world in 2020. Leaders everywhere, but especially in the public sector, were made instant entrepreneurs. They invented new policies to keep people safe and new programs to supply and support them. And if this is false—if necessity is instead and too often the mother of obfuscation and evasion—it was never more so than in the days (and years) leading up to this pandemic, and even during it. Leaders in some places did nothing when they could have tried something.

"Never let a good crisis go to waste," we have heard. But we often fail to reckon that crises are here with us all the time, and we neglect to anticipate the wreckage that will be wrought while we wait. Waiting to change was once again revealed as an empty strategy in the summer of 2020, since waiting in the United States had meant yet more Black women and men had had to die at the hands of their governments. Mayor Melvin Carter, who we meet in chapter 2, and whose St. Paul, Minnesota, office was a twenty-minute drive from where a Minneapolis police officer spent more than eight fatal minutes with his knee on George Floyd's neck, told me: "Patience is for the privileged."[30] Five decades earlier, Martin Luther King Jr. had called time one of "two or three myths that still pervade our nation." He'd said of persistent racial injustice, "They've said . . . if you'll just be nice and patient and continue to pray, in a hundred or two hundred years the problem will work itself out. There is an answer to that myth. It is that time is neutral. It can be used either constructively or destructively . . . and so we must always help time and realize that the time is always right to do right."[31] Necessity is the mother of invention, or is it not? We *can* still solve public problems, or can we not?

A prior crisis had set me on a search for answers. As I finished that search, two present crises demanded answers. The one I'd already drafted into these pages—Possibility Government—is an incomplete remedy to them all, but it is the best I have: We can help time.

We get the government we invent. We can solve public problems . . . if. We can solve public problems if we move toward possibility. The entrepreneurial spirit can still transform the public sector, even though entrepreneurship is under scrutiny, as it should be; even though much is broken in our civics and beyond. We are not yet too far gone. Possibility Government hasn't quite been pulled off, but now it's our turn to try.

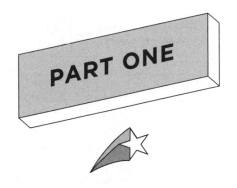

GOVERNMENT
THAT CAN
IMAGINE

1

Problems as Opportunities

The ratio was telling.[1] Just one safety check to two camera checks. It was spring 2016, and Franky Zapata was about to try a four-minute trip on the flying hoverboard he had built. It would dart thousands of feet above the ground at fifty-five kilometers per hour. Four engines, each with 250 horsepower, would give him flight, and Zapata wanted to be sure the cameras were ready. His team at Zapata Racing would later post the video to YouTube. They'd better get some good footage.

Beyond that, Zapata, a former champion Jet Ski racer turned entrepreneur, had not much of a plan. "You know when you decide to have a child, you decide to have a child because you want it. You don't decide to have a child because it will become a surgeon or a lawyer," he later explained by way of analogy to a reporter.[2]

It's possible Zapata's "child" was about to follow a decidedly differ-ent career path. A commander within one of the classified programs at the US Special Operations Command saw the clip on YouTube not long after. He forwarded it to James Geurts and Tambrein Bates along with the text, "Why aren't we doing this?"

Geurts was in charge of equipping, training, and supplying the nation's most elite warfighters: the Navy SEALs, the Army Special Forces, the Air Force Air Commandos. Bates was a former special operator himself. He had been deployed all over the globe: Soma-lia, South America, the Balkans, Afghanistan, and Iraq.[3] He ran an outpost of the Special Operations Command, called SOFWERX, that Geurts had set up (in a former tattoo parlor) to be best in class "in the future." And the two now found themselves intrigued by a 121-second video of a French thrill seeker on his flying board.

Geurts wasn't sure the flyboard was real. Bates found the music kind of "campy," but he cold-called Zapata Racing anyway. "I told them who we were and said I would love him to come talk to us . . . If it's real, let's see what you can do with it."

And with that, Zapata flew to Florida to meet with Geurts, Bates, other SOFWERX affiliates, and special operators—though without his flyboard, because it couldn't get through French export restric-tions. Reporters had wondered whether the flyboard was "the cool-est thing ever invented" or "a massive hoax."[4] Geurts and crew were about to find out.

After Geurts tipped me off to the video and I learned of his sincere interest in it, I wanted to uncover something else: Why?

Why were Geurts and Bates and the commander who had sent them the link trolling for ideas on YouTube? The US Department of Defense spends more than $600 billion a year.[5] It employs more peo-ple than any other organization in the United States. Among them are the country's bravest and most ingenious. The Defense Advanced

Research Projects Agency (DARPA), the DoD's research arm, is one of the most renowned in the world. Scientists there helped invent the internet, developed GPS, and built the ancestor to cloud computing.[6] On top of that, American defense firms spend billions on research and development every single year to invent new solutions to the nation's security challenges. So why was Geurts mining ideas for the most elite warfighters, who get sent on the most dangerous missions, in the same place you and I watch prank videos and clips of Colbert?

In chapter 2, we'll address more directly the virtues of looking for ideas among so-called nonexperts. But I wanted to be sure as I took my own trip to Tampa that we really had to go looking for them at all. When I think of most of the public problems we face—from poor nutrition to low literacy rates to crumbling roads—the argument that "we know what to do, we just have to get people to agree to do it" sounds pretty darn compelling. Too little commitment. Too much politicking. Too much partisanship. Too much red tape. Those are the reasons, we're told, why we don't solve big problems anymore. It can't really be from a lack of creativity, can it?

SOFWERX

With a few exceptions, the SOFWERX offices looked like every other startuppy "this is where new ideas are made" space I'd ever been in. It had the requisite open floor plan. Plenty of bricks, exposed beams, and cement. The cool swag. The digital monitors. Groups of young people, and some not-so-young ones, tinkered away. When I walked in, the only thing that stuck out—other than the fact that I'd just wandered into an outgrowth of the US Special Operations Command with a colleague and there were no military police, not even a gate, to stop us—

was the fitness room. It was more metal plates than Peloton. Geurts had said he wanted to create a "mosh pit." The office looked to me like Google's, but with power drills and 3D-printed explosives.

Not on the day we were there, but on many other ones, SOFWERX hosted a wide variety of activities to give life to Geurts's pit. There were rapid-prototyping events and "collaboration and collision" events, which Geurts liked to call "rodeos." At ThunderDrone, in 2017, the team had invited companies to demonstrate their drone technologies (officially, "unmanned aerial systems"), with a special focus of getting the drones to work together in swarms. A Game of Drones was scheduled for the next year, where top performers would compete for cash prizes. Earlier, SOFWERX had organized something called a Pirates Exercise, where the team worked to imagine how Special Operations Forces might be interrupted rescuing a captured tanker by the capturers using technologies they'd bought off the shelf. Spoofed GPS locations and jammed bulkhead doors were on the lists the team conjured up . . . and then published on the web. Pirates would be on Geurts's mind when he saw Zapata flying for the first time[7] (flying warfighters as counter-countermeasures to pirate countermeasures, perhaps).

The participants in these events were a motley crew. There were operators from many different Special Forces units. Government employees. Private entrepreneurs. College interns. High school students. I met some of University of South Florida's young engineers working on shoebox-sized satellites that might capture battlefield intelligence. "People are bouncing in, people are bouncing out, some stay for a while, and some go," Geurts explained. Clearly he hoped that this new generation would be among the some that stayed.

Geurts had conceived of what became SOFWERX three years before we walked in. He and a friend (a retired Air Force officer) had gone for burgers at a new restaurant in an old building in Tampa,

Florida. Geurts left with an idea about how to "reinvent the way SOCOM invents." What was wrong with the way Special Operations Command had been inventing?

Inventors from the Beginning

US special operators began as inventors. Forerunners to the Navy SEALs were the Naval Combat Demolition Units that were stood up during World War II. NCDUs raced into idea-making from the very start.[8] Hitler's army was relying on Belgian Gates along Omaha Beach and Utah Beach to thwart the Allies' Normandy invasion. These German obstacles were "three tons of half-inch thick angle iron welded and bolted together into a ten foot wide by ten foot high barricade that would tear the bottom out of a landing craft at high tide and block them at low tide." The trained warriors of the brand-new demolition units would have to figure out how to take down the gates, and in "such a way that they didn't send shrapnel from the explosions whizzing around on a beach full of soldiers and demolitioneers." More than fifty thousand troops would land at Omaha and Utah beaches, and the fate of the free world depended on inventing a means of getting through. So an NCDU Lieutenant, Carl Hagensen, did. He created a waterproof sack and filled it with C2 explosives, adding a cord and hook at each end of the sack so that it could be hooked to the gates and into other charges. He experimented with this "Hagensen Sack," and then ten thousand of them were sewed and filled and used in the invasion. The NCDUs and Army combat engineers were able to blast open "five of the sixteen corridors assigned to them" and to create three more partial gaps, and "that was enough to allow the landings at Omaha beach and the Allied forces to pursue Hitler's Army."[9]

The special operators' reputation for bravery was born on those beaches, and so was a legacy of ingenuity. It would continue via different units that also paved the way for the later SEALs, out in the Pacific Theater of the war. The Office of Strategic Services (OSS) Maritime Unit was known, "of all the forefathers of the SEAL teams . . . for pushing the limits of technology." It adopted the first one-man submersible—calling it the "sleeping beauty"—used to propel an operator along the surface before submerging for an attack. It deployed the "floating mattress," which could carry two people and was propelled by an electric drill drawing on a 12-volt battery. It hired Major Christian Lambertsen, who developed rebreathers in the 1940s for the Navy frogmen. The bubble-free diving apparatus initiated a new phase in underwater warfighting.[10]

From their inception these units attracted inventors, and that was still true—two generations later—as Geurts and his friend were brainstorming over burgers in Tampa. The special operators themselves were often inventing, and they had plenty of people inventing for them. The 2011 raid on Osama Bin Laden's compound was aided by all manner of sophisticated technologies that had been developed for use by special operators, including drones that provided air support and stealth helicopters that ferried the operators into Pakistan. The team even included a military dog that had undergone sophisticated training to sniff out explosives and booby-trapped doors.[11] In 2015, the Special Operations program under Geurts's oversight forged ahead with a list of innovations that seemed to me like it had been swiped off of Tony Stark's desk: low-cost/expendable satellites, advanced armor/materials, deployable rapid DNA analysis, unique night-vision devices, and even a Tactical Assault Light Operator Suit, a kind of armored warfighter exoskeleton nicknamed, yes, the "Iron Man suit."[12] So, what was wrong with the way SOCOM invented?

Geurts and Bates were looking for ideas on YouTube, but Special Operations seemed, at least to my eye, chock-full of them.

New Ideas

"If we had a new idea around here, it would die of loneliness," Mayor Menino used to tell us, and not happily. If he was right, I'd like to think we could be forgiven. Teams with people in their roles for a long time struggle to come up with new ideas. In government, people stay a while. We've learned since grade school the art of self-protection: We don't want to look intrusive in our organizations, so we don't offer ideas. We don't want to look negative, so we don't criticize the status quo.[13] Rare is the organization designed to allow people to take the interpersonal risks of learning and sharing, these organizations do so by generating a sense of "psychological safety."[14] Public organizations conspire to provide not a lot of that. Moreover, even if we were brave enough to share new ideas, a kind of risk-aversion-induced un-imagination takes hold (more on risk aversion in chapter 3). That is, if we won't be allowed to try it anyway, why would we even bother to think it up? And on top of all this, an acute case of Not-Invented-Here Syndrome in government means that ideas from the outside, which might help generate new ideas on the inside, are rejected.[15] In government, we even have our special idea frailties. Old bureaucracies get "ossified"; a buildup of programs leads to what one scholar has called "demosclerosis."[16] Furthermore if my mayor and others were expecting us to dream like Apple's famed Steve Jobs, well, that was just expecting too much. We weren't born Steve Jobs.

Some of these excuses would have withered under scrutiny if I had offered them to the boss. The truth is, you don't have to be Steve Jobs to be entrepreneurial. There is scant evidence that entrepreneurs are born but not made. Entrepreneurship is a "what" and not mostly a "who." You don't have to be special. It can be learned and practiced, and designed into organizations, maybe even public ones. When Menino hectored us for new ideas, he wasn't trying to get water out of a rock. He was trying to mold us into wells.

Opportunity Driven

In 1983, Howard Stevenson, a professor of entrepreneurship, described what that molding would take and foretold what was ailing—to the extent it was—Special Operations when I met Geurts. "Strengths have become weaknesses, and weaknesses strengths," Stevenson noted while describing how resources wring the innovation out of us and how we might get it back.[17]

In the early 1980s, Stevenson set out to redefine entrepreneurship. Though the term had been defined many times over since being coined by French-Irish economist Richard Cantillon in the early eighteenth century, Stevenson found contemporary definitions wanting. He felt that by the 1980s the common understanding of entrepreneurship had come to rest too much on the notion of the entrepreneur as a risk-seeking, creative, brave (you can pick the adjective) individual.

In place of a "single model of the human being who is the entrepreneur," Stevenson—later with colleague Bill Sahlman—laid out a range of six entrepreneurial behaviors.[18] On one end of the range was the "trustee" and at the opposite end the "promoter." In this conception, not all the way at the promoter end but close to it lie the entrepreneurs. Not because of some unique psychological makeup but because of the orientation they select along six different dimensions: Entrepreneurs in this formulation are driven more by the perception of opportunity than by the resources they have at hand. They commit to those opportunities often very quickly and for short time frames. They stage their commitment while maintaining minimal exposure throughout the process. They use resources only "episodically," often renting (or the functional equivalent) instead of buying. They tend to organize with minimal hierarchy and avail themselves of informal networks. And they focus compensation toward value creation. "Trustees," to an extreme, and "administrative managers," in more moderation, take the opposite orientations along these six dimensions. They are strategically driven mostly by the resources they currently control. They take longer to commit to those opportunities and then stick with them for longer. They commit their resources for similarly long durations, often after a single decision up front. They own most of the required resources. They rely on more-formalized hierarchies. And they base compensation either on scope of responsibility or on meeting short-term targets.[19]

Entrepreneurs, Stevenson told us, are opportunity driven and not resource driven. He might as well have said "entrepreneurship is the opposite of what bureaucrats do," and he and Sahlman said nearly that, but not pejoratively. Their focus, in fact, was more on private firms than on governmental organizations. Nonetheless, they identified the common features of many established organizations in which maintaining the status quo is what is tacitly and sometimes explicitly encouraged. Managers, responding rationally to what is encouraged (through compensation, promotion, etc.), happily oblige and steer clear of change. They described such managers as "classic bureaucrats," not unlike public servants, who are trustees of public resources to which they've been . . . entrusted. What such managers can do best with what they have, the thinking goes, is what they should do.

Stevenson envisioned a spectrum of management, with administrative styles of leadership on the right and entrepreneurial styles on the left. Resources—yes, among other things, but especially the availability of resources—dragged managers to the right. Stevenson wanted organizations to find ways to pull their members back to the left, where, undistracted and unpressured by bounteous resources, they would be forced to look beyond, at what they *should* do, not just at what they *could*. Menino wanted to drag us there.

Creating Choices

Design thinkers have a similar way of describing two alternate modes of thinking. Neither one is inherently better than the other, but one had come to dominate organizational thinking. Tim Brown, the CEO and president of IDEO, the innovation consultancy, described the difference between convergent thinking and divergent thinking, and the (great) need for both. "Convergent thinking is a practical way of deciding among existing alternatives," he noted. It takes inputs and uses analysis and "drives us toward solutions." Switching gears, he continued: "What convergent thinking is *not* so good at, however, is probing the future and creating new possibilities . . . The object of divergent thinking is to multiply options to create choices." He quoted the two-time Nobel Prize–winning scientist Linus Pauling: "To have a good idea, you must first have lots of ideas." He recognized the challenges of flooding organizations with more ideas but came out in favor of more ideas nonetheless, advocating a "dance" between the two approaches. "More choices means more complexity, which can make life difficult—especially for those whose job it is to control budgets and monitor timelines. The natural tendency of most companies is to constrain problems and restrict choices in favor of the obvious and the incremental. Though this tendency may be more efficient in the short run, in the long run it tends to make an organization

FIGURE 1–1

Divergent and convergent thinking

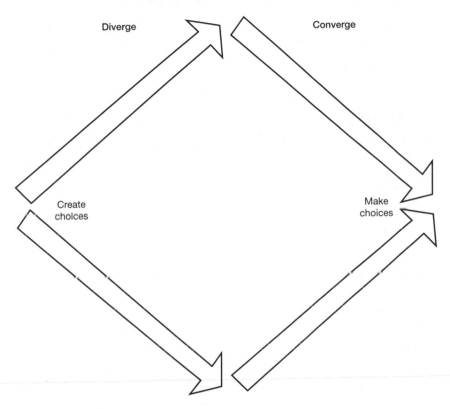

Source: *Change by Design* by Tim Brown. Copyright © 2009 by Tim Brown. Used by permission of HarperCollins Publishers.

conservative, inflexible, and vulnerable to game-changing ideas from outside."[20] Make choices, yes, but create them, too (see figure 1-1).

Geurts, in a similar vein, built SOFWERX to engineer a shift from a "scarcity" mindset to an "abundance" mindset. Scarcity is doing the best with what you have. Abundance is focusing on a problem and believing there are resources out there that can be brought to it, if you know how to marshal them. A scarcity mindset cuts ideas down before they even get thought up. An abundance mindset led Geurts to muse, "I want to create a giant bug light so people and ideas come to me." Stevenson wrote, "The best administrative practices lead to immobility and to lack of ability to respond to opportunity. The best of administrative science has contributed to closed organizations."[21] Geurts believed that. He didn't just want "new ideas." He wanted a new orientation toward new ideas. Possibility and probability. Entrepreneurship and administration. Divergence and convergence. Abundance and scarcity. It's a dance between the two, but in governments, we've forgotten half the steps. That's why any new ideas are lonely.

That we've forgotten the steps is in some ways an outgrowth of our aging. It may not be political ossification per se—program on top of program, each with its own stakeholder—but it's not *not* that. Asset on top of asset. Budget on top of budget. Resource on top of resource. Stevenson warned us it gets hard to do anything that's not making the most of those. It gets hard to pursue any opportunity beyond them. Eighty years after the SEALs had been invented, by dint of all they'd invented, it'd gotten harder to do the same.

Best Isn't Good Enough

There is a particular and much loved kind of administrative/convergent/scarcity thinking that appears so similar to its opposites that it's hard to detect. But it is limiting our efforts at imagining new solutions to sticky problems and therefore our abilities to solve them. And that's "best practices." Too often in government, the search for a new solution begins and ends with a call for finding the best of what others are doing, and then doing that. I understand the appeal: replicate what works. And we should do that. We could lift up the lives of billions of people around the globe if solutions that had been developed and successfully implemented in some places made their way to all appropriate places. But we also must recognize that in many cases, best isn't good enough. That "solutions" aren't really solutions at all, but just the things that are being done. If you asked for best practices on what's being done today to add affordable housing, reduce congestion, thwart climate change, narrow gaping inequalities, etc., you would get a list of very interesting and sometimes helpful practices. And if you, as a public leader, aren't doing the things on that list, you should. And if you, the public, aren't demanding them, you should. But the reality is, if you subjected the list to the test of "Will it be enough? Will it solve the problem?" the answer would likely be no. The best is only the best yet, so I think as *possibilitists*, we must beware best's siren call.

Following the marathon attacks, the decision was made to cancel that night's Boston Bruins hockey game, with a city in mourning and terrorists on the loose. Not long after that, Mayor Menino wanted to know if canceling had been my stupid idea, and I could honestly tell him it hadn't been, because I hadn't had an idea, stupid or otherwise, since those sobbing people had come streaming toward my home. (I think it was the right call, by the way, and I think eventually he did, too.)

An idea was forming in my head, though. And in his, and in a few others'. And the idea was that we needed to set up a brand-new fund to collect and distribute donations that were going to start coming in from around the world. The mayor was already taking the calls of people asking, "Where can we send help?"

The answer, in most US places affected by tragedy, was a local foundation. Best practices was to have an established, trusted organization collect donations and administer the funds. After the mass shootings in Columbine, Aurora, and Newtown, versions of this process had been put into practice in those locations. My mayor wasn't inclined in that direction, however. He felt that when money went into foundations (which are the epitome of Stevenson's "trustee"), it took too long to get out, and that when it ultimately did get out, it went in too many directions and not to those who most needed it. I agreed with that worry. I had, by pure chance, seen articles documenting some of the delays in disbursing funds to the Sandy Hook survivors. The shootings at Sandy Hook Elementary had happened 122 days before the marathon bombings, and still the major fund collecting donations hadn't finalized a process for distributing those donations. In Columbine, it took years for donated funds to make it to victims, and even then they received only 58 percent of what had been collected. After Aurora, it took 259 days—almost a year—for the funds to make it to victims.[22] The idea of best practices is beguiling, but it wasn't going to be good enough. The mayor insisted, with the governor joining him, that we would start up our own new fund. "You can't start something new," we were told, a statement rooted in trusteeship that left unaddressed the matter of doing better. So, I had to tell the foundation head we were going to anyway.

The Age of Surprise

Geurts had seen reasons to think government had been pulled too far in one direction, but when he looked outside of government, he saw why it was actually urgent to pull us back. In fact, it was what was going on beyond Special Operations Forces (SOF) that had him most preoccupied. In a PowerPoint presentation he made around the time he was thinking up SOFWERX, he quoted former General Electric executive Jack Welch: "If the rate of change on the outside exceeds the rate of change on the inside, the end is near."[23] He was concerned about the "exponential environment" US Special Operators were facing. The missions, he said, were becoming more dynamic. Rapid change was everywhere. SOF had more partners, and therefore more integrations to navigate. It was getting harder to provide command and control in that environment. And while it was good that they could avail themselves of incredible new technologies in the private marketplace, these advancements too were increasing the complexity of the job. The competition was more agile, and he needed his organization—made up of seventy thousand people—to be as well. And leaving aside that his competition included stateless terrorists and nefarious states, he might have been talking about the challenges we all face in our own organizations. "We are living in the age of surprise," Geurts said.

And then he laid out the challenge of living amidst surprise while trying to solve public problems. "People in government value being experts . . . their value is in what they know. The problem is, if the rules are changing, their value is waning." It was a problem made worse by a creeping division in the United States, a widening civilian–military divide. "The population that understands the military has shrunk," he pointed out. He looked ahead and thought, "As the percentage of the American public who were military-experienced or knew the military shrank, there would be an unhealthy trend where the military was revered but not understood." There were more and more people who could help defend their country and its values, but didn't know it or know how. Absent any change, it would be left to insider "experts," but their expertise was concentrated in the past, and this fostered even more concentration. "Ducks pick ducks," Geurts said, flagging the issue. "And if the world is changing, but you keep picking the same people based on the same expertise, that doesn't work."

There were other challenges, too. SOF units were the most frequently deployed forces in the post-9/11 era. They were busy. They were constantly fighting battles. And Geurts didn't buy the conventional wisdom that being pushed to the brink would force innovation. "When you are in a crisis situation, our experience tends to be that you rely on what you know best," he said. "You just try and hustle your way out of it. I don't think you think any harder because you're at war."

Geurts dug into the US Special Operations Command archives to try to find out how you could think harder. He wanted to know how his predecessors at the OSS—the ones who had ushered in the "sleeping beauty" and the "floating mattress" and the rebreathers and so much more—had achieved so many innovations so quickly during a global war. "What I came to realize was that war forced these organizations to take opinions and get perspectives from a much more diverse set of folks. Either because all of your operators were forward in the field, so you had to bring in other, new people, or since you had a burning platform, other people who would not normally think to help the military, say fashion designers and painters who invented our modern camouflage, were now incentivized to help."

What was wrong with the way SOCOM was inventing was that it was too busy with the here and now, too focused on what it knew and had seen already, and it had become too cordoned off from outside ideas. In SOFWERX, Geurts wanted a place where ducks and not ducks could come together and work together to solve the problems of the future. It strikes me now that when I watched the video of Zapata, I saw a flying hoverboard, whereas Geurts saw a not duck.

We Don't Have to Be Special to Be Agile

I hadn't thought about the flyboard for several months when, in the summer of 2019, it was all over YouTube again.[24] High above the Champs Élysées, a man was flying on a board, participating in—headlining, really—France's Bastille Day parade. After the video of the flying board circling the famed avenue below, followed by French fighter jets trailing smoke in the tricolors, came the millions of views, and then the fawning press, and the flabbergasted tweets—even a celebratory one from France's president, Emmanuel Macron: *Fier de notre armée, moderne et innovante.*[25] "Proud of our army, modern and innovative." And why wouldn't he be?

Except that it wasn't a French soldier on Zapata's flying board— it was Zapata. And the French hadn't yet bought any of the boards for their use. (Zapata told me he thought they would be the first in the near future.) Truth was, neither had the Americans. No government had. Zapata said when I talked to him a few months after, "Soon it will be 2020, and the only solution right now to climb on a captured boat is to go up to it with your own boat and climb it with a vacuum system or magnets or even with a ladder. To me, it's something from the pirates, something from 1,000 years ago. Nothing's changed."[26] What's so modern and innovative about that?

Geurts saw the whole thing as part of planning for the unplanned. He said they might buy some of the flyboards when they showed added military utility. His experiments with Zapata weren't so much about whether the device would fly or not but about whether he could train soldiers that weren't world-class athletes like Zapata, and how quickly. And he said, "I have fifty products like that. I don't need them right now. But if I need them for something unexpected, I already have a relationship. Because of the networks we built, I could call Franky up at his house right now."

He sounded, at SOFWERX, every bit the part of Stevenson's entrepreneur. Driven by opportunity and not resources. Willing to act quickly, but sometimes shortly. Staging his investments, and ideally borrowing instead of buying the capacity he would need. And comfortable operating across relationships instead of up and down reporting lines.

By the time Zapata was back in the news, Geurts was in a new role. He had been nominated and then confirmed to be Assistant Secretary of the US Navy for Research, Development, and Acquisition. It was a post with a much larger reach. There were more than half a million people in the Navy, funded by more than $200 billion for the entire department, which operated "from the sea floor to space," as Geurts liked to say. "You've been outspoken that you don't have to have *special* in your name to be innovative and agile," he remembers a very senior official telling him, working to recruit him to the role. During his confirmation hearings, Senator Elizabeth Warren said to him, "You've been the acquisition executive at Special Operations Command for a number of years, and I appreciate how you have prioritized agility and innovation in that role. But let's face it. Special Operations is near the top in the flexibility that it is given when it comes to acquisition, and you are about to move to a military department that, mmm, does not have that same flexibility . . . so here is what I want to ask: How does your experience at SOCOM inform your outlook as a service acquisition executive?"[27] Geurts called it "an excellent question" and went on to say that SOCOM had a sense of urgency, that it leveraged lots of different tools, and that it fostered a close connection between operators and the people who bought stuff for them, and that all three things were possible at the Navy, too. After being confirmed, he went and ran the SOCOM and SOFWERX innovation playbook, adapted for a department that built nuclear submarines and billion-dollar ships. He started something called NavalX to "take brilliant ideas," ones that somehow wouldn't have had a hearing or a champion, and push them forward. I paid particular note to a deputy director who said one of the goals was to allow people to get beyond "dated best practices."[28] Geurts was still, always, out looking for some novel solution to scary problems. He worried a lot about the so-called December 8th problem: How would the United States mass mobilize after an event of Pearl Harbor proportions? "If something big and unexpected happens, how will we react quickly? I am way into possibility now, because I don't want to think about it when it happens." And who did he invite to talk about it? A baker's dozen of US CEOs, only two of whom were in defense. "Lots of people want to help, but they don't know how to connect. And for me, the only cost was making the phone call." He hosted other gatherings, larger in number (thirty or so) and diverse in their composition. One was on how to completely rethink the way the Navy upgraded computers and software on its ships. Another, on the anniversary of D-Day, was to consider how to create the same level of deception that had led to the success of D-Day, given modern circumstances. He calls them "possibility sessions."

Beyond Resources Controlled

Again, Mayor Menino used to tell us that "if we had a new idea around here, it would die of loneliness." But we had ideas every day. And we were supported by an ecosystem of ideas that stretched from community organizations in Boston to global networks. The United States alone has almost two thousand think tanks thinking.[29] How could any of us in public life be short on ideas? How could any of ours be lonely?

Somewhere at a former tattoo parlor in Tampa, there was an answer, and it was this: On the whole, the ideas we have are a product of the resources we have at hand, and not of the problems in the world. They are sourced from the agencies we work in, limited by the funding we've been allocated, proscribed by the mandate we've been given. They are designed for a past that won't return and a present that isn't good enough. I heard Geurts say, "You don't want an organization to be so fragile that you have to predict the future precisely." But that's what we've become in governments all around the world. Stiff from competence, if not complacency. And fragile to whatever is coming next.

But we aren't too far gone. The pursuit of opportunity beyond resources controlled is an invitation to all of us, inside government and out, to imagine how we might help. We, the abundance.

2

Reach Out to Reach Up

On a late afternoon in 2014, Jimmy Chen walked into a food stamps office in Brooklyn, New York.[1] He remembers arriving at 3:30, or maybe it was 4:00. Closing was at 5:00. He walked up to the person staffing the entrance and said he wanted to apply for assistance. He remembers that she laughed at him. He recalls her saying that there was already a two- or three-hour wait, that most people wouldn't be seen today, that if he wanted to be seen the same day, he should come back in the morning. Chen returned the next day at 9:00 a.m., when the office opened, and waited only forty-five minutes, though he expected he wouldn't qualify for the benefits anyway.

Chen also filled out applications in several other states, where he wasn't a resident.

Chen asked mothers how to navigate the application process. He went to their living rooms and peered into their lives. He asked them how they secured benefits for their kids. But he had none.

Chen wasn't eligible for food stamps. But he wasn't a fraudster.

What was he doing then? "As entrepreneurs, we tend to solve the problems we understand best . . . you need to understand the needs of users," Chen told me. "You need empathy." Chen wasn't waiting in line for food stamps. He was waiting in line for insight.

A few months prior, Chen had left a senior role in Silicon Valley. He had parlayed a degree in software engineering from Stanford into roles at LinkedIn and then at Facebook, where he built technologies that reached hundreds of millions of users around the world. Now he had left San Francisco for Brooklyn, with a vague plan to build a startup that helped people startups weren't reaching. But he took with him a sense that understanding user experience was the key to building effective products. So when Chen decided to go looking for ideas for helping low-income Americans, he decided to go looking for low-income Americans. New ideas are why Chen was waiting for food stamps he didn't need and couldn't get.

While Chen was on Bergen Street in Brooklyn, public officials around the world were pounding the table for new ideas and were mostly looking for them around that same table—but not all of those officials. An emerging type of leader was harnessing a set of techniques to get well beyond the reach of established agencies and even that of so-called experts. Such leaders were turning toward their own citizens, using the kinds of techniques that Chen had learned, to try to identify the right problems to solve and the right solutions. They were looking to the crowd, using the web's technologies and ethos to take up "wiki government."[2] They were providing pizzas and power outlets for weekend-long hackathons, enlisting weekend warriors in the pursuit of solving public problems. They'd begun to earn both praise and skepticism for these approaches, but nevertheless a new breed of public servant was dumping old, insular traditions. The first-term mayor of St. Paul, Minnesota, Melvin Carter, told me, "My best ideas are in other people's heads."[3] (He was nothing if not consistent on this front . . . he'd enlisted a hundred volunteer citizens to help him select cabinet chiefs and department heads.[4] At his 2018 inauguration, as his community welcomed him with a standing ovation, he told them, "Don't clap if you're not going to help.")[5] I asked Carter where new ideas come from, and he replied, "I don't have a good, finite answer. Other than everyone and everywhere."[6]

Everyone? Everywhere?

From Talking to People

Chen and colleagues set out to build a company called Propel to "make America's safety net more user friendly."[7] Their first product was a benefits-enrollment app. The Propel team pulled this early tool from a bucket of user-engagement techniques that, at the time, were still only lightly utilized by people inside public office. The team had spent time in Supplemental Nutrition Assistance Program (SNAP) offices. They'd downloaded and completed application forms themselves. They had noticed things—like how many people waiting in the same line Chen was were on their mobile phones. He looked into the data, which told him that in New York City only 74 percent of eligible people were using SNAP; also that smartphone use was on the rise among low-income populations and that 45 percent of low-income Americans went online primarily with their phones, compared with 34 percent of Americans in general.[8] He had gone to a supermarket in Philadelphia on a December day and found that most of the shoppers were enrolled in SNAP there, and watched a woman (with her permission) as she checked her balance by entering a nineteen-digit number from memory into her phone . . . something she did almost every day. "We had thought enrollment was a major hurdle, but from talking to people, we came to think that there were a lot of issues with the actual delivery of the SNAP program," Chen said. A shift in insight about what the problem was (from *it's hard to enroll* to *it's challenging to use*) had prompted a shift in the targeting of the solution. Chen had grown up in a family of immigrants. He'd been through times when finances were tough.[9] But then he'd spent time in Silicon Valley, where he felt distant from the problems he was trying to uncover and fix. "A twenty-five-year-old male has technology to meet his every whim. But who is building the technology for the fifty-year-old single mother on food stamps?" he asked. And then he went to meet her, and people facing similar circumstances. He sat in their living rooms and watched them shop, so he could.

Citizen-Centered Design

You can trace Chen's time spent at a supermarket in 2015 to another supermarket in 1999 and to the core idea that informed his outreach: design thinking. In 1999, Ted Koppel and *Nightline* placed IDEO; its founder, David Kelley; and his team firmly onto the global map. Millions have since watched the episode as the group went about answering *Nightline*'s challenge: redesign the shopping cart in five days with their (then) peculiar methodology. IDEO's engineers and designers wandered Whole Foods Market aisles to observe how shoppers behaved. They cruised local bike stores for tips on design and materials. They papered walls with giant Post-it sheets and prototyped newfangled shopping carts (carts with stackable handbaskets, carts with their own scanners) from materials they'd gathered from the hardware store and welded together.[10] From there, IDEO's design-thinking methodologies—which focus on observing real people and working to uncover their latent needs—made it into best-selling books, course curricula, corporate trainings, and consulting gigs. David Kelley went on to found Stanford's design school, with these methods as its core. Chen was introduced to design thinking at Stanford as an undergraduate. He'd been to a David Kelley lecture and had been wowed.

By the time Chen was in the SNAP office on Bergen Street, that 1999 version of design thinking had been recast somewhat as human-centered design, and the new label sought not only to emphasize the empathy in design thinking ("to see an experience through another person's eyes, to recognize why people do what they do," David and Tom Kelley had written) but also to gesture at its now larger ambitions.[11] "The human-centered design process obviously works for products—that's where it originated—but the beauty of it is that it's applicable to almost anything you might want to come up with as a challenge," Diego Rodriguez, an IDEO partner, has said.[12] IDEO published a book called *The Field Guide to Human-Centered Design*, and it opened with a breath of optimism.

> Embracing human-centered design means believing that all problems, even the seemingly intractable ones like poverty, gender equality, and clean water, are solvable. Moreover, it means believing that the people who face those problems every day are the ones that hold the key to their answer. Human-centered design offers problem solvers of any stripe a chance to design with communities, to deeply understand the people they're looking to serve, to dream up scores of ideas, and to create innovative new solutions rooted in people's actual needs.[13]

All problems are solvable, they said, if we'd just work hard to deeply understand the people we served.

Across the world, there have been blooming efforts to bring these kinds of practices squarely into the public sector. The UK's Policy Lab was established in 2014 and has worked to bring "people-centered design approaches to policy making."[14] Andrea Siodmok is the deputy director there. An industrial designer by background, she had been through the same design course as IDEO's Tim Brown and Apple's longtime design chief Jonathan Ive. Siodmok and Policy Lab's head, Vasant Chari, told me their job was to "bring the outside into government" in order to "bridge the gap between evidence and the art of possible."[15] I spoke with them after they'd undertaken an effort to help the United Kingdom's housing minister address social-housing issues, on the heels of the Grenfell Tower tragedy that had killed seventy-two people. The lab engaged a thousand citizens around the country in conversations about their fears and frustrations and needs. These kinds of efforts have been a large part of the United Kingdom's other government redesign undertakings, including its Government Digital Service. In the United States, 18F, an agency charged with helping federal agencies better meet user needs, has dozens of blog posts on how to bring design-thinking methods into government.

The increasing prevalence of these practices means there is also a growing body of practical advice for how to design with the public:[16]

- If you're wondering where to start, look for work-arounds, and watch what people do.

- Write down your assumptions about the problem ahead of time. Be alert to them, but don't push them on your interviewee.

- Find people for whom the need is important, where it is important. "Target citizens with a need this hour."

- Be open about the kind of confidentiality you can and can't provide. Note any waivers required. Be honest about the time you expect to need from them.

- Having done that, don't be shy about capturing videos, photos, etc.

- Offer reassurance. Often citizens have been evaluated or tested in way too many contexts. Assure them, "This is not a test of you."

The world was now filling up with ambition and practice and advice for going to citizen "users" for new ideas, so I set out to try these tools myself. I wanted to retrace some of Jimmy Chen's tracks. I wanted to understand better why he'd gone to that SNAP office and what to make of it and what it might mean amid this wave of citizen-centered design I was witnessing. I decided in the summer of 2019 to go back to the same office where Chen had spent much of his time and to try to do some of the customer discovery that Chen had done.

The office Chen had gone to had closed. I looked into why. The press coverage I found said it was because of the advent of technology: more people were applying online, so there was less need for offices. The irony of this was the first thing that struck me. People thinking like Chen did had made it easier to access benefits from a computer but harder if you needed to do so in person.

Then a second thought occurred to me: whether the site had been closed, in part, because it had become politically toxic. Between when Chen had gone there and I tried to, something quite sad had happened.[17] In the winter of 2018, a mother had been sitting on the floor there with her crying infant, trying to comfort him. She was told she wasn't allowed to sit on the floor. She insisted that this was the only way to comfort the child. Eventually, the security team there tried to lift her off the floor and ultimately pulled her screaming baby out of her arms. The video went viral, and it's incredibly hard to watch. New York's mayor, Bill de Blasio, had to apologize. I wondered whether that also had something to do with why the office on Bergen Street was gone.

I also thought about the alternative universe the IDEO types were trying to conjure up, one where when a mother is sitting on the floor with a crying baby, it isn't security guards who approach her but instead design thinkers, who sit down next to her and begin to ask, respectfully, Why? I wondered whether—if given the opportunity to ask—they would have generated a whole list of things to try that would have had nothing to do with dragging her out of there. After a conversation with her and others like her, maybe they would have arrived at a list of new problems to tackle and new ideas for doing so. Maybe the problem to address isn't seats at SNAP offices but childcare, which is prohibitively difficult to access in the United States. Or maybe we should have toys for kids at the office. Or a TV showing *Curious George*, like a dentist's office might. Maybe we should create a special unit that enrolls people for SNAP at their own houses, or a mobile team that helps them just after they've dropped their kids at day care. Or maybe we should create different kinds of seats. Bleachers. Or lofts, like in a dorm room. Or maybe we should create a mobile app (like Chen did). Or maybe none of these things, but something else that makes applying for SNAP easier and that someday has a hope—and I realize this is a giant leap from better seats and forms—of lifting people out of poverty. But that's the exercise, and I was struck by how different that would be from what governments normally do, how generative it would be. If that's what the human-centered designers were aiming to bring about, I was warming to the idea.

Desire Lines

There are, in fact, several potential logics for designing with users.

There is historical evidence validating the approach. "The idea that novel products and services are developed by manufacturers is deeply ingrained in both traditional expectations and scholarship,"

Eric von Hippel wrote in his *Democratizing Innovation* in 2005. "Nonetheless, there is now very strong empirical evidence that product development and modification by user firms and users as individual customers is frequent, pervasive, and important."[18] He'd provided a lot of that evidence—as had other social scientists—including in one study where von Hippel had found that "users were the developers of about 80 percent of the most important scientific instrument innovations."[19] He also noted that there was a long tradition of user-driven innovation. He pointed out that no less than Adam Smith had documented so in his seminal *The Wealth of Nations*. In 1776, the same year American colonists declared their independence from a government that wasn't working for them, Smith wrote that many of the machines enabling a transformation in productivity driven by division in labor "were originally the invention of common workmen, who, being each of them employed in some very simple operation, naturally turned their thoughts towards finding out easier and readier methods of performing it."[20]

There is also a potential physio-logic to working with users. "Why fight human instinct?" Tom Kelley, an IDEO partner and David Kelley's brother, noted while explaining IDEO's penchant for "going to the source" for ideas rather than relying on focus groups and market research. He told a story about a customer—a medical-device company—insisting on a new device that could be used with one hand in the operating room, and of the reality that IDEO's team saw when they themselves went to the operating room: "Although the current product could theoretically be used with one hand, it really worked that way if you had a hand the size of Michael Jordan's. In actual practice, medical technicians used *both* hands with the device." Why not design the new device for two hands? Which is precisely what they did. By closely observing the end user, they could see how users really experienced products and services and could then come up with better ones. It was also why they'd come up with a trackball for younger kids on computers, who were confused by a traditional mouse's limited range and the need to pick the device up and reset it on a mouse pad. The point was to uncover what comes naturally to the user.[21]

I had seen what came naturally. A few years ago, Harvard Business School installed a sign just outside of my office, at one of the entrances to the school (see figure 2-1). Not a day went by without somebody being photographed standing near the sign. Newly admitted students. Graduating ones. Tourists. Executives on campus to address a class or take part in one. Pumpkins showed up around Halloween, and banners did around New Year's Eve. I'd noticed that soon after the sign was installed, dirt patches appeared to the sides of it, where the grass had been worn away. The cement strips that

FIGURE 2-1

Welcome sign at Harvard Business School

looked meant for standing on went relatively unused, because *next* to the sign (not in front of or behind it) was where people wanted to be captured beaming for Instagram. And then I noticed that the patches got resodded, and then got worn down again. In eighteen months, I watched this process repeat itself three times.

I approached Andy O'Brien, the school's amazing chief of operations, and asked him about the sign and the sod. He laughed good-naturedly and acknowledged that the cement strips—which now looked less than ideally placed—had been the product of a lot of meetings with a lot of experts. Yes, he said smiling, "There was a study."[22] I asked him why not just move some cement blocks to where the sod had been worn out? Why not put them where users seem to want to stand?

The idea of doing this—of finding "desire lines," paths created by human usage—was not one I had invented. It had been around for a while in transportation planning. Janette Sadik-Khan, New York City's transportation commissioner under Mayor Mike Bloomberg, brought desire lines to life in New York City. In one instance, her team put a new crossing between Sixth and Seventh Avenues in New York where hundreds of people crossed midblock each day to access a pedestrian arcade.[23] "Desire lines are the native operating code for a new approach to urban design," she explained. "Instead of asking why people aren't following the rules and design of the road, we need to ask ourselves why the rules and design of the road aren't following people . . . Desire lines are a road map of opportunity."[24]

Mayor Carter of St. Paul was one of those leaders who looked for "desire lines." He cited Sadik-Khan's influence on his thinking but, being from the Midwest, leaned toward the label "cow paths" when telling the story of his old high school and the debate over locating a sidewalk on its campus. "There's a cow path across the grass where students have been walking for a long time. If we ask 2,500 students to come to a public hearing on proper sidewalk alignment, most would roll their eyes. Maybe only two would show up. Most would say, I don't know what you are asking me. Or I don't belong. Meanwhile, all 2,500 know it makes more sense to cut across the grass, where the cow path is, than to go where the sidewalk is. So often we accept testimony out of a city council at 5:30 on a Wednesday instead of acknowledging that all day, every day, people are voting with their feet to tell us what is working for them." The metaphor, he said, illustrates that we should "stop forcing people to make their behavior meet our geometric sidewalk shapes or whatever public problem we are talking about [and instead ask] how do we transform to meet theirs?"[25] Carter then carried through on the metaphor in many places. He ended library fines for the St. Paul Public Library. And when he explains why, you almost forget that you thought at first that the idea sounded crazy. "Think about it," he says. "We were penalizing people for doing exactly what we wanted them to do: read books." St. Paul unfroze 42,000 library cards. And after a few months they had 43,000 materials checked out on those cards. "We fundamentally redefined our library. And it's akin to if we had opened a new branch, for $200,000 in late fees." A front-line employee had suggested the change, and Carter's library chief (one selected by the citizen process) liked it, and so did Carter.

Nothing about Us without Us

There's also justice in designing with users, the logic of fairness. It respects a "nothing about us without us" sensibility, gleaned from the disability-rights movement.[26] The mantra has spread well beyond that movement. I first heard it in a session on criminal-justice reform, from Anthony Ray Hinton, who had been incarcerated on death row before ultimately being exonerated. I later heard Mayor Carter say America is great "when the 'We' in 'We the People' truly means *all of us*."[27] If "nothing about us without us" seems obvious or even cliché, think about how many meetings you've attended about homelessness without any homeless people in attendance; about education without any students in attendance; about workforce training without any workers in attendance.

After the marathon attacks, when we set out to establish a new fund that would be a conduit for the world's generosity, people immediately and rightly wanted to know . . . what will the money be for? Ken Feinberg, whom the mayor had asked to help administer the One Fund's payouts after the marathon attacks, advised those of us shaping the fund to reserve it for the survivors and the families of the victims. There was talk of supporting the businesses affected on Boylston Street (workers would end up losing substantial wages) as well as the wider community. Feinberg was adamantly against those ideas, having been chastened by his experience administering other funds after other tragedies. "No matter how much money you raise, it will never be enough," he told us. *Focus it on the survivors and the victims' families.* It was consistent with a message we'd been hearing since the street exploded on Monday: survivors first. Friends and colleagues who'd been involved in 9/11 recovery efforts had emailed or called, having some sense of the flood of decisions that would be headed in our direction and some sense of how to wade through that flood. Their advice was unambiguous: prioritize the needs of those most affected by this tragedy, and not the needs of the agencies helping them.

Feinberg also said that once you give survivors the money, don't tell them what to do with it. If they need it for job training, let them use it for that. If they need to reconstruct their house, they can use it for that. If they want to get away and take their families to Disney World, that's their choice. The money is a gift for them to do with what they want. For the well-meaning bureaucrat, the instinct is to decide: not only to allocate the money for survivors but also what the survivors themselves should allocate it for. For scholarships? For psychological support? For housing reconstruction? We resolved that the money would be for them to do with as they chose.

A similar kind of thinking is at the heart of the direct-giving movement in international disaster relief and poverty alleviation. The organization at the center of these efforts is GiveDirectly, and it explains its outlook and findings pretty clearly. "We give cash directly to people living in poverty . . . We believe people living in poverty deserve the dignity to choose for themselves how best to improve their lives . . . Donors have given over 140 million dollars to people in need . . . and no, people don't just blow it on booze . . . in fact, research finds people use cash in impactful and creative ways . . . if you think about it, doesn't giving directly make sense? Cash allows individuals to invest in what they need, instead of relying on aid organizations and donors thousands of miles away to choose for them. Isn't this what you would prefer?"[28] The experts say it will take at least a decade to really know what to make of these efforts, in particular whether direct giving does help lift people out of poverty and whether it does so more effectively than more-typical efforts, which involve in-kind types of aid (training, livestock, food, etc.) designed, in many cases, by insiders and "experts" for the benefit of people in the world who have the least, but not always (or even often) designed *with* them.[29] It's no coincidence that when Jimmy Chen and his team wanted to support their customers faced with massive and pressing needs during the Covid-19 crisis, Propel partnered with GiveDirectly to raise and distribute cash relief to users of its Fresh EBT app.[30]

More Ideas Plus Different Ideas
Equals Better Ideas

Then there's a third logic to looking for ideas with citizens, and it has to do with the math. In design thinking, an exploration phase with users ("What challenges are we trying to address?") is meant to give way to the concepting phase ("How might we address those challenges?").[31] Problem finding lays the groundwork for solution finding. Now that we know what latent needs the users have, the questions turn to how might we solve them?

IDEO's favored technique at this point was brainstorming. The team would target a hundred ideas in a sixty- or ninety-minute session.[32] (This strikes me as more new ideas than some public agencies might have in a year.) IDEO avoided rules, generally, but had rules for this:

1. Defer judgment.

2. Encourage wild ideas.

3. Build on the ideas of others.

4. Stay focused on the topic.

5. One conversation at a time.

6. Be visual.

7. Go for quantity.

Most of the first six rules were in service of the seventh.[33]

IDEO and its ilk seemed to favor almost anything that would get you more ideas. I observed a simulation once in Copenhagen that an innovation-training company had designed with IDEO. The setup was that a city in California was trying to raise the participation rates in its recycling programs. The task was to come up with ideas to help. So one of the first jobs was to look through pictures (since it was a simulation, the participants couldn't go into people's homes themselves and meet with them) to try to develop some insight into what the problem was. Were people not recycling because they didn't care? Didn't know? Didn't have enough room to store recyclables? After some thoughts were synthesized, the challenge was to brainstorm some new ideas. And just in case you got stumped, there was a card deck with some prompts. One of those prompts actually read, "What ideas could get the mayor kicked out of office?" How was this supposed to help?

It turns out that "what ideas could get the mayor kicked out of office" is of a piece with a swelling body of research that suggests that the volume of ideas plus the diversity in those ideas (and the people providing them) can be key in arriving at good new ideas.[34] One strain of this research leans on something called extreme-value theory.[35] And the point is that traditional methods of innovation tend to get us traditional kinds of solutions, close to our current practices and capacities. But that some alternative methods for going after ideas, including the increasingly popular reliance on contests and competitions that enlist "the crowd" (sometimes a highly curated one) for ideas, are likely to produce much more novel ideas, some of which might, possibly, be extremely valuable. The point for government is that while it's true that conventional ways of arriving at new public services or new policy proposals might come up with better ideas, on average, than these new methods, contests and competitions and even the kinds of activities behind a robust brainstorm might come up with a small number of *super* ideas. And if what you really care about is the quality of the best idea—because that's the one you can run with—rather than the average quality of all the ideas, then

FIGURE 2–2

Insider versus outsider ideas

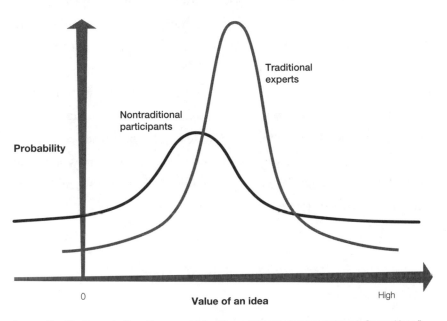

Source: Alan MacCormack, Fiona Murray, and Erika Wagner, "Spurring Innovation through Competitions," *MIT Sloan Management Review*, September 17, 2013. © 2014 from MIT Sloan Management Review/ Massachusetts Institute of Technology.

whatever you can do to get to those extremely positive outcomes would be worth the effort (see figure 2-2).

This kind of thinking isn't brand-new to government. It was behind an oft-cited episode in the 1700s when the British government offered a prize for solving the problem of tracking longitude at sea in order to save its Navy from getting lost. The financial award eventually went to a clockmaker who had solved the problem, but only after debate about whether someone unexpert in celestial bodies could really have come up with the winning idea.[36] The winner (and the debate over it) highlights the role of the outsider here. New ideas, from new fields . . . they probably won't work, but they might. I'd been involved in more mundane efforts along these lines. In Boston, we'd partnered with the company InnoCentive to crowdsource an algorithm for a pothole-sensing app. Beth Noveck, New Jersey's first chief innovation officer, had documented dozens of episodes like this, using contests and crowd collaboration to solve public stuff. She'd been intimately involved in an effort to crowdsource solutions for limiting the spread of Zika in South America. Yochai Benkler, the legal scholar and expert on peer production, had first turned me on to the potential of the crowd with his story of NASA's Clickworkers project. A decade later, when I was wondering about the wider merits of reaching out, NASA was using contests to source new ideas on everything from solar flares to space suits.[37] It had been searching for extreme values for ten years, and getting them.

One Bright Spot

The math of more ideas plus different ideas equals better ideas was behind another strategy that was gaining attention in the years since I'd left government.[38] I'd seen it up close when Annie Rittgers, a native Ohioan just out of graduate school, used it to look for new ideas for one of the newest and biggest problems. "The worst public health crisis in our lifetime," Mike DeWine, then Ohio's attorney general, had called it in 2017. "A human tragedy of epic proportion."[39] (He'd later win praise as governor of that state during its response to the Covid-19 pandemic, another epic human tragedy.) Heroin and synthetic opioids were killing ten people a day in Ohio. The question of the moment was whether the scourge was at its peak or just a new peak. That it had come to Rittgers's hometown of Cincinnati was indisputable. A May 2017 *Bloomberg Businessweek* article called Ohio's third-largest city "a center of the crisis." In one six-day stretch in 2016, 174 people had overdosed. "Everybody and their mom sells drugs these days," a local detective had observed.[40] Rittgers had been a student of mine, and I was rooting for her effort, for possibility, but even I had to face the brutal facts when I arrived at Talbert House, a large Cincinnati human-service provider. People were being brought there every weekend on death's door, I was told. The nighttime parking-lot staff were now de facto first responders. Everybody in the city was feeling heroin's effects.

Rittgers decided to wade into this horrible problem. She had grown up thirty miles north of Cincinnati. Her parents were lawyers in her small town. She had left for Dartmouth and Harvard, for Barclays and McKinsey. Now she wanted to return. "I was bothered by my distance," she said. Rittgers had spent a prior summer at a venture-capital firm that had asked her to research the addiction-recovery space. She found a few solutions to the addiction epidemic out there, but nowhere near enough. She wanted to generate some more ideas.

Rittgers had the gall, beginning in about February 2017, to think that she could do better than the existing solutions to this evolving problem, that she could triumph over the pessimistic sense of "been there, tried that." And her big idea for big ideas? A hackathon. A weekend-long event that would engage Cincinnati's tech community to spur new thinking about the city's addiction epidemic.

Rittgers reached out. She enlisted the help of a local city councilor and old friend, P. G. Sittenfeld, and his director of community affairs, Colleen Reynolds. They enlisted Emily Geiger, a managing director at a local health-care-innovation lab. Together the group ventured further into the Cincinnati community to secure the hackathon's participants. They hoped to attract a broad group: software engineers, designers, and health-care professionals; experts but also (especially?) novices. They recruited undergraduates from the University of Cincinnati, IT professionals from Procter & Gamble, and the chief technology officer of a fashion-app startup. They also invited judges and wooed sponsors. They fanned out in the community to try to under-stand what the roadblocks were for solving the problem in Cincinnati and to try to narrow them to eight challenges the solvers would work on during the two-day event. They sat with city officials and service providers, including the ones I eventually met at Talbert House, and also individuals in recovery and family members. "There will con-tinue to be a lot of preventable deaths and wasted potential if the opioid crisis continues unabated," Rittgers told me in early spring. "The biggest threat with a crisis like this is the increasing feeling of hopelessness around solving it . . . Bright spots and positive momen-tum matter."

What was Rittgers thinking? Would this effort prove to be one of those bright spots? Or would the weekend prove that enlisting col-lege students and weekend warriors for two days to generate "new ideas" was no way to address a problem of epic proportions?

The view on public hackathons is mixed. There is some evidence that hackathons can speed the creation of new ideas.[41] One expert estimated that well-organized hackathons could reduce the time for companies to bring new products or services to market by 25 to 50 percent.[42] And there was hope that in the public sector the results could be similar. Advocates said that one of the outcomes of hack-athons is simply bringing people together who otherwise wouldn't have been; that useful relationships get built. Others argued it would save the public money: Products developed during a 2015 hacka-thon for the US General Services Administration were estimated to have saved the organization more than $500,000.[43] Other supporters pointed to the civic value of public hackathons, that they built a cul-ture of cooperation among people and their governments.

Critics argued that civic hackathons produced products that were often inherently incompatible with underlying systems.[44] They also questioned whether the products generated would be sustainable. One 2011 study found that of all the apps created during New York

City's BigApps Challenge, just 35 percent were operational after a year.[45] (This actually strikes me as quite encouraging. I would have thought the number would be lower.) Other critics argued that hackathon participants were not representative of broader societal demographics. Past studies indicated that at the average hackathon, for example, 80 percent of hackers were male and most were either White/Caucasian (44 percent) or Asian/Pacific Islander (42.2 percent).[46] Finally, hackathons had elicited some strong negative reactions when proposed as a solution for deeply entrenched, complex social problems. In March 2017, a Chicago-based tech worker suggested to a local paper that the city might consider organizing a hackathon to tackle violent crime.[47] In a response titled "A Citywide Hackathon? Please. Technology Alone Can't Solve Chicago's Murder Problem," three Chicagoans argued that solutions to this stubborn problem required systems-level thinking and problem solving as well as engagement from a wide variety of stakeholders.[48]

Rittgers hoped to avoid many of the possible critiques while making the most of the weekend. She'd taken steps to balance some of the tensions in setting up a productive hackathon:

- **Settling on challenges.** If your scope is too broad, it is too hard to come up with ideas. If it's too narrow, you risk over-specifying the solutions and crowding out innovation. Rittgers had settled on eight fairly specific challenges. They included increasing networks of support for families, a way to view bed capacity at providers, new models for more effectively distributing the antioverdose treatment naloxone, ways to help people in recovery find work, and others.

- **Getting the right data.** If you have too little to go on, your participants are shooting in the dark, possibly coming up with solutions that already exist. Too much, and they may be overwhelmed. The Hacking Heroin team worked closely with

Leigh Tami, who led the city's data-analytics efforts and who had produced a heroin dashboard available online. The team also made sure participants had access to Cincinnati's open data and even worked to share raw data sets from the dispatch systems first responders had been using across the city to address overdose calls.

- **Gathering the crowd.** You have to decide whether you want only people in person, so they can collaborate better, or whether you'll leverage online platforms to get a wider range of participants. You also want a range of insiders, who can explain the nature of the problem and even give firsthand knowledge, and outsiders, who bring fresh perspectives from a diverse range of backgrounds. Twenty-four people (divided into nine teams) ultimately participated in Hacking Heroin. Twenty more brought on-the-ground experience, from the public-safety/law-enforcement communities, from the recovery community, and/or from health care.

- **Rewarding attendees.** People attend for a mix of intrinsic and extrinsic motivations.[49] Some want the satisfaction of helping, while others want to network, want credit for what they produce, or are even looking to come away with a bit of money. Public hackathons often have limited resources and need to tailor the right rewards to the right kinds of attendees. Rittgers's group was able to secure modest cash prizes, credits to Microsoft's Azure cloud-computing product, and the opportunity for the winning teams to present their solutions to the Cincinnati city council and to Microsoft's civic-technology team.

- **Evaluating submissions.** There is merit to picking judges who will allow for new, creative solutions while also providing real-world knowledge of what might feasibly be put into use. In Cincinnati, an addiction specialist, a research scientist, a public official, and the CEO of Talbert House were slated to judge the final presentations.

- **Sustaining solutions.** Attendees at public hackathons often have their day jobs to go back to. You'll need a plan for porting their solutions into (sometimes resistant) agencies or for encouraging participants to take them up in earnest, with support. Rittgers hoped the promised meeting at city hall, along with ongoing support from a local innovation group and some potential pilot opportunities, would keep up the momentum.

In the end, Hacking Heroin generated many ideas, not all of them good. A few of them were, though, and one of those grew into a company that was making a real difference in Cincinnati three years later. It was a platform that provided real-time treatment-capacity information to patients in need and to providers. Rittgers called it "just one cool bright spot" and said it was "random and lucky." She was not precisely correct about that. When contests or competitions or reaching out broadly in other ways is done well, the bright spots aren't exactly matters of happenstance. They're a matter of knowing that there are lots of potential solutions out in the universe, along a spectrum from truly bad to really good. And if you invite enough entries and get enough diversity, you are likely to get draws from all along that spectrum, including one bright spot.

We Need More Bad Ideas

When Rittgers told me of her plans to host a hackathon on the opioid epidemic, I winced. When she told me she planned to call it Hacking

Heroin, I begged her not to. I thought the activity seemed all too specious and that the name just called attention to that fact. I now see why I was wrong and why she was right to pursue it. I now know what Jimmy Chen was really doing in a Brooklyn SNAP office, even if his first idea didn't turn out to be a winner, or his second. If we are going to truly solve our biggest problems, we are going to need to go after them in ways that generate extreme-value ideas, and we are going to need outsiders to help us. And since such ideas are a product of these processes, and since they come along with all manner of ideas, in order to solve our biggest problems, we are going to have to go after more bad ideas.

When Netflix offered a $1 million prize to get outsiders to enhance its movie-recommendation algorithm, the company received more than 44,000 ideas. More than two-thirds of them did worse than Netflix's own tools.[50] That means close to 30,000 bad ideas. But Netflix was unfazed. The one entry that eventually won the competition is what mattered to the company—and that entry was 10 percent better than what the company had come up with on its own. In governing, on our most pressing issues, we're likely to want to do more than 10 percent better. (Though we might take even that.) But the point is that to get there, we'll have to be okay with processes that generate plenty of ideas that are worse.

There are other reasons, too, that in the pursuit of good new ideas we need to tolerate bad new ones. Foremost, as the famed sociologist and organizational theorist James March wrote, "Inspiration and lunacy are not ex ante so clearly distinguishable."[51] At the outset of new projects, we'll have to take the bad with the good, lest we too quickly mistake the good for the bad. Moreover, March described how a competency trap seduces us into sticking with existing practices, because we have become relatively skilled at them, and this keeps us from pursuing new ones that will take us some time to master. Even good new policies and programs can look poor until we get the hang of them. New ideas look bad at first and get better over time.

March encouraged organizations to be "impatient with old ideas, which tend to be relatively good on average, but patient with new ideas, which tend to be relatively poor on average."[52] Only after meeting Jimmy Chen in Brooklyn and watching Annie Rittgers in Cincinnati and seeing citizen-centered and citizen-fueled brainstorms and government-sponsored contests did I understand the real power in them and what working to get beyond average ideas could mean in public life.

Sometimes March wrote about this patience for new ideas and the embracing of serendipity and inconsistency as "the technology of foolishness."[53] And sometimes people bought the argument generally but begged him not to recommend it where they were. "We have enough foolishness," one colleague told him, hoping that March might not show up where he lived and worked.

We have enough foolishness these days in our politics. We have bad ideas that are bad because we disregard the truth. We have bad ideas that are bad because ideology causes us to hold on to them. I see the foolishness in making the case for more bad ideas. But we can tolerate some more bad ideas—in fact, we need them—as long as we can, ultimately, figure out a way to pursue the good ones that come alongside. We have enough foolishness these days. But also not enough.

Government That Can Imagine

What possibility leaders can do

☆ Reframe missions around problems to be solved not resources we have.

☆ Build diverse teams—pick "not ducks."

☆ Enlist outsiders and the crowd, via contests, crowdsourcing, hackathons, and more.

☆ Engage users—find those for whom the need is important, and where and when it is important.

☆ Look for "desire lines."

☆ Foster psychological safety—make clear the need for people to speak up; create forums for input; listen; ask good questions; and communicate appreciation for new ideas.

☆ Multiply options—use brainstorming (invite "wild" ideas) and other techniques to generate more choices before selecting among them.

What possibility citizens can do

☆ Hold officials accountable for their missions, not just their budgets.

☆ Demand participation at the outset of policy-generating processes; object when public opinions are solicited only after recommendations have been made.

☆ Allow and even invite observation of your experiences with government services—but insist on privacy protections and accountability for follow-up enhancements.

☆ Participate in idea-generating activities like community hackathons and provide follow-up engagement.

☆ Make known your own needs *and* the needs of others. Develop empathy for theirs.

☆ Push officials to generate lists of possibilities before settling on one approach.

What everyone can do

☆ Reject best practices when best isn't good enough.

☆ Be impatient with old ideas. Be patient with new ones.

GOVERNMENT THAT CAN TRY NEW THINGS

3

Experimenting in Public

Y'all liars," one mayor said from the back of the classroom, not lightly, as I could tell from the look on his face. And not under his breath, as I could tell from the reactions of the thirty-nine other mayors in the room.[1]

To be fair, I had possibly set the mayors up. The first time I asked the question (with a different audience), I had no idea how people would respond to it. Not students. Not citizens. Not elected officials. But this was now the ninth or tenth time, and I had an inkling how these mayors might answer.

I'd asked them to put themselves in another leader's shoes: those of Mayor Miguel Mancera, in Mexico City in 2016. His government had tried to crowdsource a map of Mexico City's tangled bus system from several thousand volunteer riders. They had mapped what was thought to be 43 percent of the city's bus routes. Mancera was going to speak to the public about this initiative. What should he say about it? I gave the mayors three options.

Mancera should declare Mapatón a success:

A. Yes, because it was.

B. No, because it wasn't.

C. Yes, even though it wasn't.

There are people who answer A because half of a bus map in a place the size of Mexico City gathered over a few weeks with only a small amount of money is surely a success. There are those who answer B because, after all, what does one do with half of a bus map? And then there are the "liars." Between the last two options on the list, the choice is either admitting failure or "lying," and people I have polled overwhelmingly picked C. Half the room had done so before the mayor called them out.

I never imagined that would be the case when I first posed the question. I'd also never thought of those who picked "Yes, even though" as liars myself. At worst, they were probably guilty of trying too hard to find a silver lining. But if they were willing to work so hard to avoid acknowledging failure, imagine the lengths to which they might go to avoid being put in a position of risk in the first place.

This is what was on my mind when the mayor called out his colleagues from the back of the room. Not what they were saying or not saying, but what they were willing to try back in their cities— or perhaps not try, for fear of failing at it. They had laid out ambitious agendas to be sure, on raising income levels or slowing climate change, on enhancing schools and making streets safe. But what if what they were doing wasn't bold enough? What if their best-intentioned actions didn't stand a chance against the magnitude of the problems, because the really creative, bold, stand-a-chance solutions were too risky?

And what if that's the bigger lie? Not the one about bus maps and crowds working or not working, but about what it's going to take to solve society's greatest challenges. What if we are all liars, and the lie we are telling ourselves is that our governments can get to where we want them to without experimenting more? Is there anything we can do about that?

It turns out, in the techniques of modern startup companies, there might be. There might be ways to take on riskier efforts, in public, with some tools made popular by entrepreneurs like Eric Ries and others. I didn't know of Ries's lean-startup methods when I was in government or when I first heard of Gabriella Gómez-Mont and her lab inside Mexico City's government. But by the time I was done with my trip to see her there, and certainly when I was in that classroom two years later to talk with mayors about it, I had a better handle on what experimenting in public was, what made it hard, and what might make it easier.

Lab for the City

In Mexico, it started with a question I already knew the nonanswer to. A colleague and I had stopped by the concierge in the hotel where we were staying in Polanco, an upscale portion of Mexico City. The neighborhood sits in the northwestern corner of the giant city known as CDMX. It was also about ten kilometers from the offices of Laboratorio para la Ciudad, the experimental arm of Mexico City's municipal government at the time.

Laboratorio para la Ciudad (Laboratory for the City, in English) was founded by Gómez-Mont in 2013. She and her team of fewer than a dozen represented the innovation vanguard in a government of three hundred thousand workers. "The hope of Mexico today is reflected in the entrepreneurs," Mancera had said at the time on his campaign website, and he meant inside government, too. He had tapped Gómez-Mont to create the new city department from scratch.

Gómez-Mont and Mancera were not entirely unique in this ambition. Bloomberg Philanthropies and Nesta, a United Kingdom–based innovation foundation, had described twenty initiatives like this in 2014, from Denmark's Mindlab to Singapore's PS21.[2] I had cofounded one of them in Boston in 2010, which we called the Mayor's Office of New Urban Mechanics. The idea, broadly, was to create spaces in government—somehow outside the normal confines of the bureaucracy—in which to try new things. In that respect, these offices weren't that different from corporate innovation arms like Xerox's PARC, founded in 1970, or more modern versions like Amazon Lab126.[3] Of note is that for all the successful products that emerged from these innovation hubs—Ethernet at Xerox or the Kindle at Amazon—the overall record on these things was decidedly mixed.[4] As it turns out, business, not just government, struggles to invent new products and services, too. Nevertheless, by 2018, more government "labs" had come to prominence, including San Francisco's Office of Civic Innovation and New York City's NYCx. And along with government digital services, which we will come to in chapter 6, the proliferation of these government innovation arms marked a key organizational shift in the move toward a more inventive public sector. The offices had different setups and different acronyms, but many were drawing to some degree on the startup techniques of private companies. I visited Gómez-Mont in Mexico to see these tools up close and try to gauge whether I thought they were fit for public stuff.

"How do we get there by bus?" we asked the concierge. After some back-and-forth about whether we really wanted to take the bus, and wouldn't we rather go by car, he confessed that there really was no comprehensive bus map to consult.

I already knew that.

Gómez-Mont's lab had run many experiments by the time I was bothering the hotel's staff for an answer I knew they didn't have. The experiment to create a bus map for Mexico City was the lab's fiftieth. Thirty thousand public buses, minibuses, and vans made up the Mexico City bus system, and there was no comprehensive schedule.

Gómez-Mont and her team had set out to change that. In the spring of 2015, they'd decided to try to create a bus map by inviting citizens to voluntarily ride Mexico City's bus routes and record them on their smartphones. It was an approach that had been tried in some developing countries but never in a developed city the size of Mexico's capital.

There were more conventional alternatives. The city could have purchased GPS technology for the buses, though that would have cost an estimated 60 million pesos ($3 million). It could have passed a law requiring the operators to record the information of the routes they drove, though that raised the prospect of a strike by the operator unions. City agencies could have hired people to ride routes and write down route information, but the LabCDMX team, as Gómez-Mont's outfit was called, estimated that that would take up to two years to complete.

The wild idea to instead crowdsource a bus map for Mexico City picks up on some of the techniques and attitudes in chapter 2 on ideas. Gómez-Mont had formed a team that included artists and designers, that welcomed in outsiders, and that held mini-hackathons. In their approach, you could sense art mixed in with the science of it all. The lab called its initial forays "provocations." Art and social progress had been intertwined for generations in Mexico City. Gómez-Mont and her team were coming full circle to some extent.

But as we walked away from the concierge—and took a car to see Gómez-Mont—I was most interested not in how the idea had come to be but rather how the project had unfolded. "A thousand things could have gone wrong . . ." Gómez-Mont told me, as she started to recount.

Probability versus Possibility

If Probability Government and Possibility Government were twin siblings, raised on a set of common ideas (that outcomes supersede politics, that data matters), this is where they decide to go their own way.

Probability Government preaches the gospel of prudence. Of what's worked before. Of best practices. Probability Government hates risk. Probability Government really hates that "a thousand things could go wrong." I've asked government groups how their organizations normally proceed in the face of the kinds of uncertainties Gómez-Mont was anticipating, and someone always says, "They don't."

Probability Government picks sure bets. Or at least surer bets. It picks the approaches that will probably work. If we don't stop to think about it very long, or perhaps even if we do, this seems to be how government should be and what government should do. Government is often the backstop in citizens' lives; a thing they need to be able to rely on, for food or for safety. Government is paying with taxpayer money, not funds we expect to be gambled away. We expect government to spend time and money on things that will work.

This is the vision of government that people have in mind when they label government risk averse. We throw those words around a lot, but what risk aversion actually means could be the key to the problem with Probability Government, to the possibility of Possibility Government, and to solving big problems.

Individuals who are risk averse prefer more-certain outcomes over uncertain outcomes, even when the uncertain outcomes have higher expected returns. A risk-neutral person will be indifferent if you offer her $50 or if you offer her a 50 percent chance at winning either $100 or $0. The expected value of both is identical. A risk-averse person will prefer the $50 guaranteed. And depending on how risk averse a person is, she might prefer that $50 guaranteed even if you raise her potential prize: say, a 50 percent chance at $120, which has an expected value of $60. But if she's someone who strongly prefers certainty to risk, she would gladly give up the chance at an extra $10 for the surety of the $50. When people say government is risk averse, this is presumably the kind of thinking they have in mind.

Are they correct? I went looking for evidence to the contrary. I had witnessed episodes that gave rise to the worst versions of this stereotype: public workers who are just showing up for the paycheck or government officials who are just biding time until they can collect their pensions. The last, absolute last thing they would ever do is take a risk on anything that would put their jobs or their retirement in jeopardy. I remember the day a city worker stepped into the elevator on the first floor of Boston's city hall and explained to a friend, who had inquired about how his day was going, that he planned to read the paper and count the days until his retirement. But my own experience gave me hope that this was the exception and not the rule. I had mostly seen brave and bold public servants, who genuinely wanted to help people, who prioritized citizen needs above their own risk mitigation strategies.

The data backs up the stereotype. Not the worst version of it, but the version where public workers are less likely to take chances. Two economists who looked at the question of risk aversion in the public sector in the 1980s found that people perceived, accurately, that government jobs were more stable than private-sector ones.[5] They found, further, that individuals who placed a heavy emphasis on job stability were more likely to seek employment in the public sector. A more recent study lent support to this notion, finding that people holding public-sector jobs, as compared with people in private-sector roles, are even less likely to buy lottery tickets than they are gift certificates.[6]

A thousand things could have gone wrong with Gómez-Mont's mapping experiment. So why did she proceed anyway? Either she had a different attitude toward risk than typical government workers do. Or she had a plan for reducing some of that risk.

A Mapping Marathon

Gómez-Mont started our conversation by naming some of the thousand things: "The politics might not work. Maybe we won't get interest from our colleagues within government. We might not have the internal capacity—the know-how—that is needed to get this off the ground. Our algorithm might not work. The gamification might not work. We might not be able to make the data actionable . . . Our backend could have failed. The dashboard could have gone horribly wrong. If no people jumped on board, we would have had nothing. If they did jump on board all at the same time, they could have crashed it."

She told me how they proceeded anyway. They started over a four-day period in May 2015 using a route-tracking app Gómez-Mont and her team knew probably wouldn't be the solution for Mexico City. If she was worried about a thousand things going wrong, picking an off-the-shelf app she was sure wasn't going to carry the load seemed like an odd choice. Twenty-eight riders participated and mapped 18 routes, but the app drained the life of the cell phones. LabCDMX decided to build its own.

The team made a second go at it in August that year. This time they recruited high school students as mappers. Thirty of them mapped

56 routes. The app LabCDMX built with collaborators functioned imperfectly, and the collected data was full of errors.

A third attempt was made in October, this time with university students. Nearly two hundred of them mapped 248 routes. There were still some errors in the data collection, using an enhanced app, but the team collected some useful feedback about which rewards for participating (cash? prizes?) were most desirable. A fourth version, in November, involved the participation of bus drivers.

On January 29, 2016, Gómez-Mont and her team launched Mapatón's finale. More than 3,600 riders took part. In all, the series of events resulted in 648 route maps. One participant even spent more than nine hours riding a bus to the outskirts of Mexico City and back. Stretched end to end, the mapped routes would reach all the way around the globe. They covered 43 percent of what the team thought were 1,500 bus routes across the city.

We know by now what the hundreds of people I've polled thought of this outcome. Approximately half thought it was a success. The other half didn't, but didn't want to say so. What did Gómez-Mont take away from it all? She told me, "We need to be thinking much more about lean methodology."

Build-Measure-Learn

"Lean" came of age in operations and manufacturing. I find it helpful to mention so at the outset, because it warns us away from thinking of the concept as a techie thing for techie people, in case we don't view ourselves that way. In the operations and manufacturing context, *lean* meant minimizing waste and reducing errors on the assembly line in order to achieve manufacturing excellence and higher productivity.

In the context Gómez-Mont mentioned, *lean* means something very similar. No doubt she picked it up from Eric Ries or one of his acolytes. Ries had been applying it in a more tech-oriented context, often for startups.[7] The idea was still about minimizing waste. But now it was about minimizing waste as companies fought their way to find products for markets and markets for their new products. The idea was to learn as much as possible while spending the least amount of time, energy, and treasure.

Ries wrote about the concept in his bestselling book *The Lean Startup*, alerting a generation of would-be entrepreneurs to the idea of "minimally viable products" and "pivots." He also wrote about it with Tom Eisenmann, a colleague of mine. The first time I really dug into lean-startup techniques, it was for reasons as far removed from government as possible. I learned about lean when it came to renting ball gowns.

Eisenmann had written a Harvard Business School case on two graduates of the school who had set out to create a dress-rental company.[8] Jenny Fleiss and Jenn Hyman figured there was a better alternative for women than buying an expensive gown they would wear on only one or two occasions. The two created Rent the Runway to rent dresses to women instead. First, the founders held a trunk show event at Harvard College, using dresses they had bought off the shelf. Later, they ran another event at Yale, this time with only dress swatches. Then came the PDF brochure they circulated, asking people to call a number to rent dresses. Then, and only then, did they really build out a dress-rental platform and the company to go with it.

And in there, in the story of trunk shows and dress styles, is the essence of the lean startup, of what Gómez-Mont was trying to do in Mexico City, and of what might be the key to Possibility Government. To allow government to try things that probably won't work.

When Hyman and Fleiss started out, building a dress-rental company was probably going to fail. Not just because back then the idea of renting dresses evoked ill-fitting tuxedos and soiled celebratory wear more than it did the newfound interest in sharing assets. Rent the Runway was probably going to fail because most startups fail. Even most startups that receive venture money probably won't succeed. First-time founders who raise venture capital fail more than 80 percent of the time. Those who buck the odds and succeed still fail on their sophomore effort 70 percent of the time.[9]

Rent the Runway's cofounders didn't try to plan or study their way out of this probability. Instead, they tested their way out. The Harvard trunk show, limited in numbers though it was, proved to them that women would rent dresses. It also showed them that women wanted different styles. The Yale event showed them that women would rent dresses they couldn't try on. The PDF demonstrated that women would rent dresses they couldn't try on, over an electronic platform. Each test resolved a key uncertainty facing the business. And each test did so relatively quickly and with relatively low investment.

Ries made the name for these kinds of testable prototypes—minimally viable products (MVPs)—globally famous. And he made the changes that naturally followed, pivots, common startup parlance. He, Eisenmann, and Sarah Dillard wrote up a handful of other examples that make the concepts clear.[10] When Drew Houston started Dropbox, he didn't start by building a complicated offline-backup-sync-and-share software but rather by creating a video about it and inviting people to sign up for it when it was developed. He answered the question about whether people wanted yet another storage solution (it was perhaps the eightieth on the market at the time) without first having to build one. When the team behind Aardvark set out to build an app that let you text in a question to be selectively broadcast to your social network for answers, they didn't build the complicated algorithm to do that. They simply hired humans to mine the network in place of technology, for the time being. They tried to answer the question of whether people would use a social-network-question-answering app before building the whole kit and caboodle.

Once I started to understand these approaches, I started to see them in other places. Including government. When President Barack Obama's administration launched Data.gov, the US open-data platform, in 2009, one of the first of its kind in the world, the platform had only forty-seven data sets.[11] To put that in perspective, there are fifteen cabinet-level agencies in the US government, and forty-seven barely allowed three data sets for each of them. Imagine how difficult it must have been for the team at the time to turn data sets (and the officials championing them) away. Don't you want to launch with a relatively complete set of US data? With something robust? I marvel at the fact that it must have been even more difficult to send out the president to announce this, when a guy named Robert from New Jersey created his own version of the site with more data than the government's official one.[12] Why do that? Why start with something incomplete, with something less than Robert can put together in his basement? For the same reason Hyman and Fleiss started with just forty students and off-the-shelf dresses. The notion of the lean startup was to learn the most—about what customers wanted, how they would use products, how you would deliver products to them—while spending the least. To try, to test, and to learn. Would citizens seek out the data? Would they be able to access it technically? Would the data they did access be kept up to date by agencies? Would the data be used to learn anything fruitful about government or to create new private businesses? To answer the early questions that the Data.gov team had didn't at first require building out the entire website with 260,000 data sets (as it has now) but rather building out just enough to put in citizens' hands to get some valid feedback.

Reflected back through the lens of Ries, of Eisenmann, of Rent the Runway, and of Data.gov, Gómez-Mont's Mapatón made a lot more sense to me. Could the LabCDMX team accurately collect information on formal and informal stops? That was the question answered by the May experiment. Could outsiders successfully contribute? August answered that. Could a game motivate engagement? Would cash prizes work? October. Could the collected data be leveraged and made useful? January's experiment and time would tell. Run all the tests at once, and if the project failed, the team would never specifically know why. But run them separately, and quickly, and the team learned something each time, and had a chance to iterate and to improve.

This is the process Ries calls *lean startup*. It's what he, Eisenmann, and Dillard called "hypothesis-driven entrepreneurship" in the paper that introduced me to the process. Perhaps its simplest formulation is build, measure, learn. Laid out like that, for government, the simplicity of the formulation can hide just how fundamentally it upends the way most of us do what we do (see figure 3-1).

In government, *build* usually comes last. And if you listen to the groups I have polled about how we normally manage risks like those Gómez-Mont faced, build usually comes after the consultants, the commissions, the conference rooms, the request for proposals, etc. Build comes after all the apparatus of Probability Government. But in the startup model, it comes first.

A PayPal Account and a Post Office Box

One other thing looked different to me in light of build, measure, learn, and it was what came after the bombs had blown up at the marathon's finish line. "You can't start something new," the foundation

FIGURE 3–1

Build-measure-learn

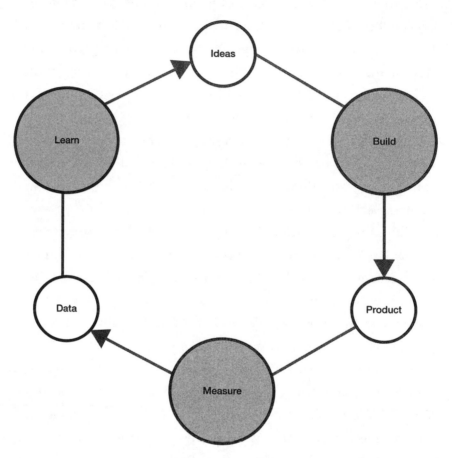

head had told me. He was probably right that among many things, people would feel skittish about donating to a brand-new fund with no infrastructure and no history. We proceeded anyway, and Mayor Menino insisted we have the fund up and running by Tuesday night, little more than twenty-four hours after the attacks. We made his deadline, barely, and with only a barebones website. It had one sentence and a PayPal link. That's it. But that night, the funds starting flowing in. People asked us for the mailing address—which we had neglected to procure or include—so the next morning I opened up a post office box, and we added the address to the website. Four days later, after a manhunt that froze a city and left one terrorist dead and another captured, I rode with the mayor back to where he was staying in Beacon Hill. We watched the president address the nation. I wandered through the Boston Common, where college students had come to sing "God Bless America," on my way to the post office on Boylston Street, which I had chosen for a bit of solemn poetry. I emptied the box's overflowing contents into a black bag that I had brought with me.

Would people give to a new fund? With nothing more than a PayPal account and a post office box, we had seemed to answer at least that question. Later, we built out the site, with how to file a claim, how the monies would be distributed, how to share with friends, who had given. Had we built everything first, we would have gotten things wrong. We also would have gotten out of the gate much more slowly and perhaps not before the world's attention had moved on to another tragedy. I wasn't thinking build, measure, learn, not in any formal sense, at the time. I don't know how clearly we were thinking at all. But One Fund Boston serves as a potentially powerful lesson in the virtues of MVPs.

Honesty, Possibly

It's a myth that most entrepreneurs like risk, and it would be a mistake to think the lesson of Possibility Government is to go out and seek it. The point is, rather, that risk is inherent in doing bold, new things. What build, measure, learn gives us is a way of resolving some of those risks without spending too much public treasure. We start with a set of assumptions about what needs to go right if some new service is to be successful. And we test those assumptions, often one by one. If we can't validate them, then we stop. And we go spend our time and the taxpayers' money on something else. In startup lingo, we "perish" the project. If the data comes back and suggests some changes to our assumptions, we pivot. Maybe it's the same service but for a different constituency. Maybe it's a different service but for the same constituency. We change some aspects of what we are doing and test again. And if the signs come back all positive, then we persevere.

It would be wrong, on most counts, to think of entrepreneurs as risk seekers. It's wrong, I think, to think of Gómez-Mont that way. She likely had more of an appetite for risk than that city worker in the elevator riding toward retirement, but that doesn't mean she was actively seeking it. It's not like "a thousand things could have gone wrong" was a magnet for her. By that logic, I suppose "two thousand things could have gone wrong" would have been even better. What allowed her, then, to go after possibility instead of probability must have been some strategy she had for reducing her risks—to get from "a thousand" potential failure points to something less than that.

Build, measure, learn also gives us, if we will take it, a way to stop lying. When things don't work out, public officials should be able to say, "We ran a test. We ran it without spending too much time and money. The test proved that either our idea or our execution was wrong. We'll learn from the failure and move on."

One public leader pushed back on me when I proposed this route. "It's not your name in the newspaper every day," she said, polite not to call me naïve and too removed from the action to know better. She also might have been right to proceed more cautiously. I know the internal narrative that gets us to where she got: If I make a mistake and admit it, the press will pillory me. The public will doubt me. My opponents will challenge me. My allies will desert me.

I think the opposite may be true, though. I believe that if we pointed out our missteps, it would be better than having the press uncover them. With trust in public officials where it is today, it is quite possible that actual honesty could increase public faith. One study illustrated that operational transparency by government increases public trust in government and engagement with it. The paper was called "Surfacing the Submerged State."[13] We should surface the experimental state, too. We'd start not by saying we want to take on more risk. We don't. What we would say is that the way we mostly build now, planning for years on end and then delivering programs or services that fall flat with the public, is high risk, too. And that there is a better way instead. That we can buy down the risk of trying new things, if we build, measure, and learn.

4

Regulating the Future

When Airbnb arrived in a city during the late 2000s, it was more with a whisper than a shout.[1] Arriving was just a matter of one host listing one spare bedroom at first, so it happened without much fanfare and often without the knowledge of the city it was in. Other technologies made a bigger splash when they came to town: Uber and Lyft's ridesharing; same for Didi, Grab, and Careem. Dockless bikes. Electric scooters. Delivery robots and robot cars. But either way, eventually, governments are pressured to react . . . or not. When possibility chases you, which one will it be?

That choice, to do something or nothing, faced Nanette Schippers and colleagues in Amsterdam's city government as Airbnb opened there in 2008 and then grew. Along with the listings, so too came the complaints: Too much noise next door. Too many hordes of tourists. Too much of turning one of Europe's gem downtowns into Disneyland. Too little tax revenue. Too little enforcement of the rules.

Too little enforcement of the rules? Schippers, who worked in Amsterdam's innovation office and became the city's adviser on the sharing economy, would first have to sort out what the rules even were. What did the city's "short-stay rental regulations"—on the books before Airbnb came to town and mainly to address longer business travel—have to say about the swell of one-night stays? And whatever they said, what did that leave Schippers and her colleagues to do?

Molly Turner faced a similar kind of sorting out. She was the global head of civic partnerships for Airbnb. She was the person the company turned to when word arrived at their San Francisco headquarters of a February 2013 article: "Airbnb Could Be Banned in Amsterdam: Local Authorities Are Now Hunting for Illegal Hotels."[2] Banned? In Amsterdam? Wasn't this one of the world's most permissive cities? Wasn't this the place where prostitution and pot were legal?

Well, no. Prostitution, yes, but the use of cannabis was not legal in Amsterdam (despite what you may have thought, or have done). The use of cannabis lived in an unusual state of existence. It was *gedogen*. Illegal, but tolerated. It was against the law, but deliberately ignored. As I came to understand *gedogen*, certain things started to make more sense to me, such as the Airbnb listings I scanned as I prepared for my trip to see Schippers: "No hard drugs." Also the necessarily euphemistic "coffee shops" I walked past as I wandered the city. But *gedogen* also seemed to explain the regulatory path that Schippers and her colleagues would eventually choose, and the negotiating dance they would end up in with Turner and hers. It could even explain how home sharing came to rival the hotel industry and how Airbnb hosts came to welcome well over one hundred million visits worldwide each year. But *gedogen* might also hold some lessons for how governments and their citizens think about regulating the onslaught of new technologies headed their way; how they think about regulating the future.

Hopes and Fears

The short-stay rental challenge in Amsterdam was a trickle and then a flood. For years before the threatened crackdown on "illegal hotels," the city's short-stay rental regulations had been circumvented. The rules were meant to permit longer business stays—a week or more—in the city, but companies like Booking and CityMundo were listing daily rentals long before Airbnb existed. Schippers's colleague Albert Eefting, who was the city's senior policy adviser for housing affairs, explained, "Even though these kinds of sites had already existed for many years, the number of houses listed on them was very small. Airbnb made it larger scale." In 2015, 575,000 inbound guests used the Airbnb platform to find a place to lay their head at night in Amsterdam.[3]

In 2012, still unsure of what the rules really allowed and what would make good public policy anyway, officials in Amsterdam began the process that would shape their response. They initiated a review of the short-stay rental regulations and organized the first of many meetings on home sharing. They invited the city's leading hoteliers and Airbnb. An Airbnb lawyer recalled the first meetings as "pretty aggressive," with hoteliers "essentially saying that what we were doing was dangerous and irresponsible." The hotel managers cited lax city enforcement for lukewarm capacity (and lower room rates) at their establishments and laid the blame at Airbnb's feet. A second meeting unfolded similarly. The Airbnb lawyer noted, "There was a lot more screaming and shouting, a lot of, 'Who do you think you *are* coming to our city?'"

Turner then entered the conversations in person. She was based at Airbnb's offices in San Francisco, where she'd worked since becoming one of the company's early employees and its first to focus on city relations. She was an urban planner by training and a believer in the power of community-based tourism as an economic driver for cities. She pitched her eventual role to Airbnb cofounder Brian Chesky, telling him, "I think you can grow the business by partnering with cities."⁴ Airbnb had gotten big enough that the regulatory concerns that would later lead to full-fledged battles in New York City and San Francisco and to the unfolding negotiations in Amsterdam were starting to need attention. Chesky walked Turner over to his recruiter on the spot and said, "Set Molly up." In 2011, she became perhaps the first person in a public-policy role at any of the new wave of sharing-economy companies that would end up tapping into cities' biggest hopes and fears. Now she was headed to Amsterdam to try to tip the scales away from "Who do you think you *are?*"

There were several tasks to accomplish across the Atlantic. First, Turner set out to learn more about Amsterdam's opportunities and challenges. The city had been investing heavily in tourism and had been attracting big industries and building an innovation economy.⁵ Quality of life was high, but that also meant that housing was in high demand—55 percent of it was publicly subsidized. The city had for generations been plagued by issues of space and had resorted to innovative means to create it. Amsterdam's iconic canal system had been dug from swampland to accommodate an exploding population in the seventeenth century. The more recent creation of artificial islands to the southeast of the city center was conceived to ease a still-chronic housing shortage.⁶ Residents were complaining that tourists were taking over their city, blocking bike rides to work with roller suitcases, and that the landlords racing to accommodate them were driving up housing prices and soaking up scarce supply. Turner and the Airbnb team also wanted to share some data in the other direction. She presented one of the company's first economic-impact studies to the city's various stakeholders and tried to convey what an economic engine the company had been for city residents and the extent to which hosts were actually attracting tourists to more outlying parts of the city. The efforts appeared to bear fruit. Hostile public meetings partly gave way to a new working relationship between city officials and company ones.

Toleration

The next order of business for both groups was to figure out whether the short-stay rentals that Airbnb's platform enabled were legal. Amsterdam's web of housing regulations made it difficult to discern at first. Eefting and a colleague, Leila Frank, continued with their meetings and also consulted with lawyers to try to sort out what exactly was allowed under current law. The city had hotel policies, which regulated hotels. There were short-stay policies targeted for business travelers, and these covered visits that were a minimum of seven nights. More conventional bed-and-breakfasts were regulated and allowed under the hotel policy, but they paid tourist taxes and reported to district councils for permitting. Where did Airbnb hosts fall? The lawyers counseled that the short-term stays were probably prohibited under this web of rules, but that a suit to curtail them might not prevail in court.

All the while, to the extent that Airbnb-enabled short stays were illegal in Amsterdam, they existed for the moment in a state of *gedogen*. (The great "hunt" for illegal hotels had not materialized, by and large.) *Gedogen* has a long and broad history in the Netherlands, tracing back to religious tolerance in the 1600s and further. It stretched from there forward over time and came to include a kind of moral, cultural, and political tolerance. One famous scholar called it "a way to defer negative reactions to things that are not morally approved," explaining how it was core to Dutch living, paving the way for things like cannabis consumption and euthanasia.[7]

Another author explained an episode of *gedogen* that took place in Amsterdam four hundred years before Airbnb arrived there, and that at least faintly foreshadowed the modern-day housing dilemma. "There was still a war on, and it was feared that any outlying buildings could be taken over by the Spanish and used as bases for attack. Thus it was against the law to build outside the city walls," he explained. "But as the city grew, people wantonly ignored the law. Look at any of the many maps and paintings that exist from, say, 1600 to 1610, and you find dozens if not hundreds of buildings of various types beyond the walls, along with neatly laid-out gardens and fences."[8] Dutch tolerance and *gedogen* had faced their share of pushback and pitfalls. Schippers and her team followed in a long tradition, but whether they were wise to do so was yet to be sorted out.

In February 2014, Amsterdam provided some regulatory clarity that was meant to eliminate any lingering ambiguity. Officials added a third category, "private vacation rental," to their short-stay policies. They formally allowed short-term vacation rentals to tourists, in groups of up to four people, provided that tourist taxes were paid and that properties were rented on a short-term basis for no more than two months a year, in aggregate. In the news, this move was widely interpreted as legalizing Airbnb. Airbnb itself hailed the development in a press release, saying, "This policy is great news for the Airbnb community in Amsterdam."

Turner and her team's relief would not last long. Now the company—which had come to represent approximately 70 percent of short-term rentals in Amsterdam, and which would be firmly blamed if short-stay proliferation led to bedlam—would have to make the new regulations work. Eefting, the housing adviser, sent Turner a post–press release email: "Congratulations. Our work is not done."

Moreover, Airbnb and its city partners would have to adapt to the new regulations amid recently muddied political waters. Shortly after the new policy was announced, municipal elections were held in Amsterdam, and the new alderman for housing affairs hailed from the only party to oppose the rental policy in the city council. Turner knew that because of this, city leaders would "ask all the same tough questions and more."

The big questions fell into three main buckets: *eerlijk*, *velig*, and *rustig*. Amsterdam officials wanted Airbnb's help in keeping short-term stays *fair*, *safe*, and *quiet*. Hotels were complaining about how unfair it was that the city collected tourism taxes (5 percent on room rental rates) from hotels and registered bed-and-breakfasts and was not making a more concerted effort to collect them from Airbnb hosts, despite the earlier announcements. Airbnb seemed inclined to give in on this request. Tanja De Coster, one of the company's in-house lawyers in Europe, explained, "For us, helping our hosts to remit taxes was a way of legitimizing our business." (This evolving interest in paying taxes became a companywide strategy and led to the odd occurrence of the company actually lobbying states, including my home state of Massachusetts, for the so-called Airbnb tax.) Capping group sizes at four and limiting short-term rentals to a maximum of two months per year would help address the "safe" and "quiet" parts of the agenda. Officials also wanted Airbnb's help doing education on the new rules. Airbnb seemed inclined to play ball on those points, too.

The two parties set out to create a memorandum of understanding (MOU) to formalize their agreements on these three fronts, but struggled to settle on one that suited both sides. The memorandum was De Coster's idea. "An MOU shows you are cooperating. You are doing something. You are agreeing to a target. But it is nonbinding. It's dating. We are not married. We are not even engaged." But over the summer of 2014, Airbnb and Amsterdam couldn't come to an agreement on even this nonbinding framework. Amsterdam officials wanted Airbnb's help on preventive enforcement. For example, they wanted the company to adjust the platform's algorithms to block illegal listings (like those that violated maximum-stay amounts). They also wanted help actively enforcing the city's rules—for example, by blocking hosts and addresses from the platform after they've been discovered to be in violation of the rules. And Amsterdam officials wanted addresses and other data from the company, so that they could enforce the rules themselves. Airbnb was wary of setting any precedents on enforcement and data sharing, which might then be sought in other cities, and said it was harder to make the platform work in the ways city officials imagined.

Airbnb was especially keen not to agree to anything that would threaten its perceived "platform" status. The company, like others in the sharing economy and in internet-based businesses more widely, had claimed legal immunity from content that users posted on its platform, citing Section 230 of the US Communications Decency Act, which was understood by these companies to provide broad—and valuable—protection from illegal behavior by their users. As summer stretched into fall and then winter, Airbnb refused to concede on data-sharing and enforcement mechanisms. Turner worried about the precedent these concessions would set for Airbnb's operations in other cities, but she also never underestimated the importance of reaching agreement in Amsterdam. "We just thought that Amsterdam is so open-minded and so visionary that if they couldn't embrace this activity, then who could?"

In December, Airbnb and Amsterdam did, finally, sign an MOU. It was billed as the most comprehensive agreement that Airbnb had ever reached with any city in the world. Airbnb agreed to prominently display the new rules on its platform and to force hosts to actively declare that they understood and would comply with them. Airbnb would send email updates twice a year reminding hosts of the regulations. In order to reduce repeat offenders, Airbnb would remove listings when Amsterdam had determined that there had been violations of the new policy at an address and had notified Airbnb. And as part of a side agreement, the company would collect and remit tourist taxes. The MOU finished with a sense of mutuality: "The parties trust that theirs will be a fruitful cooperation."[9]

If you read the full MOU, you might well have your doubts. Airbnb made no commitment on data sharing in Amsterdam's direction and no substantial commitments on preventive enforcement, except for delisting documented repeat offenders. Airbnb called the agreement "good news for residents who share their homes through Airbnb," and it certainly appeared that way. And the company wrote that the agreement "furthers Amsterdam's reputation for being a hospitable city that embraces innovation and the sharing economy."[10] On the looks of it, hospitable indeed.

More Red Carpet?

On September 12, 2016, Pittsburgh's Mayor Bill Peduto tweeted out a photo of himself and Subra Suresh, the president of Carnegie Mellon University, taken in the back of a car.[11] "The first ordered autonomous @Uber ride in Pittsburgh," he captioned it, heralding the arrival of robot taxis in the Steel City.[12] In addition to his seatbelt, Peduto was wearing an optimistic grin, and no wonder. The city had been enjoying an economic rebirth, much of it now tech-driven. Pittsburgh seemed on the way toward regaining its glory days when it was an industrial powerhouse. Peduto and others were working to make it a hub of automation and artificial intelligence and, it was hoped, a job creator and opportunity ladder. Some of the best work in the world on these fronts was being done by the robotics experts at Carnegie Mellon, and others were coming to the city to join. Uber pledged $1 billion for the development of a facility with a test track in Pittsburgh's Hazelwood neighborhood, and there was hope that other investments would follow the ones that were beginning to pour in.[13] One observer called Uber's arrival "gasoline on the fire," but meant it in a good way.

At the get-go, Uber had a more-than-willing partner in Mayor Peduto, even if his defense of the company raised eyebrows. In early 2016, the state's Public Utility Commission fined Uber $11.4 million for operating its ridesharing business in Pennsylvania without permission.[14] Pittsburgh submitted a letter of support for the company. Critics warned that Peduto was giving away the keys to the city to a company that had "a reputation for running roughshod over regulators and municipalities." Peduto defended his approach. "It's not our role to throw up regulations or limit companies like Uber. You can either put up red tape or roll out the red carpet. If you want to be a 21st century laboratory for technology, you roll out the red carpet."[15]

By early 2017, the grins were gone and Karina Ricks, head of Pittsburgh's Department of Mobility and Infrastructure, described Pittsburgh–Uber as "a love affair that went south." Uber hadn't helped the city go after a federal Smart Cities grant in ways the mayor had wanted. The company hadn't been sharing data on automated rides with the city. And it began charging passengers who received rides in the experimental vehicles without alerting the city that it was now monetizing its testing ground. Peduto made it increasingly clear that he thought Uber was failing to uphold its end of the bargain. "Pittsburgh has a really strong view of partnership," he explained, "After the Uber rollout, we saw that it was only going to be a one-way street."

A year later, a fatality on the other side of the country would further test Peduto's hands-off approach. On March 18, 2018, an Uber autonomous vehicle (AV) traveling at forty miles per hour fatally struck a forty-nine-year-old woman in Tempe, Arizona.[16] Uber immediately suspended operations in San Francisco, Toronto, and Pittsburgh. Arizona's Governor Doug Ducey banned Uber's self-driving vehicles from the state's roads. In late May, Uber announced that it planned to bring self-driving cars back to Pittsburgh. Peduto's team was caught by surprise, and Peduto himself tweeted back at the company: "You never informed us of today's announcement. You never followed up on my requirements after a fatality in Arizona . . . Time to change!"[17] He advocated for a speed limit of twenty-five miles per hour for AVs, saying, "These are our streets. They belong to the people of the city of Pittsburgh, and the people of the city of Pittsburgh should be able to have certain criteria that shows them that safety is being taken first."[18]

As it looked increasingly likely that Uber's AVs would be back in Pittsburgh, it was still unclear how welcome they should be. In December 2018, the New York Times reported that Uber was "close to putting its autonomous vehicles back on the road" in Pittsburgh, in a "drastically reduced version of earlier efforts." The company would "run vehicles on a mile loop between two company offices in Pittsburgh, and they won't exceed 25 mph," Uber had said.[19] But around the same time, reports emerged that earlier Uber AV accidents resulting in damage had gone unreported in Pittsburgh.[20] Peduto's team said they were at work crafting new incident-reporting rules and drafting a proposal that would lay out the kind of information sharing they would expect for self-driving car firms.[21]

In March 2019, Peduto announced a formal set of "Pittsburgh Principles" that covered autonomous vehicles and their testing. The five most prominent entities working on autonomous driving systems in the city joined for the announcement. The mayor issued an executive order assigning responsibility for the development of "transparent and constructive" reporting guidelines to a city department. The principles documented an ambition for new mobility technology and services that would prioritize people and human safety, advance economic and environmental sustainability, and increase data sharing and communication.[22] The city also created a new submission process around testing, outlining how companies that were pursuing autonomous-vehicle testing in the city of Pittsburgh would alert the city to their reasons for testing and their manner of testing (what cars, what areas, what times, etc.) and acknowledge the Pittsburgh Principles. Reporting would also extend past the beginning of testing, to include follow-ups that documented significant crashes, among other information. Early press coverage of the announcement noted that there were "no penalties outlined in the executive order for companies that do not cooperate." City officials replied that they did not "want to start on that foot."[23] Hospitable, again.

The Status Quo Is the Risky Choice

I had come to Pittsburgh wanting to understand how public officials could try dangerous things, or could allow them to be tried. I'd been chastened by people's reluctance to talk about bus-map failure in Mexico City, and I'd wanted to see how public leaders could manage real failure, even fatal mistakes. In my search for possibility I kept hoping to find willingness, but now I wondered if what I was seeing was wantonness. How do you explain a mayor who went from fuming to being so friendly?

Vehicle-related deaths in the United States in 2017 topped forty thousand.[24] A survey of statistics from 2005–2007 found that 94 percent of vehicular crashes were caused by human error.[25] More than one million people were dying from car accidents every year across the globe, with twenty to fifty million more getting injured or disabled. Road crashes topped the list of causes of death among people aged fifteen to nineteen. A thousand people under the age of twenty-five were dying every day on the world's roads.[26] A reason to allow robot cars in 2019 was that humans were driving vehicles and killing people.

Two RAND researchers compared the outcomes for putting AVs on the road sooner and later. They published a study in 2017 contrasting two policies that could be adopted in the United States: Allow AVs to be deployed at scale in 2020, when the vehicles were predicted to be just slightly better than human drivers; essentially once their fatality rate was one fatality per one hundred million vehicle miles traveled. Or, adopt a more stringent stance and wait until 2040, when the predicted AV fatality rate was 0.11 fatalities per one hundred million miles; nearly perfect. The researchers concluded that over the fifty-year period, from 2020–2070, the first policy would save five hundred thousand lives when compared to the second.[27]

My sense is that one reason Peduto's actions after the Arizona fatality were more bark than bite was that in some sense he didn't want to overreact to what was a statistical inevitability. It feels incredibly coldhearted to write that. Especially because the circumstances of the Arizona accident were particularly egregious, and avoidable (investigations later found that the safety driver was watching *The Voice* at the time of the incident instead of the road).[28] But people are going to die in or because of robot cars unless we wait twenty more years, in which case an extra half a million people in the United States will die from collisions caused by human-operated vehicles. Setting the new thing and the not-new thing side by side revealed that the status quo was the risky choice.

Peduto knew this. But he also knew he had a job as a politician to help usher in the future and not just let it slam the public in the face. He knew there'd be a backlash not just to him but also to the innovation if he weren't seen trying to put in some guardrails. Peduto told me, "There are two sides. One is the side of being a *mayor*. You want zero accidents. Zero deaths. The other side is being a *pragmatist* and saying that, every week, people die on our streets in auto accidents. Preventing it in the next phase for the automobile is not realistic. There will be accidents, and there will be death. You have to be mindful of that and understand that, although it is a reality, it is very hard to accept." The mayor was being a pragmatist (giving AVs room to roam in Pittsburgh) and also a politician (pushing the companies to engage community stakeholders more and to communicate more). When possibility chased him, Peduto decided to do nothing, and then something.

Revisiting Airbnb in Amsterdam

Nanette Schippers and her team in Amsterdam did nothing, and then something. When I looked at the MOU from another angle, and with the benefit of two more years of history, I could see not just what Amsterdam had granted but what it had gotten. The MOU it had originally agreed to would remain in effect for one year only, an "assessment period." Airbnb agreed to provide high-level information on rental activities in Amsterdam twice during that year. The parties agreed to meet once a quarter "to discuss the progress relating to this MOU." They also intended—"based on the experience that is gained with the MOU"—to work on follow-up terms that could be agreed upon in a more-binding cooperation agreement after the MOU had expired. Amsterdam hadn't given away the store. It had gotten a chance to experiment.

The issues in Amsterdam—excessive tourism, housing scarcity—didn't abate, and after the MOU expired, the city demanded more concessions. Airbnb began sharing some address-level data on request from the city. The company also built in a calculator so that after sixty days, hosts wouldn't be able to rent out their entire apartment anymore in Amsterdam for the remainder of the year. Over the years, Amsterdam has revised the short-stay policies further. The city began requiring registration by Airbnb hosts (and those on other platforms), with fines for violators.[29] The city cut the sixty-day maximum in half, to thirty days.[30] To those who had looked at the original MOU and thought Molly Turner had outwitted Schippers and her team, Turner remarked, "Two years later, Amsterdam got everything it wanted. Who's the master negotiator now?"[31] By 2019, Amsterdam's homestay rules were being called the "toughest laws in Europe."[32]

Looking back, the eventual acceptance, and regulation, of daily home sharing in Amsterdam appears to have gone through three stages. First, *gedogen*. Then, an experiment. Then, a revision. It mirrored what Gabriella Gómez-Mont had been doing. Build, measure, learn. And Pittsburgh and Peduto, though not all the way yet, seemed set on the same course.

Any such experiments might benefit from some more rigor—targeted results, perhaps, to go along with the tests; otherwise it's not clear what the results are being assessed against. For our wider needs at regulating the future, perhaps we might borrow an idea that economist Charles Manski developed in the context of regulating pharmaceuticals. In 2009, he proposed an idea called "adaptive partial approval" for permitting new drugs. The proposal was a solution to two problems he had seen in the drug-approval process. Both were a function of operating with only partial knowledge. In Manski's words, "Type I errors occur when ineffective or unsafe drugs are approved because they appear worthy when evaluated using available information. Type II errors occur when worthy drugs are disapproved because they appear deficient when evaluated using available information."[33] Manski cites as one of the most famous Type I errors, Merck & Co.'s anti-inflammatory drug Vioxx, which gained approval "based on data from trials lasting only three to six months and involving patients at low risk for cardiovascular illness." It was later removed from the market, but not before it had contributed to an estimated 88,000 heart attacks in the United States and 38,000 deaths—perhaps substantially more.[34] Longer trials that allowed the long-term health effects of new drugs to more fully emerge are one option for reducing Type I errors but would also delay the time to drug approval, perhaps beyond what pharmaceutical companies could sustain and even beyond the public's willingness to wait for new cures. Type II errors, Manski notes, are harder to document, because "if approval is not granted, society never learns how well a drug would perform in clinical practice."[35] Manski proposes letting the FDA "grant limited-term sales licenses" while Phase 3 trials (in which volunteers ill with a disease are given the new drug) take place. The licenses would allow a pharmaceutical firm to sell no more than a certain quantity of the new drug over a specified period. The firm would provide data to the FDA annually, and the FDA could choose to change the licensing decision accordingly. Instead of deciding no or yes, the FDA would be giving an answer that could change along with the results. As more successful milestones were reached, the drug could be made available to more patients.

Years after I had left Boston government, this was the same adaptive approach leaders there took to the question of allowing or not allowing autonomous vehicles on Boston's roads.[36] nuTonomy wanted to test autonomous cars in Boston. The city granted the company permission to do so in Boston's waterfront industrial park and offered to (and eventually did) expand those permissions as the company safely hit certain milestones. What the city called its "graduated" approach proceeded like this. In Phase A, the partner could not test on city streets and had to document or demonstrate to the city such things as ease of manual takeover from the AV, emergency-braking and emergency-stop functionality, automatic braking upon detection of an obstacle, and some other basic driving capabilities. Then and only then could the partner proceed to Phase B1. In this phase, the partner could test in the city's waterfront industrial park but only during daylight hours free of rain or snow and only with a safety driver behind the wheel. After logging one hundred miles in this fashion, the partner could proceed to Phase B2, which would expand the criteria to include some night driving and some during periods of precipitation. After logging one hundred miles in this phase, the partner could request to move to Phase C1, which would expand the allowed geography to a wider area on the South Boston waterfront. On and on the phases went, gradually expanding the geographic radius while requiring the partner to log more miles in more-varied conditions. As the graduated permissions spilled into more-residential neighborhoods, an explicit prohibition against operating on roads with speed limits of more than thirty miles per hour was layered in. The graduated testing program also required partners to provide crash reports and quarterly usage reports (including any failures or disruptions while driving in autonomous mode). Under the program, the partner was also invited to provide other insights (relating to possible infrastructural or policy needs) gleaned during the testing.[37] By late 2017, nuTonomy reported that it had, "exceeded the 600 autonomous miles required for Phases B1, B2, C1, and C2 of the Test Plan" in Boston and that the AVs had not been involved in any collisions during the testing.[38] By the spring of 2019, a second company, Optimus Ride, was working its way through the phased testing and had driven more than 2,500 miles autonomously on Boston's roads.[39]

In late 2019, San Francisco created a new administrative office that could develop and manage this type of permitting process. It was called the Office of Emerging Technology, and the city said it was designed to be "a single entrance for technology companies seeking to operate in our public spaces."[40] Its major responsibilities were to elevate the needs (equity, accessibility, data ethics, cybersecurity, privacy, and more) of the city's residents, workers, small businesses, and visitors vis-à-vis the technology companies entering and operating in the city. It was also meant to adapt policy making to fit with emerging technologies, which are "by definition . . . still being developed and are not finished products." It was conceived to help make this permitting process "certain and predictable" to the companies that might undertake them. The working group that gave rise to the office identified a bucket of emerging technologies: advanced biometrics, facial recognition, artificial intelligence and machine learning, autonomous delivery robots (these were the sidewalk interlopers said to have been the impetus for City Supervisor Norman Yee's calling for the working group in the first place), blockchain, drones, virtual and augmented reality, and more. City officials, of course, recognized that these were only examples, and that additional, newer things would come after. I was told by people who had participated that the process was one of the best examples they'd seen of bringing community stakeholders and technologists together for a real conversation about how to manage the interplay between innovation and community.

Still, I think an office like this and the adaptive permitting process like the one pulled off in Boston will be challenging to scale broadly. It is already taxing for even the most well-resourced cities to try to anticipate the new technologies, how those technologies will be deployed, and how to effectively regulate them, even adaptively, before they've come to full fruition. There are too many unknowns. It will also be too tempting to tilt these efforts against the new technologies. There is a movement afoot to strike a less permissive stance on the next wave of technologies coming into cities, and understandably so. Ridesharing has brought buckling congestion to cities. Homestays have helped accelerate housing scarcity. Governments that looked the other way feel burned. San Francisco has created a new front door, but note that front doors are meant not only for greeting visitors but also for keeping them out. Striking the right balance will be a challenge.

In our reaction to a wave of technology companies that inserted themselves rashly into our civic lives—Uber jumps perhaps to the top of the list—there is a building desire to make sure that doesn't happen again with new entrants, but I think the frustration is better directed toward the earlier bunch. The fact that we allowed Facebook, for example, and many other platforms to at first hide behind the protections of the Communications Decency Act, but now won't, is not hypocrisy. It's experimentation. Of course we shouldn't allow experiments to unfold for too long—or at all—when they have potentially catastrophic outcomes. I don't want your nuclear-powered robots roaming my city sidewalks even for a nanosecond. But we should be judicious about cutting new things off before they have started. Throughout history there have been many attempts to kill new ideas in the cradle, which would have been bad for society later, because the early stages of things are often tumultuous. We came close to prohibiting life insurance; we nearly prohibited stock trading in the wake of the panic of 1792.[41] But a government-led (and Hamilton-championed) response staved off the panic—and an overreaction—while simultaneously paving the way for innovations like the New York Stock Exchange. On balance, we should start at "possibly might be okay" rather than "probably won't." We can be against regulation at first and then for it.

Pittsburgh's Bill Peduto laid out a vision like this: "The way I view it is that if this were a football game, we haven't even started the first quarter. This is the warm-up before the game. There are a handful of vehicles. Scalability is defined now in dozens. When scalability is defined in the thousands, that is when we'll need to [implement rules]. There is still the ability to learn what the shortcomings will be and what the harms to society will be."[42] He also spoke about the personal risk that politicians had to be willing to take on: "If you are not going forward, who is?"

Then the question becomes, if we can try things or allow them to be tried, can they scale and make a positive difference in the world?

Government That Can Try New Things

Possibility leaders

☆ Identify key assumptions/uncertainties in new projects. Test them in minimally viable ways where possible.

☆ Prioritize for testing first: things that are most uncertain, things that are most essential to success.

☆ Use staged budgets. Stop what's not working, or change it. Scale what is.

☆ Build portfolios of experiments. Then aim high so the wins cover the losses.

☆ Separate "people" from "projects" so you can build objective reviews. Projects may have failed, but employees may or may not have. Did they deliver learning efficiently?

☆ Experiment *with* the public, not *on* the public.

☆ If "pilots" are tests, describe them that way. Promise *learning*, not *success*.

☆ Be candid about results. Before and after, express that some failure will be required on the way to breakthrough successes. Communicate this to the press and the public.

Possibility citizens

☆ Elect officials that promise (modest) failure and maximum learning. Look for possibility in their campaign platforms. Be skeptical of candidates who express certainty about the outcome of new efforts. Ask at candidate forums, endorsement meetings, etc.: What amount of failure will you tolerate? How will you manage it? How will you react to it?

☆ Ask officials for "possibility" dashboards along with their performance dashboards: What have they tried? What has succeeded *and* failed? Question "success" only—it may suggest obfuscation or a lack of ambition, or both.

☆ Provide "possibility" accountability. Don't immediately trash failures. Ask: Was the expenditure of time/money minimal? Was learning maximized? Are there other efforts also being tested to solve the same problem? (Then strongly criticize efforts that overspent, underlearned, and underinvested in a portfolio of efforts.)

What everyone can do

☆ Communicate that the status quo is often the less safe choice.

GOVERNMENT
THAT CAN SCALE

5

Government as a Platform

The irony was not lost on me that I was late for my meeting at Waze, stuck in traffic in Tel Aviv.[1] To make matters worse, when I finally did arrive, and I finally did get to asking Gai Berkovich about his company's ability to grow its free data-sharing program with cities, I seemed to have put my foot in my mouth. "In two years," I asked, "how many cities will the Connected Citizens Program be in? One hundred?" Waze had gone from zero partners to fifty over the program's first two years.

"I think that's the wrong question," Berkovich replied. "How many cities won't we be in?"

The Connected Citizens Program (CCP) was an extension of the core Waze navigation product that more than sixty-five million commuters used each month in 2017 for routing and real-time traffic updates.[2] Waze called those users "Wazers" and described them as the world's largest community of drivers. The basic idea for CCP was that Waze would share with cities traffic data it was gleaning from its users (the app passively collected speed and congestion data as drivers used it to navigate their commutes), and cities would share with Waze planned special events, street closures, street construction, etc. Win-win. CCP had a religious origin of sorts: The impetus for the program was a visit by Pope Francis to Rio de Janeiro in 2013 and a suggestion by Rio's mayor that his staff reach out to Waze to learn how to incorporate the company's data into the city's planning for the momentous visit. Rio was the company's first data-sharing partner, and nine others joined in October 2014. Now, two years after that, I was wondering how many more were coming, and Berkovich, the chief operating officer at Waze, was chiding me (with a grin) for being skeptical.

My doubt wasn't totally unfounded. There was much interest in CCP at Google (Waze's parent company) and in the world, but there weren't many resources dedicated to it. More than eighty cities and groups were asking to join the program. More than fifty had. But each new partner had needs: how to join the program, how to make sense of the data, and how to turn that sense into action. The cities didn't have the spare talent—not the data analysts or data visualists or traffic engineers—to do all that. And neither, it seemed, did Waze have the people to support them. Inside the behemoth that was Google (and then Alphabet), there was something close to seventy thousand employees at the time, and yet CCP was supported by just three of them.[3] Within Google, where the culture was to build things and then build them "10x" bigger, these three people were expected to grow the program to five hundred cities—or, in Berkovich's conception, to every city on the planet. I felt not totally stupid wondering how?

I wasn't the only one wondering. Paige Fitzgerald was curious, too, and she had more than a passing interest. Fitzgerald was CCP's program manager. She led and made up one-third of the scant team. She was seeking more full-time help on the project, but Di-Ann Eisnor, CCP's founder and the head of growth at Waze, had demurred. For the time being, Fitzgerald borrowed resources from inside Google where she could. "We basically operated on goodwill," she recounted. Fitzgerald considered whether the time had come to charge for the free program. Maybe then the team would have the resources she felt they needed. "We can't work hand-in-hand if we scale," she had told me in the summer of 2016 in the face of the growth demands. "Our biggest challenge is just trying to hang on for dear life."

If my doubts about the ambitions for CCP were well founded, they were more broadly founded, too. Hanging on for dear life was a professional hazard of program management in public work. CCP wasn't the first time a sleek new program had been thought up, and even tried, in order to solve a public problem. But too often we observe that the press releases, the ribbon cuttings, and the celebratory launches are followed by . . . not much. Can we solve public problems anymore? is a question in two parts: Can we come up with new ideas? And can we try them? But then comes a third part. In the wake of too many experiments that lead nowhere, or "shiny objects" that deliver acclaim but no results, or that do deliver but are starved of resources nonetheless, we also have to ask ourselves: Can we scale those new solutions so that they make a transformative difference in people's lives?

If I'd faced as much traffic heading home, maybe I would have had the time to fully recognize the rationale for Berkovich's confidence. He was facing the age-old question of how to take a new solution and make it a big one, and he didn't seem fazed. Maybe I wouldn't have attributed his self-assurance to mere ambition. It took me some time—

and some visiting of other tech companies with similar appetites for growth, and a rereading of the history of government ventures that accomplished things at large scale—before I recognized the thing (and then worried about it, too) that gave Berkovich confidence. It wasn't blind ambition he was channeling. It was "platform thinking."[4]

The Drivers' Wikipedia

Waze began as a community project in 2006 called Free Map Israel, led by Ehud Shabtai.[5] Shabtai was joined in creating the company by Amir Shinar and Uri Levine as they built what one of them described as "the drivers' Wikipedia."[6] Over its first ten years, Waze developed into a free, real-time, crowdsourced navigation app. Waze could be used anywhere in the world but required that there be enough people providing data to make it useful. In the spring of 2016, while CCP was getting off the ground in just a handful of cities, 186 metropolitan areas globally each had more than twenty thousand active Wazers using the main app.[7]

In addition to the Wazers, the company had relied on more than 360,000 volunteer map editors around the world who updated maps and verified local edits to improve Waze's accuracy. One journalist commented on Waze editors and their "almost missionary zeal" to improve the quality of the app. He described a top editor, Jesse May, who spent "hours on the computer every night, making sure the world that Waze presents to drivers is the world that is really out there. 'It's my hobby . . . Instead of playing Doom or watching the boob tube, I'm going to do something that's more beneficial.' Sometimes he will even drive out of his way to check on a user report in person. 'My wife just shakes her head.'"[8]

In November 2012, Waze began monetizing the app by offering resellers and advertisers a web interface to advertise based on location. The next year, Google bought the company for a reported $1.3 billion amidst rumors of a counteroffer from Facebook and interest from Apple.[9] Waze, with its community of sixty-five million users, had something of interest to these tech giants. It also had something in common. Like Facebook's core offering, like Google's search, like Apple's iOS for its iPhone, the Waze app was more than a product. It was a platform.

Platforms Bring Users Together

A definition is a useful starting point for understanding how Waze got to where it did, how CCP might, and what that has to tell us about how we might scale efforts to solve public problems. Platforms "bring together individuals and organizations so they can innovate or interact in ways not otherwise possible, with the potential for nonlinear increases in utility and value."[10]

Consider two types of platforms. The first, innovation platforms, "consist of common technological building blocks that the owner and ecosystem partners can share in order to create new complementary products and services."[11] Apple's iOS is a platform of this type. An entire ecosystem of app developers has grown up around the smartphone operating system, all adding value to the phone itself. Google's Android is, too. So is Microsoft Windows for the PC, and Amazon Web Services for the cloud. Transaction platforms, the second type, "are largely intermediaries or online marketplaces that make it possible for people and organizations to share information or to buy, sell, or access a variety of goods and services."[12] Google's search is a platform of this type, allowing advertisers to target searchers. So is Facebook's social network, allowing individuals to share information with each other. So are Amazon's Marketplace, Tencent's WeChat, and many other platforms. Airbnb and Uber, which we came across in chapter 4, are transaction platforms. So is Waze.

These platforms all bring users together, but there is something very particular about them that gives them their astronomical growth: They bring users together in ways that create value for other users. I found the case of Waze so illuminating because with one use of the app, this power is easy to see. If I were the first user of Waze, the app would be of no value to me. But as soon as other drivers started downloading and using it on their way to work or home or school, it became more valuable. The more users there are, the more traffic information there is, which makes the app's route suggestions better. And because of this value, more and more people join and fewer and fewer leave, which compounds the usefulness further. The power is in the network of users. These effects have come to be called *network effects*.[13]

Not all products and services have these network effects. If I buy a Ford car, it's not as if another buyer of a Ford creates much value for me in my car. I'm mostly indifferent, really, as to whether others buy a Ford or a Toyota or any other brand. Not so for Waze or for any of the other platforms we came across. The same effects are at play for Facebook and Twitter. Also for Airbnb: The more guests, the more value for hosts. The more hosts, the more value for guests, who can choose among a wider array of apartments. The more guests and, consequently, the more guest ratings, the more reliable the platform is for other guests. Same for Lyft and Uber. Drivers bring passengers. Passengers attract drivers. Passengers make it better for other passengers with their ratings. Users add value for other users. (See figure 5-1.)

FIGURE 5–1

Network effects in a two-sided platform

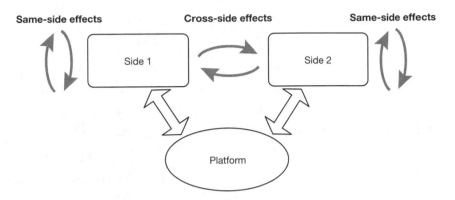

Same-side effects　　　　**Cross-side effects**　　　　**Same-side effects**

Side 1　　　　Side 2

Platform

Source: Adapted from Thomas R. Eisenmann, "Platform-Mediated Networks: Definitions and Core Concepts," Module Note 807-049 (Boston: Harvard Business School, 2006; revised, 2007).

These effects are in play both for users of similar types and for those across the platform. When the effects involve users on the same side of a platform adding value for each other, they are called "same-side" or "direct" network effects. Wazers making the app more useful for each other is an example of direct network effects. When it is users on different sides of a platform adding value for each other, these are called "indirect" or "cross-side" network effects. When more iPhone users attract more app developers, that's a cross-side network effect. Some platforms have both. Same-side network effects are at play when Facebook users create content for each other. Cross-side network effects are in action when developers build apps that work on Facebook's platform.

Network effects can be positive—the addition of the second user or partner adds value for the first—but they can also be negative, where users degrade the value of the platform for others. More users on Airbnb means more ratings, but it also means more competition for that prized rental for a vacation weekend. If fraudulent reviews swamped Amazon's Marketplace, there would be large negative network effects at play.[14] The same goes when Facebook fills up with haters and harassers, and the rest of us leave.

The same goes when your commute to work grinds to a halt on a highway. The next time you want to pound your fist on the steering wheel and curse being late for your 9:00, feel free to blame "the platform." Roads have giant network effects—positive and negative ones—and are a great reminder that platforms existed long before Amazon and Facebook and Microsoft and even before fax machines and telephones. A road that connects one person to nothing is of no value (unless it is solitude you seek). But as soon as a friendly neighbor or a useful business pops up alongside, the road's value has increased for everyone. Waze and the roads its users ride on demonstrate that it's not just the tech companies that build platforms that leverage network effects. Governments do too.

Government as a Platform

Tim O'Reilly is one of the chroniclers of the internet and has been writing about government as a platform for at least a decade. He drew on the roadway analogy: "The Federal-Aid Highway Act of 1956, which committed the United States to building an interstate highway system, was a triumph of platform thinking, a key investment in facilities that had a huge economic and social multiplier effect. Though government builds the network of roads that tie our cities together, it does not operate the factories, farms, and businesses that use that network: that opportunity is afforded to 'we the people.'"[15]

O'Reilly observed a similar phenomenon in many other aspects of public life. "The launch of weather, communications, and positioning satellites is a similar exercise of platform strategy. When you use a car navigation system to guide you to your destination, you are using an application built on the government platform, extended and enriched by massive private sector investment. When you check the weather—on TV or on the internet—you are using applications built using the National Weather Service (or equivalent services in other countries) as a platform."[16] He contrasted this approach with "vending machine government" and explained what he meant: "We pay our taxes, we expect services. And when we don't get what we expect, our participation is limited to protest—essentially, shaking the vending machine. Collective action has been watered down to collective complaint . . . What if, instead of a vending machine, we thought of government as the manager of a marketplace? . . . In the vending machine model, the full menu of available services is determined beforehand. A small number of vendors have the ability to get their products into the machine, and as a result, the choices are limited, and the prices are high." A marketplace, "by contrast, is a place where the community itself exchanges goods and services."[17] O'Reilly suggested that if we look hard enough and long enough, we might find this strategy in action all across public stuff. "The idea of government as a platform applies to every aspect of the government's role in society."[18]

Where could we look to find these platforms? We could start in our own neighborhoods. We would, for example, find them in community policing and neighborhood watches. These approaches were getting new looks in 2020 in the wake of the Black Lives Matter movement and calls to reduce funding to police departments or to reimagine public-safety approaches altogether. In the vending-machine model, how do cities and towns provide public safety? When crime goes up, more police officers are promised; more services are delivered by the government. And in a platform model? The community is invited in to play a role. The city, instead of (or in addition to) providing more patrols, provides what? Maybe it's a folding table and some chairs in a community space on a Wednesday evening. Not too long ago, it might have been access to an email list to share information. Nowadays, it is access to open data on everything from the status of streetlight repairs to the rate of car break-ins to camera feeds. But whatever the tools, the idea is the same—connect people so that they can share information (a transaction platform) or so that they can create "complementary products," such as a teen basketball league (an innovation platform). And all the while, exploit the fact that more users make other users better off. If more of my neighbors join and share, my family is safer. (Except when neighbors start using the meetings to pester other neighbors, or when community policing is a guise for vigilantism or worse, or when digital versions of the neighborhood watch become platforms for racial harassment, as they have on more than one occasion, and then, decidedly not.)

We could also look to national government. In 2010, at the urging of and under the leadership of one of India's famed internet entrepreneurs, Nandan Nilekani, the country undertook an initiative to provide Indians with a universal identification. (It was akin to an American Social Security number.) Indians didn't have a national ID, which meant they didn't have a way to prove their identity, which meant that getting access to government services like subsidized food or to private ones, like a bank account or mobile phone, was difficult. That, Nilekani observed, left a public system rife with fraud and abuse, marginalized the poor, and hampered the economy.[19] Nilekani assumed a senior government post, set up shop in Bangalore, and issued the team its own sort of "what cities won't we be in" mandate: reach 600 million Indians in five years, and ultimately all 1.2 billion of them.

Achieving that scale that speedily would be extraordinary. It took Facebook eight years to reach a billion users around the world and WeChat just over seven to get its first billion, and neither required a user to sign up *in person*.[20] Each twelve-digit, randomly generated ID number would be linked to all ten fingerprints of a person and to iris scans of both eyes. That meant collecting 2.4 billion iris scans and 12 billion fingerprints across more than four thousand cities and towns. India's people speak at least 121 different major languages, and actually many more, and every person would have to be spoken with.[21] India had at the time something close to 75 million homeless people, a population on its own that would have made it the twentieth biggest country in the world, and they all had to be reached.[22] On top of that, Nilekani and his government made this seemingly impossible task even *impossibler*: they made the program voluntary.

Then Nilekani did the thing that tells you much of what you need to know about his plan for getting there. He gave the ID the name *Aadhaar*. *Aadhaar* means "foundation" in Hindi. He branded the thing as a platform, and then he built it that way. "There are two big things we have to do. We have to constantly focus on enrolling the unenrolled and make sure there are useful applications for the enrolled," he said as they got underway, alluding to two sides of the platform.[23] On the one side: 1.2 billion people if they could be enticed. And on the other: government agencies and businesses that had subsidized food and fuel and the private mobile phones and bank accounts they wanted. "Think about it like a flywheel that has to be put in motion so it gains acceleration. The real strategic challenge is how do we create a virtual flywheel which spins faster and faster, and gains so much momentum that it is unstoppable," Nilekani had added.[24]

How do you? It's a chicken-or-egg problem that all platform launchers face, and it is "probably the most difficult challenge for platform strategists . . . When side A's volume depends on side B, and side B's volume depends on side A, how do you get started?" There are three broad approaches: "(1) Create stand-alone value for one side first, (2) subsidize one or both sides, and (3) sometimes bring two sides on board simultaneously."[25] Three platform scholars offer up a list of eight maneuvers for dealing with the dilemma:[26]

1. **"Follow the rabbit."** "Use a non-platform demonstration project to model success."

2. **Piggyback.** "Connect with an existing user base from a different platform and . . . recruit those users to participate in your platform."

3. **Seeding.** "Create value units that will be relevant to at least one set of potential users."

4. **Marquee.** "Provide incentives to attract members of a key user set onto your platform."

5. **Single side.** "Create a business around products or services that benefit a single set of users; later convert the business into a platform business."

6. **Producer evangelism.** "Design your platform to attract producers, who will induce their customers to become users."

7. **Big-bang adoption.** "Use one or more traditional push marketing strategies to attract a high volume of interest."

8. **Micromarket.** "Start by targeting a tiny market that comprises members who are already engaging in interactions."

Amazon used the first strategy when it opened its traditional business (selling goods it held in inventory) to its Marketplace business and allowing other small businesses and vendors to participate. PayPal used the second strategy (among others), as it got started and grew. The authors explained, "PayPal's marketing team . . . simulated customer demand on eBay by creating a bot (an automated software tool) that bought goods on the site and then insisted on paying for these transactions using PayPal. Noting this apparent growth in demand, many eBay sellers signed up for the PayPal service—which in turn made PayPal even more visible and attractive to consumers . . . within three months, PayPal's user base grew from 100,000 to one million."[27] Adobe pursued a seeding strategy and launched the PDF document-reading tool "by arranging to make all [US] federal government tax forms available online. The size of this instant market was huge, encompassing any individual or business that might need to pay US taxes. Adobe induced the IRS to cooperate by suggesting that millions of dollars in printing and postage costs could be saved. Taxpayers, in turn, got fast, convenient access to documents that everyone needs . . . Impressed by the value provided, many adopted Adobe as their document platform of choice."[28] Nintendo used the marquee strategy by signing up major video-game designers to release games on its new consoles. OpenTable, the reservation platform, adopted a single-side strategy by first using the app as a seating inventory software for restaurants, and only later opening it up to restaurant guests. Kickstarter turned its creators into evangelists by giving them the tools to host and manage their campaigns, and thus attracting crowdfunders to the site. Twitter tried the big-bang approach with success when it launched at South by Southwest in 2007. Facebook fell into the last strategy when it started at Harvard College.[29]

What did Nilekani do? He started by evangelizing himself: "I visited 25–26 state governments. I went to Raipur, Lucknow, Patna . . . I met chief ministers and chief secretaries, made presentations, got everybody on board, met banks, insurance companies and oil companies. We had talks at industry associations. I spread the message." Nilekani and his team built partnerships with registrars to enroll residents. They went to big organizations that already interfaced with huge populations, including federal agencies, state governments, the

India Post, and telecom companies, and sought to piggyback on their enrollments. They built a training system for operators who enrolled residents and then improved it when it was too slow. They ran pilot projects to test authentication for banks and telecoms, and they got regulators to agree to accept Aadhaar "as proof of both identity and address, enabling investors to . . . buy mutual funds." They even had a budget to spur application development by state governments and federal ministries. They gave awards to district collectors who developed interesting apps. They supported business-plan competitions for private Aadhaar entrepreneurs. They did all of this with the notion of getting that flywheel started, so that the growth would then occur on both sides, exponentially, and also with the notion of tamping down the doubts. "The best way to deal with [opposition] is to show [Aadhaar's] usefulness . . . to give unmatched benefits . . . that is what will win the debate."[30]

It looked for a while like this wouldn't be enough, like Aadhaar would miss its goal. In 2012, three years into the program and two years since the first person had been signed up, 190 million had enrolled.[31] But that meant more than 200 million to go to meet the 600 million target in just two years' time. The team hit those numbers and more. By December 2014, more than 700 million had signed on. By December 2016, there were well over a billion. By the end of 2017, the team had hit 1.2 billion. By the summer of 2019, they were providing almost 1 billion authentications a month.[32] They'd provided more than 32 billion overall. They'd achieved their "which cities won't we be in" goal.

What could Waze do? It was at fifty cities, with every other one to go. Paige Fitzgerald, the CCP program manager, was hanging on for dear life, yet meanwhile the program seemed to be a boon for Google. Waze's parent company had come under fire for tax avoidance, antitrust violations, privacy violations, and censorship—the kitchen sink of tech scrutiny—but every time CCP came to town, it generated positive headlines for the company. A student of mine, a former Googler, observing that CCP was worth "$100 million" in good PR to the company, said that she would ask for a $5 million budget were she Fitzgerald. I agreed that in terms of PR, in terms of the groundwork it laid for Waze's next big effort in cities (its carpool service), CCP was worth—if not $100 million or even $5 million—at least two or three more engineers and a few program administrators. What Waze could do was fund them. Provide the resources. From Waze. From Google. Di-Ann Eisnor, CCP's founder, told me, "We put a video of CCP up at TGIF, the Google weekly meeting. Sergey [Brin] pulled us aside and said, 'I love this.'" So, find the money? Isn't that what you do to support programs that work? Build the case with data, go to the higher-ups, get the goods?

Or . . . what Waze could do was what Waze always did and what Google had done with Search and YouTube. Turn CCP, the program, into CCP, the platform. Connect people on and/or across a platform. Create and strengthen ways for them to add value for each other. Get the flywheel going by getting one side started, or the other, or both.

And that's what they did. "Waze built a community portal so the cities could help each other," Fitzgerald explained. There the cities exchanged case studies and analytical tools they had created on their own. Waze held summits in New York, in Paris, in Mexico City, where transit leaders shared tools and techniques. The CCP team piggybacked onto an existing platform, inviting super-Wazers to help in the cities where they lived. Fitzgerald and her small team—still three full-timers—created some marquee wins that would attract others to the platform. They turned their best cities into evangelists. "We couldn't continue to hand-hold all of these partners," Fitzgerald confessed. "We focused on high-profile partners as well as innovative partners who were engaged, who would create tools that could be shared with other partners as well . . . We had those summits and we figured out even giving out just speaking spots was a big motivator for people to present their work. What we chose to highlight, what we knew was key, was cities building an analytics solution that could be shared with other cities." "That's what enabled us to scale," Fitzgerald reported back, two years after I'd asked how fast CCP would be able to grow. In 2019, the program was in one thousand cities. Not every city on the planet (there are more than four thousand with populations in excess of one hundred thousand), but a long way from fifty, and with practically the same tiny team.[33]

What Would We Do without Each Other?

Platform thinking underlay the One Fund Boston, too. I didn't know to call it that at the time. For weeks after I brought home that first black bag of money, the contributions poured in. What John Hancock, the marathon's signature sponsor, had started with a $1 million contribution was echoed in numbers large and small. I had opened some of the envelopes early on, before the volunteers swelled in number and the bankers came in and automated the process. Each check or handful of coins was salve on a broken city's wounds. But for all the gifts that came in (from individuals, from corporations), the ones that struck me most were proceeds from lemonade stands and local running races and other initiatives people had taken upon themselves to organize as complements to ours. Mostly by accident, and maybe with a sliver of prescience in a week full of quick decisions, we too had created an innovation platform.

In fact, there was a crush of requests to build other side efforts in order to support ours. We heard from local groups and national retailers. We fielded plans to put the One Fund Boston logo on garbage cans and to use the fund's name for a concert full of headliners. There were two possible reactions to these requests. The first was to lean toward control and ownership. That is, it's our logo, our name. We want to protect the integrity of both. We want to ward off fraud. Don't say your work is part of ours. The second approach was to cede that control. It's a scarier approach. It says, Go ahead. Plug in. It says that even though you don't work for us, we are working in the same direction. It says that even though we don't know you, we think you'll have something to add. In the early days of the marathon response—and probably due more to the limits on our own time and capacity for screening all the potential partners than to any special wisdom—we chose the second reaction. We chose a platform approach, and a rather open one at that. In all the hundreds of activities that sprang up to support One Fund Boston, there was hardly a contract or memorandum of understanding to be found.

One Fund Boston was a platform in another way too, a way that was more subtle and that touched the heart. The fund was, in a pretty straightforward manner, a transaction platform; straightforward in that it was an intermediary that made it easier for companies and individuals to donate and for survivors and the families of the victims to receive those donations. At One Fund Boston, we weren't fundraisers. We didn't ask for money. We just made sure it went from where it came from to where it should go. And it's easy to see in that way the cross-side network effects: the more contributors there were on the one side, the more donations to the One Fund Boston community on the other side. But there were same-side network effects, too. The members of that One Fund community helped each other. Of course, we all hated that anyone at all had been killed or hurt in the attacks, but it was true that the many survivors provided value to each other. This was a lesson imparted to us from those who had helped after the 9/11 attacks: that for all the ways the money helps, the bringing together of the community through the process is really what *heals*. And so there were small things and important things we did to support those on that side of the platform, to help make sure they could help each other. On the one-year anniversary of the attacks, and around the same time that those two survivors had told me "you have to show people that government can do new things," one of them, Patrick Downes, told a gathered audience and the world: "We chose to love, and that has made all the difference."

He continued: "To our fellow survivor community, what would we do without each other? We should have never met this way, but we are so grateful for each other. We have shared our despair, sense of loss and challenges, as well as our hope, gratitude, and triumphs. We have been there for each other, and we will continue to be there to pick each other up and celebrate milestones for years to come. Most of all we will cherish the bonds of mutual admiration. And to those who continue to struggle through despair, ongoing medical care, and the prospect of heart-wrenching surgical decisions, don't forget for a second that we will be there for you at a moment's notice. . . . I am so proud to be a Bostonian, because I am so proud to be connected to all of you." Downes closed his address, choking back the tears he had for the "fallen angels" who didn't survive that day, while expressing his love for the bonds of his city.[34] Boston Strong was the post-attack rallying cry. Boston-as-a-platform would have been a lot less eloquent, but no less accurate.

Platforms Fail, Too

"The idea of government as a platform applies to every aspect of the government's role in society," Tim O'Reilly said, and we should look for places to apply it.[35] On balance, there is evidence that platform businesses grow faster, more profitably, and more productively; they do more with less.[36] Which is what we'll need to do by necessity, if not also philosophy, to address the long list of public challenges we face.[37]

But the same evidence shows that most platforms fail. Three scholars compiled data on platform efforts dating back to 1995, and analyzed not only the 43 that survived but also the 209 (or 83 percent) that didn't.[38] Platforms are exercises in possibility, too.

Worse yet, platforms can succeed in ways that hurt the public. Even the ones that have survived can lay only contingent claim to success. Think of broken laws, violated trust, concentrated power, double-edged swords. Platforms may leave out ecosystem members, drive up resentment, and antagonize government agencies if they "don't keep their power or ambitions in check."[39] Governments as platforms can—and will, and have—too.

I witnessed a platform that failed in many of these senses. In the summer of 2018, I was in Beijing to try to understand how ofo had gone from being a school-based startup to a bike-share behemoth in a matter of months, topping an all-out market-share battle with its rival Mobike. The company had provided billions of bicycle rides in pursuit of its own "what cities won't we be in" mission: "Anytime, anywhere, a bike to ride." It had put 6.5 million bikes into the streets of China in its first year and a half—and since, millions more.

Bike sharing wasn't new when ofo launched on the campus of Peking University in 2015, but its dockless model mostly was. That model gave riders the convenience of leaving bicycles practically anywhere they wanted in the city. And they did. Soon the bikes were everywhere. Blocking sidewalks. Showing up in rivers. Stopping up alleyways. The city of Hangzhou confiscated twenty-three thousand of them over a short period, and the staggering pictures were only previews of more to come.[40] Thousands of bikes piled up in Shanghai, thousands more outside a factory in Xiamen. There shouldn't be such a thing as a "bike graveyard," and the photos of them were haunting.[41]

Looking at them, you can't help wondering how something like this could ever happen. How could it? On the list of reasons: The network effects were never as strong as the company thought they were, especially given the presence of so many other bike-share companies. Sure, it helps me, if I'm a rider, that some other user has ridden a bike to the building where my meeting is letting out, allowing me to pick it up from there. But given the presence of so many other companies, and given how easy it is to switch to any other of many competitors, it's not *that* helpful. So on the same side of this platform, there wasn't considerable power at play. Moreover, the company and others like it operating at the same time failed to cultivate a second side of the platform early enough. The bike maintainers, the reallocators . . . there could have been a whole ecosystem of people engaged to keep the bikes functioning and where they were supposed to be. But the efforts at this, while eventually substantial, were too little, too late.

There were initiatives to use financial inducements to get riders to leave bikes in better places. And there was even talk of integrating ofo's data with the government's, so they could both weed out problem riders, repeat offenders, and the like—shared data and application programming interfaces (APIs) being the toolkits of platform players. And what if the company had pursued such integration? If it had, I suspect it would have ended up as part of China's social-credit system—a government platform, really—for monitoring and ranking China's citizens.

Six months after my visit, ofo was essentially over. Now the pictures were of users lining up outside headquarters trying to claim deposits they had provided at sign-up. The company was headed for bankruptcy.[42]

Platforms as Government?

It may seem relatively clear that platforms for monitoring and quashing dissent are bad and platforms for channeling money to attack survivors are good, but one of the things that makes government as a platform so challenging is that many of the cases feel more gray. Aadhaar is not China's social-credit system, but it has raised significant concerns about big-brother government, about privacy, and about disenfranchising people without the ID numbers. Efforts to make an Aadhaar number mandatory for accessing certain services generated substantial pushback that reached all the way to the Indian Supreme Court.[43]

Even Waze's CCP raises deeper questions, questions Paige Fitzgerald tackled the first time I met her. Ostensibly for the purposes of better urban planning, some cities had requested that CCP share data involving speeding trends. Waze declined to share the data with governments, and Fitzgerald explained why: "Even my father teases me that he will soon be getting speeding tickets in the mail because tech companies work with police departments. He won't because of us; we won't share it." She added that her father seemed slow to believe her. Waze providing CCP as a platform with cities as one side, and Wazers and editors making up another side, raises a related squeamishness. One student of mine put these words to it: "Do you want city hall to be one side of the platform, or do you want government to be at the center? I think that's where the tension is. Are we ceding governments to now just be part of a platform that other people run? Or do we want government to be the platform?"

Indeed, these questions won't always come in headline form. Occasionally they will be on the order of the Facebook–Cambridge Analytica scandal accompanied by congressional and parliamentary hearings and promises of reform. But more often they will be in the form of looming policy questions. How will we manage the e-scooters that have arrived in town? Should we, government, create an API to help gather data on their status and location? Should we, tech companies, participate? These were the questions in the air in Los Angeles in the spring of 2019.[44] Should we, government, partner with Uber on public transit, as Denver's authorities and those in twenty other cities had by the summer of 2019, so that the company might sell public transit tickets through its app or even provide "public" rides where busses didn't reach?[45] When Uber's CEO says he wants the company to become the Amazon of transportation, a platform for much of the transit sector, we should take him seriously, and literally, and have the tools for deciding.[46] Which brings up a final case in point: Amazon's overlap with government as a platform gets headlines when it's about a $10 billion cloud contract for the US Department of Defense, or when it's about the company's Rekognition facial-recognition tools, and especially when it's in connection with surveilling neighborhoods or identifying immigrants.[47] But Amazon has more than five thousand government agencies using Amazon Web Services (AWS) for everything from police-records management to identity solutions to election tools, and that number will grow, as will the number of underlying functions.[48] Competition from Microsoft's Azure and others will make that growth not completely unchecked, but it's possible that within a decade AWS will be a sort of de facto operating system of government. How many cities—and small towns and large states and federal government agencies—won't they be in? Amazon as government as a platform will offer tremendous efficiency, reliability, and security, and yet it will continue to reraise the questions of who, when it comes down to how government works and what it does, is really in charge. It is time we relearn the techniques of government as a platform and past time we raise the scrutiny on platforms as government.

How Many Kids Won't We Save?

"How many cities won't we be in?" is a rallying cry. It says, "no more" to programs that start and stagnate, that dwindle, or that grow only in line with the resources they are given. It's the answer to the question in a spring budget meeting about growing that new program for the homeless or the one that's cutting down on school absenteeism. "How many corners won't we reach?" "How many kids won't we save?" It's money. It's roads. It's identity. It's reach.

And that kind of ambition for scale comes with a set of tools. Waze's Gai Berkovich told me, "I think it's kind of witchcraft to manage a community."[49] He meant—I think—that it's part science and part art; what you do as the platform provider and what you leave to the ecosystem. But government as a platform comes with a set of earthly tools, too: hardware, software, rules, and processes that can accentuate positive network effects and mitigate the negative ones. And it comes with, if we hone them, a set of strategies for governments' getting there, involving building platforms or, on occasion, borrowing them from private partners or lending them out.

6

Trisector Entrepreneurs

A senior official in President Donald Trump's administration told me, "If it can survive the Trump–Obama transition, it can survive anything."[1] I don't think he meant it as an exaggeration. He told me this at around the same time the *Washington Post* reported on Trump's efforts to "review, revoke and overwrite key parts of his predecessor's legacy."[2] After year one, the country's forty-fifth president had issued seventeen executive actions to roll back rules and regulations championed by its forty-fourth. Ninety-six cabinet-level agency decisions had been promulgated to push back on the Obama era, and more were in the works. Trade. Environmental policy. Foreign policy. Where President Obama had zigged, President Trump now zagged. And yet somehow, this new piece of the bureaucracy, this part of the Obama agenda, had managed to survive. It still does as of this writing.

It was the United States Digital Service (USDS), and I had become curious about the new operation's survival before Trump even announced his candidacy.[3] The USDS had been born out of HealthCare.gov's debacle of a rollout; a tech mistake that had threatened one of Obama's signature policy achievements. President Obama and the people he brought in to rescue the downed site decided to start up a new agency—one that could draw into government the country's best software engineers, designers, and related experts—with a goal of making sure something like that never happened again.

The US leaders had modeled it on a similar effort in the United Kingdom, the Government Digital Service, which had likewise been born out of a giant technology failure in the government health care space. I wondered if the USDS could survive past the burst of energy delivered by its founders in its early, heady days. Would it last? I had visited the USDS as it finished its first year, to ask its founders what they planned to do for its second, while Obama still had eighty weeks to go. What could they do to make sure their efforts to build more-agile government outlasted them? Three years later, the USDS remained. And the administration official was telling me that this was all very encouraging. Because the effort to modernize government would require a "generational" effort. And he is right that it will.

Will possibility last? Will the efforts that need to be rallied be rallied? The methods tried? The chances taken? I am hopeful. But the ties that have been built over the last decade between private entrepreneurs and public officials are threatening to fray during the next one. The reasons for that are complicated. One solution, I think, lies in the USDS and agencies like it around the world, for reasons that go beyond the improved services these agencies will deliver.

What most threatens the possibility project in the coming years is a brewing animus between techie entrepreneurs and government types. Some of that stems from a fear of what things like artificial intelligence can do and what government can do with such things. The protest of thousands of Google employees about their company's involvement in AI on behalf of the US Department of Defense was but one episode that foreshadowed the growing tension. So were the Facebook hearings in the spring of 2018—a real Rorschach test for possibility if ever there was one. Techies thought it was government ignorance that was on full display; government types thought it was techie hubris. Things have not gotten better since.

What the USDS and agencies like it do in the face of all this is subtler than their main mission. Their main mission is to help their governments deliver software that works for citizens and under contracts that don't swell to the hundreds of millions of dollars. But what they might do that's as important, and increasingly so, is generate leaders with experience starting things in both the public and private domains. Techies come into government, and they leave, carrying the sensibilities of each sector to the other. There is a version of this that we should be wary of, yet another revolving door that enriches a few and fosters distrust. But there is another version, one that I am cautiously optimistic about, where what's created with this kind of movement back and forth is a generation of entrepreneurs, of possibility artists, who have experience working in the private, public, and not-for-profit domains. If we can pull that version off and cultivate a new network of trisector entrepreneurs, we might get possibility that lasts.

Coming Together

The launch of HealthCare.gov was one of possibility's dark moments. President Obama had swept into office under a banner of optimism. The audacity of hope. Change we can believe in. Yes, we can. And the president in his second term was indeed going to deliver what had seemed improbable—what had been impossible at least since the 1960s—and that was a sweeping expansion of health coverage that would bring the United States as close to universal coverage as it had ever been. On the day the site launched, Obama announced that HealthCare.gov would allow Americans to shop for health insurance with the ease of buying a book on Amazon.[4] As it turned out, only six Americans were able to sign up for health insurance on the site that day, while tens of thousands were unable to access it.[5] In the early weeks of October 2013, as the site was crashing around them, no one in what had been regarded as a tech-savvy White House knew the full extent or cause of the problems. In high-level discussions, leaders considered scrapping the original site (which had taken years to build) and starting over from scratch.[6]

The effort to rescue the site fell in part to a small group of people who hailed from the startup world, and the tech world more broadly. President Obama tapped Jeffrey Zients, the country's first ever chief performance officer, to lead the operation to fix the website, along with Todd Park, the country's chief technology officer. Park had been a health-technology entrepreneur (cofounding his first company at twenty-four) and then was persuaded to become the CTO at the US Department of Health and Human Services before serving in the same role on a government-wide basis. The two quickly pulled together a small, ad hoc team of highly skilled tech managers from inside and outside of government. These included Mikey Dickerson, a Google site-reliability engineer; Ryan Panchadsaram, who'd worked at Microsoft and Salesforce before becoming a Presidential Innovation Fellow; Jini Kim, a Google product manager; and a few others.[7] Over the course of approximately two months, the team led the repair of the website (and its underlying IT systems) to the point where the vast majority of users could shop for health insurance online. The site was ultimately instrumental in allowing eight million Americans to sign up for health insurance in the program's debut year.

HealthCare.gov demonstrated that a small group of highly talented entrepreneurs and tech workers from outside the normal government-tech ecosystem had the ability to fix problems and also revealed the misaligned incentives in the government's IT-procurement process that had created HealthCare.gov-style implosions.[8] Park had seen the potential for what this kind of talent could do in two other programs that had invited technologists and entrepreneurs into government: the Presidential Innovation Fellows program, which he had cofounded in 2012, and 18F, which some of those fellows had gone on to create in 2014 to extend its work. "The most important rule of startups is if you get the best people, you win. Full stop. These early programs were alphas for getting lean-startup talent and thinking into government," he said. Park, with Obama's support, refocused his time and energy on recruiting more of that kind of talent into government. Panchadsaram began coordinating teams to create space for a new bureau that could house this talent. Park persuaded Dickerson to lead the new bureau. Dickerson recalled, "I returned to California after working on the team to fix HealthCare.gov. I slept for a couple of weeks, and I began the task of processing what I had seen and done. I knew that HealthCare.gov was the most important work I had been a part of. I saw that technology in parts of government was in bad shape." He went on, "But there was hope. When asked, some of the very best engineers and troubleshooters in the world willingly put their lives on hold to dedicate their time to this very difficult problem. When they got there, they found government officials and contractors who also wanted nothing more than to fix the site and who were ready and willing to work together to make it happen. There was limitless opportunity to do more."[9] Dickerson moved back to Washington to lead the new USDS. Erie Meyer joined him to get it started. She'd been the founding member of the tech and innovation team at the US Consumer Financial Protection Bureau, which was itself a startup within government, having officially been created in 2011. Haley Van Dyck was named deputy administrator of the USDS. Van Dyck was optimistic about what it would mean to bring new perspectives into government; both for the people that were brought in and for the delivery of public services. "The work of the engineers and designers that we're pulling in from across the country will actually have a chance to influence and change the way government is operated," she'd told tech journalist Stephen Levy.[10] The subheadline to the article, "Stock Options? Don't Need 'Em! I'm Coding for Uncle Sam!" captured the brewing esprit de corps. By 2015, the new service counted more than a hundred employees on its team. It also began standing up digital-service teams within the Department of Homeland Security, Veterans Affairs, and other parts of the government.

This new government agency followed on models that had been tried elsewhere, and it has been emulated since. The United Kingdom formally opened its Government Digital Service (GDS) earlier, in 2011. It was initially led by Mike Bracken, who before that had been the director of digital development at the *Guardian*, in charge of its digital transformation. He'd been involved in several other technology ventures, too. One of the first projects the GDS took on was GOV.UK, a single landing page for all online citizen-government interactions in the United Kingdom. GDS used lean-startup methodologies to iteratively build the site. In 2019, Senator Kamala Harris proposed a bill in the US Senate that would give state and local governments grants for standing up digital-service teams. California, Kansas, Colorado, Georgia, New Jersey, and Massachusetts were all said to be working to launch and sustain their own digital-service teams.[11]

Other countries, cities, and states have adopted different models, but also with related goals—attracting entrepreneurial talent into government and inviting entrepreneurship from the talented people already serving there who may have felt it wasn't welcomed or even

allowed. John Paul Farmer, who had cofounded the Presidential Innovation Fellows program with Todd Park, was appointed CTO in
New York City in 2019 and started recruiting for a variety of startuppy tech roles: deputy CTO for digital, product manager, deputy
CTO for innovation, innovation coordinator, director of NYC AI lab,
director of NYC design lab, UX designer, director of research and future planning, and more. Shireen Santosham led a very active group
of innovative thinkers as chief innovation officer of San Jose, California. In 2014, Rudi Borrmann became director of innovation and open
government in Buenos Aires. Two years later he became undersecre-
tary of public innovation and open government for all of Argentina.
David Moinina Sengeh was appointed chief innovation officer in Si-
erra Leone—the first in his country—leaving his role working on AI
research in Nairobi for IBM.[12] All around the world and at every level,
governments were bringing themselves closer to the skills and tools
of modern entrepreneurship and to contemporary entrepreneurs.

And all around the world, great leaders were helping usher entrepreneurial and civically minded talent in their direction. Code for
America, which Jen Pahlka had started in 2009, created fellowships
that drew designers, software engineers, and their ilk into city governments. And before the organization had branched out in more
directions, it had started a global trend. Soon enough there were
Codes for Canada, Mexico, Ghana, Kenya, Japan, Germany, India,
Australia, and others.[13] And it had also started a generational cascade.
Rachel Dodell and Chris Kuang, two college students, launched
Coding It Forward to create pathways for young people to do something "mission-driven" with their technology skills and to make
sure many of those pathways led into government. In the summer
of 2019, fifty-five students from thirty-four colleges and universities
in the United States spent ten weeks of their summer at six federal
agencies "putting their software engineering, data science, product

management, and design skills to use serving the American people."[14] The Ford, New America, and Hewlett foundations set out to cultivate a field of public-interest technology and to help universities work together to "equip tomorrow's computer scientists, information architects, engineers, data scientists, designers, lawyers, policy experts, and social scientists with the skills to create public policy that centers the needs of people and their communities."[15]

It was a bull market on "Tech for Good," and it seemed likely that #techforgovernment was set to be a big part of that.

This rise of interest and activity was mirrored in the private sector. The preceding decade had seen a boom in private companies coming to market with "govtech" and "civictech" solutions. There were new private ventures trying to solve housing problems and security problems and climate problems and health problems. Two collaborators at MIT, architect Newsha Ghaeli and biologist Mariana Matus, founded Biobot Analytics. They figured out a way to measure opioids in sewage (excreted by humans) and map this data for cities looking to tackle the opioid epidemic in real time.[16] And they figured that would be on the way to transforming wastewater infrastructure into "public health observatories." They were accepted into the highly competitive accelerator Y Combinator. They got their first pilot with Cary, North Carolina.[17] Seasoned entrepreneurs were flocking to the space as well. Ralph Clark took over as CEO of ShotSpotter in 2010.[18] He'd spent his career in finance and high tech and had sold his cybersecurity company. Why did he step into the role of leading a gunfire detection and location provider? Why wade into a morass of new technical hurdles and government selling? "I liked the mission and saw that I could make a difference."[19] Many others were thinking and acting similarly.

Moreover, they found willing investors. Ron Bouganim, a serial entrepreneur who'd also been civically active, made the case to big venture-capital firms that they should be investing more fully in

this market, and when they were slow to take him up on his suggestion, he decided to launch his own fund. Bouganim did 562 pitches
in 2013–2014 and raised $23 million for "the first-ever venture fund
focused on startups that are transforming the trillion-dollar global
government-technology market."[20] He's gone on to raise more. Shaun
Abrahamson and Stonly Baptiste, two reformed govtech entrepreneurs, started their own firm in this direction as well. They launched
Urban Us in 2012 and aimed to invest in hardware and software companies solving city problems.[21] Julie Lein and Clara Brenner had created Tumml, a startup hub for urban tech, and then launched their
Urban Innovation Fund. The *Wall Street Journal* observed, "More venture capitalists are seeking ways to support startups in sectors with
heavy red tape."[22] And it wasn't just the funds focused in these areas
anymore: Andreessen Horowitz, Highland Capital, and General
Catalyst were each in on the solve-public-problems action in some
fashion. Vista, a private equity firm, scooped up GovDelivery and
Granicus, two companies that helped governments inform their citizens. Berkshire Partners acquired Accela, a government permitting
and licensing company. *Government Technology Magazine* catalogued
more than six hundred unique investors—"from individual angel investors to large private equity companies"—investing in and shaping the govtech market.[23] I remember one thirty-day span in 2018
when almost $50 million was invested by venture capitalists in just
three firms selling technology to government in the United States:
$3.5 million for Seneca, a company that intended to help govern-
ments manage citizen complaints; $7.5 million for SeamlessDocs,
a company that was helping government create web forms; and
$38 million for Mark43, a company I had come to know that built
police-records management software. It was a lot of money being invested in not particularly flashy stuff. All of this might have been
kind of shocking, except that that spring looked a lot like the spring
before it, when $25 million had been invested in Neighborly to build

technology to help governments raise municipal financing, and $30 million was poured into OpenGov, a company that built software that helps with public budgeting and planning. These trends were evolving elsewhere, too. Daniel Korski had been deputy head of policy at 10 Downing Street and afterward launched PUBLIC with Alexander de Carvalho, a venture investor. They put together a suite of programs to help startups transform the public sector, which included advice and also capital, with an early focus on Europe and an eye toward the global govtech market.

I had set out in 2010 to chase possibility myself in Boston's city government. I had joined Harvard Business School to teach it in 2014. I set out to write this book about it as the decade came to a close, and as I did, possibility seemed within our grasp. The image that all the activities—the digital services and innovation offices; the incubators, accelerators, and fellowships; even the capital investments—conjured up in my mind was of a wildlife crossing, those green underpasses or overpasses that allow animals to cross safely from one area to another. Habitat fragmentation, it is called when humans build roads and canals and power lines that divide wildlife habitats, and these bridges and tunnels are meant to alleviate the division. And I thought that whatever it was that had fragmented our own habitats—hiving off government from entrepreneurs—whether it was political philosophy or the march of technology or just the burdens of bureaucratic buildup over time, that all this work individuals were doing all over the world was giving us a means of finding our way back to each other.

Coming Apart?

Then I wondered whether it would be enough. Would it last? That had been my question of the USDS and, by proxy, of the movement, and there were worrying signs. Some of the reasons seemed more mundane and even fixable, and others were more profound.

On the more banal side, govtech-startup enthusiasm did begin to meet with the reality of starting up at all (the most likely outcome being failure) and of starting up to sell to government. One CEO of one of these types of companies told me, several years into the job, "You would have to be an idiot to start a company that sells to governments." Another CEO was more generous, but clearly felt burdened by the high expectations that came with raising venture capital in this space (expectations for growth at high speed) and by the vagaries and vicissitudes of the government sales cycle. I wanted to beg both not to throw water on the whole enterprise in front of my students. Not because I wanted to hide the truth from my would-be public entrepreneurs, but because there were two truths. Selling to the government or starting up to solve public problems was challenging. And some companies were able to get quite good at it.

There are strategies for overcoming these more practical challenges and the frustrations that come with them. I have a few simple ones, and they come from my time observing startups in this space and especially from my time watching one of them: Shield AI, which was founded by Brandon Tseng (once a student of mine), his brother Ryan (a serial entrepreneur), and Andrew Reiter (a technologist).[24] Brandon had been a Navy SEAL and, at one point, a human building-clearer. He'd seen one of the most dangerous operations in modern warfare—entering a building—and imagined a better way. He, his brother, and Reiter, along with the team they built, developed autonomous flying robots that could enter buildings first, self-navigate and map buildings, and provide video intelligence to protect service members and civilians inside. More than twenty venture capitalists at first declined to fund the startup. Several said they would if only Ryan and Brandon would pivot to oil and gas companies or to making selfie drones. Eventually the two found investors who bought into their plan to sell to the military, and then the task was figuring out how to do so. Ryan understood the challenges of selling to programs within the US Department of Defense and similar customers, but felt it was more doable than selling-to-government pessimists thought, and I feel the same way. He said it was a matter of getting down to the building blocks, and I agree. Almost all government buyers are undertaking three (often separate . . . yikes!) processes: planning, funding, and acquiring. Governments assess their needs. They source and appropriate money. And they choose among possible providers and ultimately deploy the new products or services. In each of these phases there are biases for the status quo that good providers can overcome. The status quo of endowments affects governments assessing their needs: they are likely to overvalue their incumbent providers relative to their merits.[25] Therefore, new providers should work to deliver benefits well in excess of those of their often entrenched competitors, and those benefits should go well beyond just saving money. The status quo of the budget (it mostly rolls over from prior years, in many places) means that, among other techniques, strong providers must work to make sure the benefits they do offer get the attention of people in positions of budgetary authority. The status quo of behavior means that deploying any new product or service will run into serious obstacles if it requires public workers to alter very much how they do their work. New providers can seek to find ways to still deliver their new innovations, but should minimize the required behavioral change for public workforces. There are, of course, many other techniques that sophisticated government sellers are deploying, and I hope companies in this arena will get better at them. I do believe that one of the ways to scale possibility is to have companies build great products and services for governments and then to sell them skillfully.

Then there is, of course, frustration running in the other direction. I often advise companies selling to governments to realize that before you walked in with your really well-meant and well-thought-out and well-produced innovation, the official you are meeting with had a meeting with someone selling snake oil (maybe because the snake-oil salesman was related to someone "important"), and she has to spend all day keeping snake oil out of government, and she's not wrong to think you might be selling it, too. Frustration was born of fraud. It was also born of instability. Among the companies started up in this new wave, many have come and gone. Neighborly—which was going to revolutionize municipal debt financing for localities, and which was part of the investment spree I mentioned above, and which had piloted in Cambridge, Massachusetts, in 2017 and in Madison, Wisconsin, in 2018, among other places—was on its way to dissolution by 2019.[26] Some governments were being bombarded with promises of new this and new that (blockchain! virtual reality! machine learning!), and then jilted when the companies making these promises came and went. And frustration was born of hubris, too. Government officials were chastened by startups promising to solve complex problems with simple solutions. The officials were growing tired, to turn a phrase of a former US president, of hearing, "I'm from Silicon Valley, and I'm here to help."

Above and beyond these growing pains of govtech selling and buying, an even more profound anxiety was settling in. Mass automation loomed as a potential jobs killer. Mass observation (by cookies, sensors, etc.) made an awakening public feel like it was living amidst "surveillance capitalism."[27] People were worried that they were being exploited by their social-media platforms, and that their democracy was, too. And startup-driven ecosystems that had seemed a panacea a decade earlier ("we want to be more like San Francisco") were adding to inequality in cities. Skyrocketing housing prices, rampant

evictions, and rising homelessness in the Bay Area were three warning signs for cities elsewhere. There was a growing sense among
some that technology was not the solution to our problems—technology was the problem. Public officials justifiably felt that entrepreneurial types who'd promised to solve the problems on their plates
were filling them up with more.

If there was a growing enmity, the feeling was mutual. Tech workers were increasingly uncomfortable with the uses to which their
work product was being put. Five thousand Google employees wrote
to the company's CEO that "Google should not be in the business of
war." They specifically singled out Google's participation in Project
Maven, an artificial intelligence effort. Ash Carter, a scientist himself and a former US defense secretary, published an open letter in
reply. "Dear Googler," it started, before making the case for Google's
participation: national defense is an "inescapable necessity"; AI is
an "increasingly important military tool"; human involvement is
still required "in any decision to use lethal force"; making sure that
stays true and technically possible "takes specialists like you"; "your
very survival rel[ies] on the protection of the United States. Surely
you have a responsibility to contribute as best you can to the shared
project of defending the country"; and so on.[28] But AI for war wasn't
tech workers' only beef. Amazon employees protested the company's
work with Palantir, a big-data company that had been working with
US Immigration and Customs Enforcement (ICE). The protests came
amid ICE's detention of families at the US borders and raids in US
cities.[29] The workers also called on the company to "stop selling facial
recognition software to law enforcement." Their 2019 letter to CEO
Jeff Bezos concluded: "Our company should not be in the surveillance business; we should not be in the policing business; we should
not be in the business of supporting those who monitor and oppress

marginalized populations."[30] Amazon told its employees it would continue selling Rekognition to law-enforcement agencies. Then, in June 2020, the company put a one-year pause on letting police use the tool, "in a major sign of the growing concerns that the technology may lead to unfair treatment of African-Americans."[31] The company expressed hope that the pause "might give Congress enough time to put in place appropriate rules" for ethical use of the technology.[32]

A bridge had been built between two worlds, and now it threatened to come down. There are no simple answers for how to make sure that it doesn't or, conversely, for how to know when in fact it should. Governments will regulate technology companies in the ensuing years, but with which motives, and precisely how? Some wary techies will keep their talents from governments, but to what effect? And in many places, a circumspect public will ask them both to keep their distance from each other (facial-recognition bans are one example; so is the battle over encryption), but by how much? Some questions seem easier for me to answer. Yes, companies should help the United States protect itself from its adversaries. No, software engineers should not be compelled to help authorities separate parents from their children. No, they shouldn't be violating civil liberties and human rights. Many questions can be answered only on a case-by-case basis. Take just one: The Waze app we came across in chapter 5 led an elderly couple into a Brazilian neighborhood where they became the victims of a deadly shooting.[33] In the wake of that tragedy, Waze could incorporate data about neighborhood safety into its app. It could give the app the technical capability to route people around "dangerous" places. But could the company do that without discriminating against particular neighborhoods (digital redlining) and their residents? Where should the company and the governments it works with strike a balance between safety and equity? Answers to that precise question and the thousands just like it raised by this modern marriage of startups and governments are mostly beyond the scope of this book, though we have addressed some strategies for beginning to tackle them: designing with users, testing and iterating, and mastering platform mechanics. And I do think there is one other strategy that can help.

Trisector Athletes

Joe Nye, a professor at Harvard's Kennedy School of Government and its former dean, described a unique kind of leader with the ability to "engage and collaborate across the private, public, and social sectors."[34] He called them trisector athletes. What we need today more than ever are trisector entrepreneurs—leaders who can invent and build across all three sectors.

In 2013, Nick Lovegrove and Matthew Thomas, two private sector consultants who had also worked in public organizations, expanded on Nye's definition. They pointed out that the world's biggest problems all required government, business, and nonprofits to cooperate. They acknowledged that the challenges to developing trisector leaders were partly owing to "a widening disparity between business, government, and nonprofit incomes, the onerous confirmation process for senior government jobs, and the differing incentives and cultures of the three sectors."[35] I'd say these obstacles are still present, wildlife bridges notwithstanding. Nevertheless, Lovegrove and Thomas argued that the world needed to nurture these types of leaders and that leaders could cultivate a trisector mindset in themselves. Aspiring trisector leaders could set out to balance competing motives, acquire transferable skills, develop contextual intelligence (seeing difference across the sectors and translating across them), forge an intellectual thread (I call this having an idea), build integrated networks, and maintain a prepared mind.[36] Theirs is a wise list.

I shared it with my MBA students on a day when I invited them to consider their own career choices by stepping into the shoes of five students who had come before them. One of those five was Henry Tsai. He had been an early employee at a tech startup that was later sold to Yahoo. He had worked for Marissa Mayer. He then came to Harvard Business School, and I was fortunate to have him in class. He spent a summer during business school working in the San Francisco Mayor's Office of Civic Innovation. On leaving business school, Tsai wondered whether he should return to private-sector tech or take on a more public role.[37] He ended up accepting a one-year fellowship in the office of San Jose Mayor Sam Liccardo. From there he went to Facebook, where he worked on the civic-engagement and elections-integrity team for several months, and then moved on to help manage the platform's antiharassment strategies and tools. The kinds of questions Tsai wrestles with in that role are not the kinds that lend themselves to easy answers. But I'm supremely confident that he is better at working through them for the time he spent in government. Moreover, I suspect that someday he will find his way back to public service, and that if/when he does, he will be even better in that role for the time he spent at Facebook. Now, Tsai is a special person; by makeup he could never be the kind of person who simply leveraged his government role into a private-sector gig or who would reenter the public sector to do his former employer's bidding. And I recognize that there are people like that, and that we should be on the lookout for them and even have policies that prevent them from abusing a revolving door. But I know Tsai takes questions of public value and public purpose into his private-sector work these days. And I know that if he goes back to serve publicly, he will take a sense of what is and isn't technically possible and commercially sustainable into the public work he does, and that the people he serves will be the better for it. And I believe that if more people pursued careers like this, we all would be better off.

Trisector entrepreneurship is not a method for solving all the riddles, but of giving us at least a fighting chance at solving them well, and it's something more than that, too. It's a method for arriving at a life well and interestingly and meaningfully and adventurously lived. We can, by inventing and building in each sector, develop a set of skills for doing so across them. Then all we have to do is decide what to use those skills for.

7

Inventing Democracy

Chuck Rhoades was the attorney general in New York.[1] Harvey "Hap" Halloran was the commissioner of the board of elections there. And in the spring of 2019, they got into it over possibility. Rhoades wanted to allow people to vote over their mobile phones. Halloran was not having it. The US attorney general was objecting, allegedly over "cybersecurity concerns," and Halloran was, at least at the moment, firmly on his side, telling Rhoades, "I share the attorney general's objection."

Rhoades rebutted, "I have an equally pressing concern: Democracy. And inclusiveness. This is why it's vital we approve mobile voting. This is about more people voting, which is the American ideal. It's about what's right, which is your board's mandate. Hap, let us seize this opportunity to be true patriots to bring a voice to those without one. I propose a pilot program to test the efficacy of mobile voting."

Halloran turned snarky: "We are all moved. Our hankies are damp." Then, seeking to end the discussion, he confessed, "We are looking to rule against, but thank you for dropping by." Later, when Rhoades again reached out to Halloran, the recalcitrant elections commissioner asked, "What do you want?"

Rhoades, restating his case, said, "Open and fair elections."

Halloran bent toward sarcasm again: "Yeah, well I would like to tap-dance like Gregory Hines, but I have neither the shoes nor the rhythm to pull it off."

Indignant, Rhoades shot back, "No, you don't have the will. But I do. Time to get my blockchain voting pilot program out of the gates."

Halloran was unmoved: "You are not going to get a fucking pilot program."[2]

Many of us who've labored at one point or another in public service can imagine ourselves as Rhoades in that moment. The fact is that even Rhoades had to imagine himself as Rhoades, because he wasn't real. He was a television character played by award-winning actor Paul Giamatti on the sensational Showtime television show *Billions*. How the cast captured the back-and-forth among bureaucrats so granularly (and profanely) is simple to grasp. Just ask any of us who have been there. But how a storyline on the arcana of blockchain voting ended up on a Showtime hit, well, to understand that—and to decide for yourself whether some real-life Rhoades should get a real-life blockchain-enabled mobile-voting pilot to fix our real-life democracy—you have to reach further. You have to go back to an Indian polling place in 1984, to an Afghanistan hillside in 2012, and to the real New York City in 2015.

Nimit Sawhney remembers the first time he thought about protecting the vote. It was not long after India's Prime Minister Indira Gandhi had been assassinated. "It was a . . . tough time," he recalled, delicately. "There were elections immediately after, and while I was too young to vote, I did see people forced to vote at gunpoint."[3] Sawhney declined to reveal more about that day to me. But when I read reports of "booth capturing" back then, where armed gangs would attack a polling place and "shoot it out until one party takes command of the ballot boxes,"[4] I began to understand why he said, "Maybe someday we'll find a way to make sure that doesn't happen again," and why someday might be someday soon. Sawhney went on to build a career as a software engineer and worked in digital security. He moved to the United States. In 2014, he started prototyping a mobile-phone-based election system with coercion-detection and coercion-prevention capabilities. He began building a platform that would leverage blockchain technologies to make voting tamper-resistant. It was the kind of thing that Giamatti, as Rhoades, was advocating for on *Billions*, and it was, by 2016, available from the company Sawhney had turned his project into: Voatz.

Mac Warner's first visions of mobile voting came when he was watching a shepherd tending his sheep. Warner was a US Army officer, on one of two tours in Afghanistan, and had had trouble voting. The obstacles that get in the way of voting while abroad—relying on snail mail to remote locations, tracking down fax machines, voting by email without privacy—had bedeviled Warner. He was frustrated. Then he felt frustrated for his kids, all four of whom had followed in his footsteps to serve their country abroad. And then he felt . . . possibility? Warner was on a mission and saw an Afghan shepherd on the side of a remote mountain tapping away on his mobile phone. The logical leap wasn't too large: If the shepherd could be on his mobile phone out there to take care of his responsibilities, why couldn't Warner? When the former army officer became the secretary of state for West Virginia in 2017, he told his team to fix overseas voting for West Virginians serving abroad. Mobile phones became the centerpiece of that initiative. "These people are putting their lives on the line. They have skin in the game, and they should be able to vote in our democracy." A year later, West Virginia paired up with Voatz to try mobile voting for overseas voters for the May 2018 elections, which included the US congressional primary. Two West Virginia counties participated. Thirteen citizens stationed abroad voted from their mobile phones. Rhoades hadn't yet gotten his "fucking pilot program," but Warner had gotten his.

Bradley Tusk was doing battle of only the metaphorical sort when he first homed in on the power of mobile phones in voters' hands. He had, after a career in politics, become Uber's first lobbyist, its self-described political "fixer."[5] In 2015, New York Mayor Bill de Blasio was backing a plan that would have limited the number of new Uber drivers per year to less than what the company, at the time, was adding each week. Irritated, Uber added a "de Blasio" feature to its app in New York City, so that customers would see what New York might be like, in the company's view, under de Blasio's plan: long wait times or no cars at all. And Uber invited its customers, directly from inside the app, to email the mayor and the city council to "say 'no' to de Blasio's Uber."[6] The customers did. De Blasio backed down, and Uber removed the feature.[7] But Uber's use of its app—and of the phones it resided on—didn't start or end in New York City. Time and again, taking the lead of the company's cofounder, Travis Kalanick, and with Tusk's early help, the company activated its customers to text and tweet and talk on Uber's behalf. Tusk explained, "The reason ridesharing is legal in all the jurisdictions in the US. . . . is because, over time, a couple of million people weighed in with elected officials, and that won the day. What that said to me is that if you give people the tools to advocate from their phones, they will vote." Tusk dedicated much of his post-Uber time—and some of his post-Uber fortune (he had taken stock in the company as his consulting fee)—to the prospect of mobile voting. Tusk, with Sheila Nix, a political strategist who he'd tapped to lead his philanthropic efforts, would tell anyone who would listen (and many who wouldn't) about mobile voting and its potential to increase voter participation and, therefore, to tilt democracy away from extreme voters and special interests. Tusk even extolled the virtues of mobile voting to one of the creators of *Billions* over dinner one night,[8] but not before he had made it happen in real life. Tusk had funded the West Virginia pilot.

The Sawhney/Warner/Tusk experiment had come together hurriedly in the spring of 2018, but it had apparently gone off without a hitch. Plans were in place to open it up to overseas voters from all West Virginia counties for the upcoming November election. Tweaks were underway to make it even more robust. Then, on August 6, 2018, Kevin Beaumont, a self-described "EU security tweeter," tweeting as @GossiTheDog, retweeted a CNN article about Voatz and the upcoming November election with his own commentary: "This is going to backfire." He accused Voatz of operating with out-of-date security for remote logins. He added, "If a startup (I'm sure they're nice people btw) with 2m in funding approaches and says they have biometric security and Blockchain it still need[s] independent vetting . . . There needs to be oversight here." He went on, "I'm a foreign dude with an avatar of a cowboy porg riding a porg dog on Twitter who appears to have done more investigation of the security implications of this than anybody. Bonkers, America."[9]

Bonkers, America? Sawhney and his team, Warner and his, Tusk and Nix—they had demonstrated that citizens and leaders, entrepreneurs and elected officials, could together experiment with the apparatus of democracy. But ought we? It's not just a question on television. Once we've come to develop the tools for Possibility Government, what should we use them for? @GossiTheDog had a view on it. What should the rest of us think?

Democratic Recession

Around the time that Sawhney, Warner, and Tusk were making their visions a testable reality, three books came out that sounded the alarm bells on democracy: *The People vs. Democracy*, by Yascha Mounk; *Can Democracy Work?*, by James Miller; and *How Democracies Die*, by Steven Levitsky and Daniel Ziblatt. Their titles foreshadow their conclusions.

Mounk relays a trove of dire data on democracy. Less than half of young Americans are likely to say "that they take an active interest in politics."[10] Only 48 percent of those born in the 1970s do, and these aren't kids.[11] These are people (like me) with kids. It gets worse. Less than one-third of American millennials believe "that it is extremely important to live in a democracy . . . close to one in four millennials now think that democracy is a bad way of running the country."[12] One in six Americans "believe that army rule is a good system of government."[13] "The good news," Mounk ventures, "is that the number of people who say that army rule is a good way to run America is indeed smaller than the number of people who hanker after a strong-man who doesn't have to bother with Congress or elections." If that was the good news, I was afraid to learn what the bad news was, but Mounk gave it to us anyway. "The bad news is that [the number who say army rule is a good way to run America] is rising rapidly."[14]

Mounk also reminded us what two renowned political scientists, Martin Gilens and Benjamin Page, had found in their research into the question of who rules? The economically elite, along with narrow special interests, had the most influence, they showed. "The preferences of the average American appear to have only a minuscule, near-zero, statistically non-significant impact upon public policy."[15] Near-zero? No wonder a majority of Americans distrust people in public life.

There's apathy about our way of life; openness, even enthusiasm, for strongman rule; and antagonism toward our elected leaders. Then there's antipathy toward our fellow citizens. Levitsky and Ziblatt offered the following observation: "Consider this extraordinary finding: In 1960, political scientists asked Americans how they would feel if their child married someone who identified with another political party. Four percent of Democrats and five percent of Republicans reported they would be 'displeased.' In 2010, by contrast, 33 percent of Democrats and 49 percent of Republicans reported feeling 'somewhat or very unhappy' at the prospect of interparty marriage."[16] Also bonkers, America?

And bonkers, world? The democratic retrenchment—a "democratic recession," as political scientist Larry Diamond has called it—is present across the globe. "In much of Europe . . . citizens are less likely now than a few decades ago to believe their elected representatives prioritize the interests of the general public," Mounk reported.[17] He described a 2017 poll that showed rising support of strongmen leaders in Germany (33 percent), France (48 percent), and the United Kingdom (50 percent), double the numbers there from a similar poll in 1999.[18]

James Miller relayed another depressing, and global, trend:

For many years, the best-known such index was that produced by Freedom House, an American government-funded nonprofit organization dedicated (in its own words) "to the expansion of freedom and democracy around the world." Ever since the late 1970s, it has graded countries on a scale of one to seven, measuring 10 indicators of political freedom and fifteen indicators of civil liberties, and then sorting 195 countries into three categories: free, partly free, or not free. Its annual report for 2018, titled "Democracy in Crisis," found that a total of 71 countries had suffered net declines in political rights and civil liberties, compared with only 35 that registered gains: "This marked the 12th consecutive year of decline in global freedom."[19]

If Possibility Government is Mayor Peduto and testing robot cars and "the status quo is the dangerous choice," then the case for possibility democracy seems, by these measures, open and shut. Doing nothing looks to be awfully risky.

Blinking Red

The problem is, as it almost always is, that doing something is risky, too.

If democracy in 2018 was atrophying where it resided, it was also under assault from its adversaries. "Today, the digital infrastructure that serves this country is literally under attack," the US director of national intelligence, Dan Coats, warned in July of that year. "I'm here to say the warning lights are blinking red," he said, using the same language that had been deployed, unsuccessfully, ahead of the 9/11 attacks on the United States. He named several "offenders"—China, Iran, and North Korea—but he said that Russia was the "most aggressive foreign actor, no question. And they continue their efforts to undermine our democracy."[20] Continue . . . because what was widely understood, if not universally acknowledged, was the Russian intervention in the 2016 presidential election. The colloquially named Mueller Report was actually a "Report on the Investigation into Russian Interference in the 2016 Presidential Election," and the conclusions on Russia's role were damning. "The Russian government interfered in the 2016 presidential election in sweeping and systematic fashion," reads the report's second sentence.[21] Then, in great detail, that sweep is spelled out. Coats was worried in 2018 about what the Russians had done in 2016 and were still doing and were likely to do. And the fear extended beyond presidential elections and particular campaigns. US intelligence agencies had also concluded that Russia had hacked state election systems. Three days before @GossiTheDog wondered if anyone in America was paying attention to the cyberthreats to mobile voting, the *Wall Street Journal* had reported that the American security apparatus was paying attention to cyberthreats to voting writ large. General Paul Nakasone, director of the National Security Agency (NSA), said US Cyber Command and the NSA were "tracking a wide range of foreign cyber adversaries and are prepared to conduct operations against those actors attempting to undermine our nation's midterm elections."[22]

Given these vulnerabilities, @GossiTheDog wasn't the only one sounding the alarm about the West Virginia pilot, now slated to expand for the November general election. Computer scientists, legal scholars, and other observers wondered aloud whether the time was really ripe to be experimenting on the vote. A *Vanity Fair* article gathered some of the building objections and wrapped them up thusly: "Should those votes be compromised, or should the app glitch, it would have a non-zero impact on overseas voters. Furthermore, other, similar, companies are testing their own versions of blockchain-backed mobile voting . . . These companies argue that their systems could help increase voter turnout. But an atmosphere in which the 'warning lights are blinking red' seems a less than ideal testing ground."[23] The article cited Joseph Lorenzo Hall, the chief technologist at the Center for Democracy and Technology, who called Voatz "a horrifically bad idea." He went on to say, "Imagine if you're a uniformed military serviceman stationed abroad, excited to be able to cast a ballot in, say, the West Virginia primary, where they plan on using a remote blockchain voting system . . . then imagine that in 20 years, the entire contents of your ballot are decryptable and publicly available . . . It's not something we should throw to the [venture capital] wolves or allow bleeding-edge technologies to mess with, without serious and deep inquiry and interrogation."[24]

Resistance to mobile voting was a contemporary strain of already established resistance to electronic voting and internet voting. In 2017, fourteen countries used some form of internet voting. Estonia was the first to introduce permanent national internet voting.[25] But political scientists worried about all the risks. "Security threats to internet voting exist in the form of internal actors (i.e., voters, election officials, service providers) or outside actors (i.e., individuals, organizations, or even hostile countries)," one warned.[26] These actors could launch denial-of-service attacks to prevent access to voting websites, they could imitate other voters, they could hack into systems to steal or otherwise modify votes, they could dupe voters via phishing attacks, they could infect the voting software with viruses or malware. Any or all of this could break confidentiality of the vote, compromise its integrity, make the vote unavailable, or make it impossible to know who had voted. It could swing elections. A thousand things could go wrong, some of them cataclysmic.

Imagining, Trying, and Scaling

In light of the risks of doing nothing to fix our democracy and the risks of doing something, Tusk came down firmly on one side. "It's not that the cybersecurity people are bad people per se. I think it's that they are solving for one situation, and I am solving for another.

They want zero technology risk in any way, shape, or form. So, paper maybe solves the problem for them. But in my view, when you can't resolve the issues on guns, on climate, on immigration, because the middle 70 percent doesn't participate in primaries—where I don't see a world where the U.S. still exists as one country because we are this polarized—well, if you don't want that to happen, you have to solve the dysfunction a lot, lot faster. I am solving for the problem of turnout. If turnout were actually 82 percent and going to paper-only ballots would reduce it to 80 percent, well okay, that's not an unreasonable tradeoff. But when turnout in a primary election is really only 12 percent, I argue that even if you win the battle, you lose the war." He held his view about the potential of mobile voting not only strongly but also optimistically: "At a certain point, the future always wins."

Not always. Sometimes, on some issues, the future takes next to forever in arriving or never does. And sometimes it arrives, but dangerously or unfairly. The techniques of Possibility Government should be for occasioning the future and for helping to get it right. By that bar, how did Tusk, Sawhney, and Warner do?

Ideas don't get actors to play them in Showtime dramas, but if they did, the Sawhney version of mobile voting would have needed one right out of Possibility's central casting. It was born in Sawhney's own experience as a citizen, when he was troubled by what he had seen in India. It was kindled, at a hackathon at South by Southwest, the film, media, and music festival in Austin, Texas, in 2014. It was there that Sawhney and his brother brainstormed areas around creating tamper-resistant technology via blockchain and landed on voting, walking away with $10,000, one bitcoin, and thirty minutes with a venture capitalist as their winning prize. The venture capitalist then promptly told them not to pursue it: It was too hard of an industry. They had too little knowledge of US elections or elections anywhere.

Sawhney spoke to people across the technology industry. "Interestingly, almost every person we talked to said, 'Don't do it. It will be a giant waste of your time.' Everyone kept telling us there were so many hurdles. Legislative issues, political challenges, regulatory matters . . ." Unswayed, the team spoke to politicians, to town and city clerks, to election auditors across the country. And they met with voters, and they thought like them—pondering the obstacles they faced to vote and the lines they waited in—and they made the leap. Create choices before making choices. Widen the aperture for ideas. Design with the users. Every problem is solvable, and the people who face them hold the key to their solutions.[27] If "government that can imagine" is the first step toward Possibility, here, in the form of hackathons and techniques of design thinkers, was that first step.

How Voatz built from that idea, and how it unfolded into the West Virginia test, had many of the hallmarks of "government that can try new things," too. Before the Voatz team rolled out mobile voting for congressional primary elections, they tested it on college campuses in student-council elections and in the Democratic and Republican party conventions in Massachusetts. These venues had similar(ish) characteristics, but lower stakes. Build, measure, learn. And when primary time did come, Warner's team had limited the test to only two counties and without too much fanfare. "We didn't push for the military agencies to send out email blasts; we didn't have the Federal Voting Assistance Program advertise on our behalf; we didn't do social media," said Donald "Deak" Kersey, Warner's general counsel. "We had no problem pulling the plug; we weren't too bold or too proud to stop doing what we are doing just because it provides a solution to a problem. We can always find other solutions." The results of the primary had been reassuring. The thirteen ballots were cast; none appeared tampered with. "The safeguards worked. We felt a lot more confident to move forward to the general," Kersey explained. His team and Voatz planned to put in "more stuff" for the November election. (For example, the West Virginia election officials wanted voter-verifiable ballots emailed to the voter and the state without sacrificing the voter's anonymity.) Build, measure, learn, again.

The question that lingered—lingers for us—now that blockchain-enabled mobile voting had been thought up and tried was, How should it be scaled? *Should* it be scaled? The November election, really? . . . The congressional election? And if that, then what? Then where? More than just overseas voters? Voters with disabilities, who have a harder time getting to the polls? All voters? (Voters during a pandemic?) Other cities and states? (Voatz had been in discussion with several states.) The 2020 presidential? How big could it get, and how big should it get? I was told that India's Prime Minister Narendra Modi might be interested in mobile voting. Close to a billion voters all on their mobile phones someday? What do we think about someday soon?

Democracy has been the architecture of one of the world's great scaling experiments: How might we allow the people to self-govern? In Athens, self-rule was invented and then spread. (Though some scholars have said it might also have existed in India, China, and Japan; later in Africa and Iceland; and among the native populations of Australia and America.)[28] It has spread inconsistently and imperfectly, but it has spread nonetheless. Perhaps sixty thousand citizens lived in Athens in 431 BC, when democracy made its "surprising appearance."[29] Today, more than four billion people live in democracies.[30] Government as a platform thinking offers insights into how that happened. At its best, democracy passes our "does an additional user make me better off?" test; at its best, democracy creates giant and positive network effects. The more people who come together, who vote, who participate, who rule, the better our society. Out of difference, strength. This was the central insight behind America's unofficial motto: "*E pluribus unum.*" Out of many, one.[31]

The question of whether and how mobile voting should scale thus becomes a platform-architecture question. Voatz had made a series of hardware choices (e.g., limiting its offering only to more-modern phones with certain identity-confirming biometrics) and software choices (e.g., leveraging a public-permissioned blockchain) that aimed to preserve the platform. With West Virginia, the team arrived at a nine-step process (application, authorization, authentication, voting, transmission, voter verification, preparation, tabulation, postelection auditing) in accordance with rules (e.g., the system is intuitive, it works for users with screen readers, it does not allow mismarking of ballots, it protects personal data, etc.) to protect each vote's integrity. The question is, At scale, will these components—the software, hardware, rules, and process—hold up? Sawhney is confident that in time they will. Alex Halderman, a University of Michigan computer science professor who made a name for himself by successfully hacking into voting machines, remained a skeptic. He worried about the risks to voter anonymity. As the November elections creeped closer, Halderman called blockchain voting "mostly hype."[32] Possibility Government imagines, tries, and then scales. Sawhney, Warner, and Tusk had availed themselves of its tools. Time will tell us how well.

Democracy Entrepreneurship

There are many ways of answering the question of whether mobile voting should exist. We can weigh the risk of not doing versus doing.

We can assess, as we just have in part, the way of going about it. We can also ask, as some mobile-voting skeptics have, about alternatives. With so many pieces to an election, why not focus elsewhere? Somewhere safer? Why not registration? Or why not some other angle on participation? (Why not a voting holiday?)[33] Maybe work on making democracy more open, more representative. Change who runs. Reinvent redistricting. Expand the franchise. But do you have to experiment on the vote itself?

This, broadly speaking, was the view of Larry Schwartztol. He was counsel at an organization called Protect Democracy, which had been watching Voatz with considerable concern. "Tech and voting?" I had asked him, "Is there any combination of those two things that you would be okay with?" He replied, "I have a hard time seeing a vision for voting and technology that doesn't increase the attack space for interference. I don't know that that will be the governing principle for all time, but for right now, that should have some weight."[34] ("Right now" was his version of "the warning lights are blinking red.") He continued: "There is an intense threat from Russia and others. It's not clear that the federal government is taking sufficient steps to mitigate those. The states are a patchwork of voting systems, which means there are multiple pathways of attack but no unified defense. This is important because attacking any one state could undermine the country's confidence in election outcomes more broadly." As for Voatz in particular, he felt that the biometrics and blockchain gave a false sense of security. And he worried, as others had, about the risk of even false claims of intrusion. "Voting is like currency," he elaborated. "Its value depends on the confidence of the electorate. So when confidence takes a hit, democracy declines."

What made Schwartztol's reaction so fascinating to me, and a little confounding as I tried to decide what I thought about Voatz, was that although Schwartztol and his organization objected to *this* experiment, they didn't object to the notion of testing and experimenting on democracy. In fact, they built their whole organization around that very core. I learned about Protect Democracy in the first place from Justin Florence, who had cofounded the startup in 2017. We become friends after he had moved to Boston from Washington, DC, where he had been in the Office of White House Counsel. He had seen up close how rules and norms in the executive branch protected the democracy, and he worried they were in retreat. Florence and Ian Bassin, who had also been a White House lawyer, started Protect Democracy to halt that slide. But they didn't start it in the mold of the traditional not-for-profit. They injected novelty and innovation into their culture. "We default toward action and we are willing to fail," their principles read in part. "We do unconventional things to address unconventional challenges . . . We would rather try ten things and fail on seven . . . ."[35] It was a culture of possibility. Bassin told me how this was playing out in 2019. "We have set up an entire stream of work . . . little beta projects. They are meant to be lean. They have gating tests. We give them limited time and limited resources. And we have set targets, so we will have clear signals on did we hit them or not. And if we do, we invest more. The goal is that we will come up with twelve of these. We will test five or six. And we will have two that show enough traction that we will invest in next year."[36]

Schwartztol said to me, "I think we should ask: What's the problem Voatz is trying to solve? Is it participation? Well, are there other ways to solve it?"[37] He wasn't just asking hypothetically. He and his colleagues were actively experimenting with other ways to protect democracy. They had engaged software engineers (unusual for an organization that was otherwise made up mostly of lawyers, with Democratic and Republican pedigrees) to develop VoteShield. The idea behind the technology was to layer some data analytics on top of the voter-registration lists made public by the states each month and to monitor for aberrant changes: fifty thousand address changes in one month, say, instead of a more typical one thousand.

Bassin remarked,

People more typically think of the vulnerabilities of voting machines. But when we asked about their biggest fears on elections security, the voter-registration databases kept coming up. Voter-registration files are online all year long . . . the vulnerability is that much greater. And they are a centralized file containing every latent vote. Unlike voting machines, where you might get access to just one or a few . . . access the voter file and you now have access to the entire state. You could make very small changes in them that would be very hard to detect, and maybe then only months later. What would happen is someone's address might have been changed from 100 Main Street to 1000 Main Street. On election day, they will be told they are at the wrong polling place. They will be told to go across town. And maybe they will, or maybe they will have to go back to their job before their lunch break ends and miss the chance to vote. And if a particular demographic were targeted, it could change the outcome of the election.[38]

VoteShield could compare voter files from month to month and track the differences. Using machine learning, it could compare those differences to all other historical differences and find the changes that stood out. Protect Democracy built VoteShield the same way it built the organization. "We said, 'Let's do a beta,'" Bassin explained. "We said, 'Let's pick one state.' It was lean startup. 'Let's do the smallest possible version to see if it works.'" In less than four months—between September 2017 and January the following year—the team had a beta for Ohio that "absolutely spotted when there was a change in a voter file that went outside of standard deviations." While Sawhney was piloting his software with Mac Warner, Bassin and team were experimenting on theirs in Ohio, and later with Iowa's Secretary of State Paul Pate, and others.

"Are there other ways to solve it?" Schwartztol had asked. There is a small wave of democracy startups trying to answer just that. For-profit and not-for-profit. With tech and otherwise. On voting and more broadly. You can find more than a handful of new organizations working on democracy, even if we take a minimalist view of what democracy is: where "almost all adults have the right to vote; almost all adult citizens are eligible to hold office; political leaders have the right to compete for votes; elections are free and fair; all citizens may form and join political parties and other kinds of associations; diverse sources of information about politics and public policies exist and are legally protected; and government policies depend on votes, or other expressions of public opinion."[39] David Moss, a historian and a colleague of mine, started an effort that I find most hopeful: the Case Method Institute.[40] He and his team were training teachers to teach democracy by the case method all across the country. He and collaborators wrote twenty-two cases that "each explores a key decision point in the history of American democracy," and they invited the students to step into the role of president, senator, judge, citizen.[41] Over the question of the federal negative. During the battle for women's suffrage. Amidst the debate over referendum government and jury trials. "Faith in the democracy and in the essential principles of self-government has long been what united most Americans—what most bound them together. Yet sustaining and nourishing that faith, particularly in the face of unending crises, scandals, and transgressions, has always been part of the grand struggle of democracy," Moss wrote in an introduction to a compilation of those cases.[42] Each invites younger (and all) Americans to struggle. I'm astonished by what the early results (achievement test scores, but also measures of willingness to participate in democracy and even run for office) say about the ability of this effort to lift up teaching and learning, and I am made optimistic about our democracy. I believe Moss is onto something invaluable when he says engagement with the democracy, in the deepest and most active sense, is what we all need. Through each case, in each session, students are asked to reinvent a bit of America. Not always differently, but again.

"Are there other ways to solve it?" Schwartztol had asked about repairing our democracy, and Yordanos Eyoel was underway supporting a slew of organizations exploring just that. Eyoel led Civic Lab, itself a new effort as of 2019, and its work to support "democracy entrepreneurs."[43] A first cohort of seven organizations ran the gamut from promoting new models of civic organizing to supporting a new generation running for public office.[44] Their leaders were people like Katie Fahey, who had successfully led a grassroots campaign to prohibit partisan gerrymandering in the state of Michigan. Fahey was now attempting at her new organization, The People, to bring together Americans across deep political divides and "from all walks of life," to empower them to get more involved together in the political process.[45] Civic Lab was also supporting Darrell Scott, who'd cofounded PushBlack. Among the organization's aims: "to transform Black voting rates by building deep, daily relationships with millions of African-Americans through their phones."[46] By the summer of 2020, PushBlack was sending daily black-history stories and news stories via mobile platforms to more than five million subscribers.[47] Scott and his team were "huge believers in experimentation, constantly testing, innovating, and changing," Eyoel said. "That's what's made them nimble and successful."[48]

What does Eyoel say to those who tell her none of this can work, that democracy is too delicate for trying new things? "The thing I would say is that we can't afford not to try," she told me. "Our democracy *is* very delicate. And it cannot be left up to the political parties, the political elite, the academic elite, the economic elite, to define how our democracy works and who it works for. Every single person has a legal and moral obligation to contribute to refining and developing our democracy . . . And let's not forget, this entire republic we have"—she said, about the one her family had brought her to from Ethiopia at thirteen—"has always been an experiment. And when only 17 percent of people say they trust their government, there is something fundamentally flawed. We have to use everything at our disposal, including experimentation and innovation, to make this an inclusive and responsive and healthy democracy. I just don't see any alternative options."

Not all of the democracy-startup efforts will succeed. We know statistically that most of them won't. Not all of them will have the right idea. Most will try to make things better; some might make it worse. Ian Bassin says that generally speaking, and given the scope of the challenge, "the more the merrier." Eyoel has called on Americans to match every dollar they give to political campaigns with twice as many for democracy entrepreneurs, and she has called for philanthropists to invest in civic culture at the scale they invest in things like education, workforce training, and public health.[49]

In June 2020, as Americans took to the streets to protest in support of Black lives and against racial injustice, and as people around the world did the same, I asked Eyoel how she saw democracy entrepreneurship in that context. "One reason Civic Lab exists is because of my own personal experience," she replied, referring to the Boston Women's March she had helped organize in January 2017. The march ultimately brought out more than 175,000 people in Boston, as marches like it brought out millions across the world in support of human rights.[50] "I saw a lot of people who had never marched before; they'd never done anything 'public' besides vote. They marched and said, 'What do we do now?'"

Government That Can Scale

Possibility leaders

☆ Build government as a platform; places where government acts as a connector for other parties to (a) innovate and provide services and/or (b) exchange information and goods and services.

☆ Harness network effects to grow platforms. Maximize positive network effects—where each member makes the others better off—and minimize negative ones.

☆ Address "chicken or egg" issues in getting platforms started. Look to create value for one side first; subsidize one or both sides; or bring two sides on simultaneously.

☆ Share data, use application programming interfaces (APIs), etc., to enable platforms. But think beyond software. Also use hardware, rules (laws), and processes (operating plans).

☆ Create talent magnets for people from other sectors—entrepreneurs and others—to serve "tours of duty." Use fellowships, internships, and term-hiring practices.

☆ Think broadly about talent. Look for individuals with high humility. Avoid helicoptering know-it-alls.

Possibility citizens

☆ Look to create complementary services to government platforms (e.g., a teen basketball league as part of a community public-safety effort).

☆ Be watchful for who owns the platforms: government or business. In either case, retain democratic governance; you are the platform sponsor.

☆ Look for privacy, equity, autonomy, incumbency threats of platforms. Platforms can fail in many ways; they can concentrate power.

☆ For govtech entrepreneurs who want to help scale solutions with new products and services: selling is buying. Learn to break down the building blocks of government buying.

☆ Develop careers as trisector entrepreneurs. Rotate in and out of public service. Learn differences across sectors and how ideas translate across them. Build integrated personal networks. Then leverage these relationships and your contextual intelligence with integrity, not greed.

What everyone can do

☆ Work to solve problems at "population scale."

WE GET THE
GOVERNMENT
WE INVENT

8

Possibility or Delusion

t was April 2020 in Singapore, but still March in the United States for another hour, when I was on a video call with Ping Soon Kok and Jason Bay of GovTech Singapore.[1] Kok, Bay, and colleagues in Singapore's government-technology agency, along with their counterparts at Singapore's Ministry of Health, were leading the unfolding effort behind TraceTogether—an app that used Bluetooth technologies in smartphones to support community-driven contact tracing to slow the spread of Covid-19. The approach, still in its very early stages, had been praised as a part of Singapore's heralded virus-fighting efforts and had also generated questions about its potential privacy implications. Weeks later, Google and Apple would jointly announce plans for their own Bluetooth-based contact-tracing protocols, generating similar hopes and worries. (The two tech giants would later scale their plans back.) But in Covid-19 time, that was still eons away as Bay explained to me over Zoom how important it was to understand that the technology wasn't a panacea; how the technology needed to be built with users in mind; how much more effective it would be as it scaled (if it scaled). Kok chimed in, telling me that they hadn't been sure whether or not it would work, or whether they'd get buy-in on this as just one of a thousand and one possible solutions. I lay awake for a while after our call. Sleep hadn't been coming easy as Covid-19 swept the world. But this night, as I waited for dawn, what struck me was how fascinating and fraught Bay's approach had been. And how much of what he was leading looked like the other exercises in possibility I had come to know in writing this book.

Meanwhile, leaders everywhere were trying new things to slow the spread of the disease, to save lives, and to protect cratering economies, and not all—but some—of those efforts looked like something else entirely to me. The US president mused out loud about injecting disinfectants to kill the virus.[2] His comments were met with swift derision, and he later claimed to have been speaking sarcastically. Nevertheless, the manufacturer of Lysol and Dettol felt forced to put out a statement: "We must be clear that under no circumstance should our disinfectant products be administered into the human body."[3] There were reports that calls to US poison-control centers about drinking the disinfectants were up. One public-health official recounted a woman asking "if, for a child, it was better to inject or ingest."[4] Those episodes notwithstanding, I think it is safe to say that *most* people knew swallowing Lysol or bleach was no way to stem a pandemic. It was delusion.

But what about other new efforts to fight Covid-19 and its wreckage . . . possibility or delusion? Recall Jim March's observation in chapter 2 that inspiration and lunacy are not ex ante so clearly distinguishable.[5] Amid the crisis there was a flood of new suggestions to officials, all over and at every level. Ideas came from experts and outsiders. Email inboxes were swamped with offers for aid from long-trusted helpers and from possible swindlers. How could officials know which to try and which not to? How could we know which attempts to support and which to scorn?

And what about efforts to try new things to solve public problems overall? In more places and at more times, the public and its leaders should move on from probability—from doing things that "work" but achieve mediocre outcomes—and toward possibility. But we don't want to move past Possibility Government to something else entirely. And we seem, in places, at risk of that, too.

As I watched the unfolding events in Singapore and around the world, I wondered whether and where we could draw the line.

Contact Tracing Commenced

By the time Singapore's government first confirmed a case of Covid-19 in the country, on January 23, 2020, it had already deployed a key public-health tool in fighting infectious diseases: contact tracing. "The case is a 66-year-old male Chinese national from Wuhan who arrived in Singapore with his family on 20 January 2020," the Ministry of Health (MOH) press release read that day. The release described the circumstances of his arrival to Singapore, and it shared the results of traditional contact-tracing efforts that would later involve hundreds of human contact tracers in Singapore: "MOH has initiated contact tracing and nine close contacts of the case, who are his travelling companions, have so far been identified . . . The health status of all close contacts will be monitored closely. As a precautionary measure, they will be quarantined for 14 days from their last exposure to the patient."[6]

In deploying trained contact tracers so swiftly, Singapore was following on long-standing practice. Tracing has been a common strategy used around the world to fight the spread of sexually transmitted infections, dating back to the 1500s, though not without controversy.[7] Singapore officials were also drawing on their own experience containing prior viral outbreaks that had affected the region, like SARS in 2003, H1N1 in 2009, MERS in 2015, and Zika in 2016. Contact tracing had proved useful elsewhere, as well. For example, it had been used widely in Liberia during the Ebola epidemic in 2014–2015.[8]

Some experts viewed Covid-19 as a potentially good candidate for contact tracing because of the way it spread. On average, people with the virus began to show symptoms 5.5 days after being infected. During this presymptomatic period, they were capable of spreading the virus to others. Even more worrying, it appeared that people who never exhibited symptoms could spread the virus, too. The number of people that an infected person would go on to infect looked relatively high.[9]

So by February 10, Singapore's MOH had seventy contact tracers working in shifts seven days a week and following an orderly protocol. When a person was diagnosed with Covid-19, hospital staff first conducted an interview with that person to ascertain his or her movements during the period prior to the onset of symptoms.[10] Using this information, the hospital staff drew an activity map, which identified the places the infected person had visited, recent activity, and close contacts. Then, the hospital sent this activity map to the contact-tracing team within Singapore's MOH. Leveraging experts in communicable diseases, epidemiologists, and volunteers from various departments, they sought to create a full map of a patient's movements within twenty-four hours of diagnosis.

Contact tracers then verified the information in the activity map by calling all the places and people the infected person recalled visiting. During these calls, contact tracers gathered additional details about the patient's movements and generated a list of anyone who had had close physical contact with the patient, had lived in the same place, or had recently spent at least thirty minutes within two meters of the patient. These people—identified as close contacts—were deemed to be at high risk of infection. After the team interviewed these people, those experiencing symptoms were hospitalized and tested for Covid-19.

Close contacts exhibiting no symptoms following contact with the patient were given a choice to quarantine at home or at a government facility. Close contacts staying at home were required to stay in one room and use a bathroom that no one else used. If the MOH could not reach or identify a close contact, it enlisted the police to assist in the search.

Experts from around the world took notice of Singapore's early efforts.

"Got a Question for You"

While Singapore's MOH was scaling up the manual tracing efforts, Jason Bay was beginning to conjure up something new. On January 24, the day after his government had notified the country of the infected sixty-six-year-old male and his nine close contacts, Bay pulled over to the side of the road while driving home and started texting a friend at the MOH. Bay began his message with a greeting followed by an idea:

[2:52:22 PM] Happy new year! (Kinda) Got a question for you

[2:53:27 PM] Are you aware of any contact tracing mobile app solution currently?

[3:28:56 PM] 5 years ago i was in a convo with some others during another health scare. they wanted to use telco location data to help contact tracing.

[3:29:12 PM] but a mobile cell is too big. 300m radius in some cases. too many false positives.

[3:30:06 PM] if you think this is worth looking into, some of my devs are trying to figure it out

[3:30:51 PM] but we need to integrate it with a privacy-respecting db or some way to roll up the contact tracing tree

. . .

[3:32:28 PM] Ok. Here's my use case hypothesis.

[3:32:45 PM] I assume that a critical mass of Singaporeans download this contact tracing app.

[3:33:06 PM] This app continually scans for other users of the app using bluetooth.

[3:33:25 PM] When it finds another user, it takes a hashed identifier of the other person (for privacy) and stores a log.

[3:33:39 PM] I don't know if this log is to be stored centrally or locally.

[3:34:31 PM] But if the user is identified as a patient, that log can either be sent or inspected, and the list of other similarly equipped app/devices and timelogs of when the patient came into contact with them, can be downloaded and made available to MOH Ops.

[3:35:16 PM] Either that or we update some kind of "bulletin board" that other app users can check, and if they see that someone else they were in close proximity to has been infected, the app pushes a notification to ask the person to go see a doctor.

[3:35:52 PM] (Said bulletin board is a virtual metaphor. Just something the app auto checks in the background.)

[3:36:07 PM] Can you help me to check/validate this broad concept with the relevant people?

[3:37:08 PM] If it's useful, I'll ask some volunteers to take a spike on this over the next couple of days.

[3:37:58 PM] Let me know soon can?

Bay's MOH contact texted him back that it would be useful to find solutions to help with contact tracing. She sent Bay contact information for a colleague who could work with him. That was enough for Bay for the moment.

Bay's idea had a much shorter history than traditional means of contact tracing, but it wasn't brand new. In 2014, a researcher named Katayoun Farrahi had published an article with two other computer scientists suggesting the use of mobile phones to help recreate activity networks for use in contact tracing.[11] In 2015, two sixteen-year-olds, Clarissa Scoggins and Rohan Suri, both of the Thomas Jefferson High School for Science and Technology in Alexandria, Virginia, won Third Prize and $1,000 in the International Science and Engineering Fair for their project "Development of a Rapid, Accurate, and Private Contact Tracing System Utilizing Smartphone Proximities."[12] Suri had thought of the idea during the Ebola crisis. As a high school sophomore, he had read of the impact contact tracing was having, but also the challenges of scaling it, given the potential perils of face-to-face interviews amid such a virulent outbreak.[13]

To Bay, the Singaporean context seemed potentially well suited to a digital contact-tracing tool like the one Suri had thought of. There was precedent there for use of technology in the public domain.[14] Mobile penetration was high, with over 90 percent of Singapore's adults owning a smartphone.[15] Singaporeans were said to have a high degree of confidence in the government. Compliance with government requests was largely expected. Per one survey, some 75 percent of respondents said they trusted the way in which the government managed their personal data.[16] Wrote the BBC, in Singapore, "[W]hen the government calls and asks you questions, it is a near-certainty that everyone will cooperate."[17]

Still, Singaporeans had reason to worry. Recent data breaches in the country loomed large.[18] A government-initiated data-security review, which concluded in November 2019, yielded a number of recommendations to improve data security, which the government had begun to implement but had not yet completed.

Bay wanted to try to build a solution robust enough to address these concerns. On January 24 and over the holiday weekend (it was the Chinese New Year), Bay recruited his colleague Joel Kek, a GovTech software engineer. Soon they pulled several other volunteers into the effort. Bay told them, "The app will not be a 'silver bullet,' nor a replacement for Singapore's manual contact tracers." By February 8, the group had tossed around the idea and completed some bare-bones proofs of concept, which they then raised with others outside the division. Bay told Ping Soon Kok, GovTech's chief executive, about the idea, saying, "This is just something we are toying around with." Bay remembered, "We didn't want to promise too much. I just wanted to establish that we weren't wasting effort and that nobody else had already put together a turnkey solution."

Kok responded flexibly, if not overly hopefully. "With agencies clamoring for digital solutions to support their Covid-19 response, I needed to redirect Jason's resources to deliver more-immediate needs. We were tasked to develop digital tools to support the mask-distribution exercise, chatbots to handle Covid-19 queries, enhance our Gov.sg WhatsApp capacity, and many more. His was one of many ideas. But he was able to find some resources to get started, and as a senior director, Jason has sufficient autonomy in organizing and managing his division. So if he thinks an idea is worth pursuing, and it's not too much of an impingement on resources, he should do it."

Meanwhile, also on February 8, Prime Minister Lee Hsien Loong addressed the nation. "We have faced the new coronavirus situation for about two weeks now . . . Every day brings new developments, and we have to respond promptly and dynamically."[19] He spoke of contact tracing's value and its limits: "So far, most of our cases have either been imported from China, or can be traced to imported cases. When we discover them, we have isolated the patients, done contact tracing, and quarantined close contacts. This has contained the spread and helped stamp out several local clusters. But in the last few days, we have seen some cases which cannot be traced to the source of infection. These worried us, because it showed that the virus is probably already circulating in our own population." Because of this, officials raised the national risk-assessment level from yellow to orange, the second-highest level.

Building TraceTogether

With the knowledge that no one else in Singapore's government was creating a digital contact-tracing solution, with a proof of concept behind them, and with the go-ahead from Kok, Bay built a growing team to create TraceTogether. They also worked closely with the MOH during the development process. The TraceTogether team shadowed a group of contact tracers to understand their work and challenges, and began to gain what they felt were important insights. They learned that the manual contact-tracing process was designed to reduce false negatives, at the expense of producing many false positives. Bay understood that Singapore was issuing quarantining notices for 30 times to 40 times the number of confirmed Covid-19 cases. "If that's the case already," he thought, "TraceTogether shouldn't add more false positives to the mix." The focus would be on finding the people that human-led tracing efforts would miss: people the infected individuals might not recall being with, or strangers they might have been in proximity to, but did not know personally.

The plan for TraceTogether was that it would rely on "Bluetooth handshakes," or the wireless exchange of data between devices over short distances—typically up to ten meters. When a user downloaded TraceTogether, the app would attach a random ID to her phone number. This random ID would then be used to generate temporary IDs that were constantly refreshed. When two users' phones were close to one another, the app would exchange their temporary IDs, time-stamping the occurrence and logging the length of the encounter. The app would not track location, just proximity to other users and the duration of that proximity. By now, the team had settled on the idea that information would be stored locally on the person's phone and not uploaded to any central server or to the cloud. Bay described the decision to utilize Bluetooth technology: "Because it is a low power signal that degrades very quickly over distance, we can use signal strength to figure out the distance between two phones within a reasonable margin of error."

When someone within the TraceTogether system tested positive for Covid-19, the MOH would send the person a code and request access to her encrypted contact logs for the preceding twenty-one-day period. "It takes that long to establish upstream linkages," explained Bay. "You need one to two days of information to determine who the infected person might have exposed, but you need fourteen days to determine where the infected person herself may have been exposed." The user would then send the encrypted logs to the MOH, which would decrypt the code to access the "contacted" mobile-phone numbers. "At that point," said Bay, "we would do some post-processing to determine the distance between the person and all of her contacts." This information would then be passed on to Singapore's contact tracers, who would determine which individuals to contact and what action to take (e.g., testing, quarantine, issuing a stay-at-home notice, or isolation). The TraceTogether team still needed to find a way to help the MOH's tracers integrate the data into their current workflows; they planned to provide data to the contact tracers and activity mappers at first via either a dashboard that allowed them to segment data by day or in a table of close contacts.

The developers began conducting user surveys as they moved from theories to practice. "The design team went around the neighborhood," said Bay's colleague Joel Kek, "and asked people for their feedback on the wireframes we had put together. An overwhelming majority of people were positive about the app, but they raised two key concerns: battery life and privacy."

Policy and technical obstacles pushed the potential deployment into March. "Because we weren't asking for a government mandate that Singaporeans download the app, and we had positioned it as a voluntary action taken by socially responsible individuals in support of the community, our stakeholders were generally supportive," Ping Soon Kok recalled. "But some wanted to see that the app could work and that it would be secure." Kok worked to open up those paths for Bay and his team, while the engineers worked to sort out technical hurdles. One complication was that not all Bluetooth signals were created equal: different devices would transmit at different signal powers, complicating distance estimation. To sort this and many other lingering uncertainties out, the team embarked on a series of tests. These included static trials, where they placed multiple de-vices within range of each other and allowed them to run overnight; an indoor office trial, where GovTech's workers simulated common daily interactions; and field trials.[20] Tuning the app's algorithm for various devices and other tweaks resolved some issues the tests had surfaced. But one hurdle remained confounding and threatened even a March launch: the iPhone.

The operating system for Apple's iPhone created technical barri-ers to deployment of TraceTogether, given the way the iOS had been designed. Bay explained that in order to preserve battery power, and likely also as a privacy-protection measure, the operating sys-tem running on iPhones did not allow apps to run in the background and collect Bluetooth signals. This was in contrast to Google's An-droid operating system, which did. And while Bay understood that Google's operating system had about a two-thirds penetration rate in Singapore among mobile-phone users, that still left one-third run-ning Apple's iOS. The TraceTogether team built a potential work-around: if users kept the app running in the foreground but put their devices in power-saver mode (by putting their iPhones face down on a desk or upside down in their pocket), the app could function with-out draining the battery.

But that was a lot to ask of users, the GovTech team knew, and their field test bore out their concern. Even though users were briefed on how to handle their iPhones, they did not comply in practice, and the data collected was spotty. Entreaties to Apple executives both in Singapore and at the company's California headquarters in early Feb-ruary to change the restrictions had not borne any fruit. Now here they were, almost two months down the road and thousands of engi-neering hours into the project, and with the country's Covid-19 cases still creeping upward. Bay and his team decided to proceed none-theless. The app was submitted to the Google Play app store and to

Apple's App Store in mid-February. By March 16, TraceTogether had made it through the first, but not the second. A decision was made to target a March 20 launch date.

The TraceTogether team discussed whether to proceed if they could only launch for users of Android phones. Doing so would dramatically reduce the potential effectiveness of TraceTogether. The app's usefulness depended on deployment and adoption rates. The notion of sending a letter from Singapore's government with a high-level signature to executives at Apple—presumably the company's CEO, Tim Cook—was also floated. In the end, neither step proved necessary. The app made it into the App Store on March 18. On March 20, TraceTogether officially launched.

Ready for It?

On March 23, three days after TraceTogether's launch, Singapore's foreign minister (who was also a medical doctor) took to Facebook to announce that the underlying technology would be open-sourced and made available to the world.[21] He felt it would build trust in Singapore's efforts and lay the groundwork for potential interoperability across borders. Bay and his team put together a white paper and a policy brief on what they had built and how it might be used. I was struck that right there on their website, they spelled out the risks: "The biggest and most important caveat is that we are still in the very early stages of using TraceTogether to help with Singapore's contact tracing operations, and **it is too early to tell how effective Trace-Together actually is**."[22] (Bold and underline in the original.) They laid out, in their own words, that this was an exercise in possibility: "These are big dreams, and success is not guaranteed. There are both technical and non-technical challenges that stand in the way."

This, they said of a project they had promoted via the government's messaging platforms, that they had enlisted trade unions and privacy companies to promote, and that they had generally tried to rally the nation around with the following tagline: "Protect ourselves, Protect our loved ones, Protect our community."

The day I first spoke to Bay, the app reached 1 million downloads, in a country with a population just over 5.5 million. While adoption had exceeded his expectations for the moment, it fell short of optimal. And though close to 20 percent of Singaporeans had TraceTogether on their phones, Bay and his team had very little data about how well it was actually working. Three weeks after launching the app, Bay noted, "We have not had any interesting results so far from a clinical perspective." The team had identified twelve close contacts. Of these, nine had already been identified by the manual contact tracers. "We had one false positive," Bay continued. "This person lived in an apartment complex and was sitting on the opposite side of a wall from a person with Covid-19."

On April 3, Singapore's Multi-Ministry Taskforce announced that an "elevated set of safe distancing measures" would go into effect on April 7.[23] The task force was acting out of significant worry about a growing number of locally transmitted Covid-19 cases over the preceding week. Now the country would move toward full home-based learning for schools and close most workplaces. If people would be interacting less, it meant that TraceTogether, still in its infancy, might not have a chance to grow up very much, at least over the coming month.

It would be hard to walk the foreign minister's promise back. This left it to Bay and his team to get the app ready for the world. And it left leaders in countries all over the world to decide whether they were ready for it.

Possibility or Something Else?

What struck me amid all of this was how much the effort to shepherd TraceTogether from idea to reality in eight weeks' time looked like all the efforts at Possibility Government I had witnessed. There was the idea from outsiders. (A high schooler on the other side of the world?) There was the designing with users. There was the building and testing. (They'd built "device farms" to test Bluetooth signals and experimented by placing phones around the office in their backpacks and briefcases.) There was the leveraging of platform thinking.

Not everyone thought TraceTogether was something worth trying. Bay had promised that TraceTogether was designed to support the work of Singapore's human tracers, not replace it. But his promise meant that a data-collection effort, albeit with privacy protections, was now linked to a centralized government interviewing, identifying, and quarantining effort. This moved some observers and researchers to advocate against systems like TraceTogether categorically, and others to advocate for alternative approaches.

Digital-tracing strategies had led to concerns that such tools might compromise individuals' privacy and violate legislation, especially in European Union countries subject to the General Data Protection Regulation. One expert said that Covid-19 had opened the door to invasions of personal privacy that could last long after the pandemic, warning of a "9/11 on steroids."[24] Another noted the risk of contact-tracing apps becoming "vehicles for abuse and disinformation."[25]

Bay and his team had tried to anticipate these concerns. Downloading the app was voluntary at the outset, and Bay said they prioritized collecting only the minimum essential information for TraceTogether to achieve its purpose. Phone numbers between contacts were not exchanged within the app, no geolocation data was shared, and no personal-identification data was exchanged. Contact logs were also deleted after twenty-one days. The decision to attach a random ID to users' phone numbers rather than storing the encrypted phone numbers themselves was made to enable users to revoke consent and have their data erased. A TraceTogether FAQ stressed these points.

This did not allay all the privacy and governance concerns. One alternative strategy was to still use smartphone-based apps and still track proximity-duration information (either with GPS or Bluetooth, or both) but not share that collected information through centralized authorities. Researchers at the Massachusetts Institute of Technology (MIT), in collaboration with others at Harvard University and the Mayo Clinic (and with software engineers at companies such as Facebook and Uber), had developed an app called Private Kit: Safe Paths.[26] In its early development, the app tracked a user's GPS location/movement every five minutes and kept the encrypted data stored on the user's phone for up to twenty-eight days. This information was not shared with third parties without the user's consent.[27] Within the app, a user could self-report that she had tested positive for Covid-19. Other users would then receive notifications if they had been near that individual during the infectious period. The notification would contain no personal information (e.g., name, age, etc.) about the user with Covid-19.

As Singapore was rolling out TraceTogether, MIT and its collaborators were in discussions with a dozen cities around the world to run pilots.[28] A March 26 column in the *Economist* labeled these approaches "bottom-up," and called their civil-liberties risk "low."[29] The same column characterized Singapore's approach, by contrast, as "top-down" and its civil-liberties risk as "high." A *New York Times* article the same week featured TraceTogether and other tech-driven tracing approaches with the warning: "Tracking entire populations to combat the pandemic now could open the doors to more invasive forms of government snooping later."[30]

Jason Bay, Joel Kek, and five teammates at GovTech had written of these alternative approaches that moved government officials out of the loop: "In theory we appreciate the privacy and scalability benefits of doing so. In practice, our ongoing conversations with public health authorities performing epidemic surveillance and conducting contact tracing operations compel us to recommend otherwise."[31] Singapore's foreign minister had said of TraceTogether: "It's a hybrid system based on public support, keeping trust, and maintaining privacy. I think it's important to have those features because otherwise contact tracing will not work." He also explained that the Singapore government wanted to "avoid a false dichotomy, between a completely centralized government system where Big Brother knows it all, or a decentralized anonymous system where it is a free-for-all and no one really has an overall view of the data."[32]

There were more than privacy concerns about TraceTogether and apps like it. There were worries that the apps might provide a "false sense of security." There were concerns the apps might simply be ineffective and a drain on attention and resources best spent elsewhere. Alarms were raised that because of uneven smartphone use, the apps might leave certain populations, "the aging or the under-resourced," beyond the reach of possible benefits.[33] Three experts painted an especially dire picture, writing in April 2020:

> The issue of malicious use is paramount—particularly given this current climate of disinformation, astroturfing, and political manipulation. Imagine an unscrupulous political operative who wanted to dampen voting participation in a given district, or a desperate business owner who wanted to stifle competition.

Either could falsely report incidences of coronavirus without much fear of repercussion. Trolls could sow chaos for the malicious pleasure of it. Protesters could trigger panic as a form of civil disobedience. A foreign intelligence operation could shut down an entire city by falsely reporting Covid-19 infections in every neighborhood. There are a great many vulnerabilities underlying this platform that have still yet to be explored.[34]

This swirl of opportunity and peril played out quickly in places beyond Singapore. Daniel Korski, who we came across in chapter 6, made the case, of sorts, for the United Kingdom's own Covid-19 app, after it had already been abandoned. National Health Service (NHS) officials had, since March, worked to build an app similar to Singapore's TraceTogether, but in light of Google and Apple's subsequent rollout of "exposure notification" interfaces, as well as technical struggles with the app in development, the NHS shelved its original app in favor of another using the Google/Apple Application Programming Interface (API). But where some saw this, yet again, as proof that governments should steer clear of new technologies, Korski saw something else. "That's the wrong lesson to take," he said. "The story of the NHS app is the story of ministers and officials trying to buck the worst instincts of government." He wasn't arguing for a return to the original app, to be clear, but rather for more of the NHS's experimental approach in government, and not less. After it was all said and done, he could look approvingly at how NHS and its collaborators had tried (built prototypes, tested them in limited fashion on the Isle of Wight, expanded the tests to more real-life scenarios, and yes, abandoned the effort when more testing uncovered more problems and "when the original app was found to be wanting when compared with the Google/Apple version"). The hoped-for solution hadn't panned out, but "this process," he wrote, "is a model of how government must work."[35]

So where Bay and his team saw possibility, others saw fantasy. Where Korski saw possibility, others saw waste. And it raised the question for me, how would we know which it is? Across the thousands of efforts being tried to fight Covid-19, and the infinite list of things that had been tried or would be to solve all of our public problems, where was the line between possibility and delusion?

If you ever had to find the line before or during a project, and not simply after it finished, where was it? If you thought in the spring of 2020 that pursuing chloroquine and hydroxychloroquine as Covid-19 treatments was a fool's errand, it couldn't just be because you didn't like President Trump, who was the old drugs' main champion. For starters, he wasn't the only one pushing them. The state of Utah ordered $800,000 worth and contemplated buying millions of dollars more, following the recommendation of a Utah physician who touted the drugs' efficacy "in test tube studies," reports from ICUs, and, most publicly, a study (not a randomized control trial) from southern France that suggested that 80 percent of patients on hydroxychloroquine had "cleared the virus," despite these claims being "without any rigorous evidence the drugs can help patients recover faster from Covid-19."[36] What's the basis for not liking that chance-taking, yet liking others? And what to make of leaders who had shut regions down early in the pandemic: Fast-acting *possibilitists* for slowing the spread, or *delusionists* for locking down entire jurisdictions without knowing spillover consequences? How would you have judged their efforts *at the time*? And what to think of the leaders who moved to open up their cities or states or countries early . . . like Georgia's Governor Brian Kemp, who announced that certain businesses could reopen in April 2020, defying public-health warnings and the timelines of some of his peers, or Las Vegas Mayor Carolyn Goodman, who also in April wanted to reopen that city and offered it up as a "control group" to measure the impacts of easing restrictions.[37] Could you, surely, have known then whether they were being foolhardy? Or whether they were simply following in the spirit of Louis Brandeis, the famous American jurist, who'd made popular the notion of individual states as "laboratories of democracy"?

Possibility versus Delusion

I went back in light of all of this and asked the people I'd met along the way what they thought about distinguishing between possibility and delusion, and I asked some others as well.[38] I went back to James Geurts, Jimmy Chen, and Annie Rittgers, who'd labored to open up organizations and systems to new ideas. Back to Gabriella Gómez-Mont, Bill Peduto, and Molly Turner, who'd tried even when trying was perilous. Back to Paige Fitzgerald, Bradley Tusk, and Yordanos Eyoel, who'd thought about possibility at scale. I asked scholars of entrepreneurship and of social change. (See the box "Some Signs You Might Be Deluding Yourself and the Public.") I asked Eric Paley, a venture capitalist who'd seeded this particular riddle in the first place, with an article he'd written in 2016.[39]

Some Signs You Might Be Deluding Yourself and the Public

- If your idea **isn't tied into a bigger mission**.

- If your idea targets symptoms of a problem and **you haven't spent any time uncovering what the underlying causes** are.

- If you are trying to bring about systemic change and **you haven't mapped the system**.

- If you **haven't raised your idea with the people you think you are trying to help**.

- If **the rewards don't substantially outweigh the risks**.

- If **those affected by your potential failure are not in a position to bear the risk**.

- If the **risks are substantially borne by parties different than those that would benefit from the returns**.

- If you are **introducing systemic risks you have not accounted for**.

- If you have **not thought about how others might use your new thing with ulterior intentions**.

- If you **ignore evidence that exists already that your idea can't work**. It's not that ideas tried before can't succeed on a second or third attempt under new leadership or in new contexts or with more practice. But you can't take concrete scientific or technical barriers and throw them out the window.

- If your idea **isn't testable** at all or not testable in reasonably short cycles.

- If your **tests aren't observable or measurable**.

- If you **ignore negative data** that comes back from your tests.

- If your **tests aren't reversible** and for reasons of politics or intransigence, budget processes or resource commitments, you can't dial your project back even amid overtly negative signals.

- If your **tests are not bounded** at all; if you are trying something new on everyone, all at once, at all times; if you are committing too much capital (energy, money, goodwill) before proving that what you are working on is possible.

- If your new thing requires partnership and you **haven't thought about how to get the other partners to try what needs to get tried**.

- If your test is **not part of a portfolio of experiments**; if it's the one and only new thing you have going on.

- If you **haven't earned the credibility to experiment** by building trust and fostering relationships.

- If you **haven't practiced experimenting** with new things in lower-stakes contexts.

- If you've **ignored the difficult parts of what you are trying to do**.

- If you **haven't sought out others already partway up your learning curve**; if your team is entirely made up of people new to the issue/problem.

- If what you are doing is **inconsistent with your values and your community's (appropriate) values**.

- If your new thing **compounds inequities and discriminates explicitly or implicitly**.

- If you have the **wrong motives**.

- If you've **promised success at the outset**.

On ideas, I heard broadly that people agreed with James March—i.e., that it was difficult to tell up front which proposals were genius and which were something else. But I also heard that there were clues. Motives matter. Turner had invited leaders to ask themselves: "Are you pursuing this possibility because it will make you *look* good, or will actually *do good*?" Getting to the real source of the challenges matters, too, she said. "Is this a solution to the symptom or to the root cause of the problem? If it's really getting at the root cause, when nothing else is able to, that feels like a good opportunity to go for possibility. But too often the urban tech world goes all in on solutions to symptoms. They're not worth the effort and often have unintended effects."[40] Rittgers and Eyoel both reiterated the importance of real listening to frontline workers and end users. Eyoel believed that a good indicator would be whether the idea conceivers had gotten "proximate" to the problem they thought they were trying to solve.[41]

On the "politics" of ideas, I'd also picked up that impossibility was ephemeral, that boundaries stayed fixed until they didn't. That political logjams stayed, until suddenly breaking. So it would be useful to have some nonpolitical way to pick out the delusions from the not delusions. Only the naive would ignore politics completely, but only the timid would use politics as possibility's sole indicator.

Often I heard that the question—possibility or delusion?—put too much onus on the ideas themselves. Rather, it was the process that determined the outcome. Geurts said, "The difference between a great idea and great innovation is execution."[42] This is both a matter of getting the good stuff done and sifting out what's ultimately not. Paley said, "The very best entrepreneurs are not evangelizers of nonsense. They are truth seeking, and there is a truth."[43] So how leaders seek out that truth makes a world of difference. I heard over and over again that running good tests was essential. Make things "trialable, reversible, and divisible."[44] Bound the tests; limit them in time, space, geography. Ideally, test in a way that gets you quick feedback. Geurts warned, "Be on guard for cycle times to get the answer that are longer than the circumstances for which you need the answer."[45] Then learn from the evidence that comes back. And I was told to bear in mind how the risks of these tests compared with their rewards (a familiar formulation), and that who bore the risks was a key line of demarcation. Don't try new things where the risks of failure fall heavily on the people who don't benefit from the fruits of the potential successes. And be wary of trying things where the risks of failure fall on people who are least in a position to absorb them.

The question of possibility or delusion, at scale, was especially on people's minds. Rittgers pointed to one subriddle here: "One reflection I have over the last several years is how easy it is to sell an idea about some great potential in comparison to how hard it is to keep people engaged in operationalizing that potential, once the work to bring it to fruition begins. We see failure too soon."[46] We do often see failure too soon. This is a version of what March had called a "competency trap"—where organizations abandon new initiatives they are inexperienced in, because they aren't good at them *yet*—and a consequence of "Kanter's Law," which is that "everything looks like a failure in the middle. Everyone loves inspiring beginnings and happy endings; it is just the middles that involve hard work."[47] So while delusion is ignoring evidence that your new intervention won't work, so too is giving up on your new intervention before people have been given time and experience to make it work. Effective possibility leaders communicate and rally people through these "messy middles."[48]

Possibility at scale also means watching out for systemic risks. (These systemic risks were the reasons Protect Democracy was critical of mobile voting.) It means looking out for the consequences of your new thing being used in ways you intended *and* in ways others might use it with *other* intentions. It requires warding off explicit or implicit racial, gender, and other kinds of discrimination in new programs. Delusion is taking the worst aspects of our society and concentrating them on platforms and letting them grow.

March had said it's difficult to distinguish ex ante between inspiration and lunacy. The strong advice here then is for leaders and the public to reserve judgment, to try to tamp down the reflex to object to ideas that sound strange and novel. What I heard over and over was a reinvitation to be impatient with old ideas and to be patient—and observant, experimental, and communicative—with new ones. There is a truth, and it is that in many places the status quo is not working. And there is an alter-truth, but it's not that your new thing will work—it's that your new thing only *might* work. What you do with that humility makes all the difference. We need possibility, but not delusion. We need a politics of foolishness, but not *foolishness*. There is a line, and it may be difficult to see, but truth seekers will find it.

9

Helping Time

Can we solve public problems anymore? A decade later I had my answer. We can, possibly. What history and the present show us is that there is a set of tools and practices for trying new things to solve pressing problems. We're able to have government that imagines, that tries new things, and that scales those things to make an impact. That kind of government, Possibility Government, would be very different from what we expect or witness in most instances, but it has existed and does and can exist.

Governments Are Not Just Giant Startups

Granted, there are many reasons to doubt this kind of government. People will argue that *possibility is best left to others*. They will say— or maybe you will tell yourself—that someone else, some other entity, some other part of society, should be in charge of novelty. Not government. Not me. The private sector is an entrepreneurial engine, one version of this argument goes. Private entrepreneurs have mastered the techniques and tools of risk-taking. They are playing with private money. Let private companies explore the unexplored. And in fact, as we saw in chapter 6, there has been surge in govtech and civictech startups. It's foolish, however, to leave this work to the private sector entirely. Private companies won't, on their own, solve truly public problems. Private markets left entirely to their own devices are not perfect. It's been well established that one of government's key roles is to step up when there are market failures. Everyone acting in their own self-interest—the self-interest that private companies are serving—will not create the outcomes we need. Each of us on our own won't invest in or protect the commons. Free-riding (not paying our fair share for shared resources) and externalities (generating costs, like air pollution, that we don't bear) are why we have governments provide for public parks and public health. And if the government shouldn't cede those roles (and I think it shouldn't), it can't cede exploring in those areas entirely either.

Moreover, to suggest that government should cede possibility to startups ignores who the startups need as willing partners and customers. We won't have a robust ecosystem of private entrepreneurs in this space unless they have public counterparts willing to look past incumbent providers toward something and someone new.

An appealing alternative to "leave it to the private sector" is "let the foundations do it." We are living in what observers have called the "second golden age of philanthropy." By 2014 there "were nearly 100,000 private foundations in the United States with total capitalization close to $800 billion."[1] The Bridgespan consulting group pointed out in 2019 that there was much new capital coming in behind what had already been set aside. "More than 180 wealthy donors (with an estimated net worth of nearly $1 trillion—and rising) have pledged to give away at least half their wealth, meaning that at minimum $500 billion will flow to established charities or new foundations in the coming decades."[2] Couldn't we look to philanthropy instead of government to try new things? Wouldn't it be better to try and fail on the Rockefeller Foundation's dime or on Mark Zuckerberg and Priscilla Chan's than on the public's?

This is the argument that Bill Gates lent some credence to at the end of 2019. Wading into the argument of the wealthy and taxes, Gates said, "I think the rich should pay more than they currently do, and that includes Melinda and me," and this is what generated most of the attention to his comments. But Gates also said:

> In addition to fair taxes, Melinda and I think there's value to society in allowing the wealthy to put some money into private foundations, because foundations play an irreplaceable role that's distinct from what governments do well. In particular, philanthropy is good at managing high-risk projects that governments can't take on and corporations won't—for example, trying out new approaches to eradicating malaria, which is something our foundation is working on. If a government tries an idea for improving global health that fails, someone wasn't doing their job. Whereas if we don't try some ideas that fail, we're not doing our jobs.[3]

Rob Reich, a Stanford political scientist who is a skeptic on the role of private foundations in a democracy, carves out a place where they can exist that mirrors Gates's point. Reich thinks generally that foundations lack accountability and transparency and "subvert democratic aims," and he finds it particularly hard to justify the tax deductions that subsidize them. But "the case for foundations," as he calls it, in a democracy is to be discovery engines for solving public problems. "Because of their size and longevity, foundations can oper-ate on a different and longer time horizon than can businesses in the marketplace and elected officials in public institutions, taking risks in social policy experimentation and innovation that we should not routinely expect to see in commercial firms or state agencies."[4] The billionaire philanthropist and the philanthropy skeptic agree on this.

But the argument for leaving the innovation to philanthropy rests on several justifications. The first is that private donors are making or will make these kinds of "risky" investments. And Reich points out the poor record on that. He cites a 1949 article written by a foun-dation leader, titled "Timid Billions." The clear implication is that the article could run again today. Reich quotes another, two-time foundation leader who more recently said, "Courageous risk-taking is not what most people associate with foundations whose boards and senior leadership are often dominated by establishment types."[5] Reich points to others with similar concerns. Bridgespan does, too. As it was pointing out just how much philanthropic money was com-ing, it was also warning of a growing sense that institutional foun-dations weren't living up to their "full potential" and that "stasis" was core to the problem. New money might be more adventurous than old money, and given that much of it comes from startup types, there are some early signs that it might be. So far, the Bill & Melinda Gates Foundation's investments in innovation, including in unique responses to Covid-19, are the philanthropic exceptions, not the rule. The Bloomberg Philanthropies' abundant investments in govern-ment innovation are as well. Many other funders often seem more probability-oriented in giving their wealth away than they were in making it. I am not betting on a wholesale revolution here.

The second thing a "leave possibility to philanthropy" argument is betting on is a willing set of partners in the public sector. It's hard to imagine testing new solutions in public health, say, without public-health workers. I am skeptical about broad new solutions on hunger, poverty, or sustainability that don't engage government officials to a large or even moderate extent. It may be, as Reich says, that foundations can be the "seed capital" on public issues. He points out the role philanthropic capital played in gestating public libraries, and Pell Grants, and the national 911 emergency number, allowing these programs to "audition" for public support.[6] But all startups need more than just capital. Addressing public problems is most likely to require that public workers help, participate, or at least tolerate new approaches. This means there is no such thing as "leave it to philanthropy." And it means that entrepreneurs and generous philanthropists should want public workers to be skilled *possibilitists*, too.

There are two other potential arguments embedded in the philanthropy-as-the-innovator approach, which you will hear people say if you suggest that government should try new and therefore riskier things. Either they will tell you *government shouldn't take on risky projects*, or they will tell you *government can't take riskier projects on*. One is a question of what ought to happen. The other is a matter of what does. Let's take them in turn.

Government shouldn't take on riskier projects? Tax dollars shouldn't be spent on things that will fail, the objection begins. But Robert Lind and the Nobel Prize–winning economist Kenneth Arrow laid the groundwork for us to believe otherwise. They argued that government should be risk-neutral in theory, and especially as the populations they are responsible for grow in number. (That is, you can imagine this principle applying more soundly to the US federal government than to the government of the town you happen to live in.) This is the basic logic of diversification and the thesis behind insurance. David Moss wrote an entire book about government's role as "the ultimate risk manager" and explained the long tradition in this kind of thinking. As far back as 1601, the first English insurance act justified marine insurance because "the loss lighteth rather easily upon many than heavily on the few."[7] Government is better situated than any other entity in our society to take up and take on the risk of trying new things. It has the largest coffers. It can spread the cost of failure across the largest numbers of people so that the impacts on individuals often are relatively minuscule. Some of the most momentous public policies (Moss cites Social Security as just one) have been efforts by government to shift and spread risk. We should see product and service innovation in government in the same light. What we are doing in not taking up new things is leaving the risk of being hungry or poor or undereducated on individuals. Government isn't eliminating risk when it decides not to take a challenge on; it's just leaving that challenge with the people—often vulnerable individuals—who are least positioned to address it.

In addition, the "no tax money for risky stuff" argument has some other holes. Because foundation money in the United States is tax-subsidized, it is also partially public money.[8] It's strange in that sense to be for innovation by private foundations and not also for innovation by government. Moreover, plenty of venture capital is public money, too. Take just the largest US pension fund, the $372 billion California Public Employees Retirement System (CalPERS).[9] Approximately 7 percent of its investments are made into private equity, including some into early-stage ventures. There are distinctions between allocating some portion of a diversified financial portfolio into early-stage investments and allocating some portion of a state's operating budget into new projects, but they are not so wide as to merit a sweeping claim that you shouldn't take risk with public money. We already do. The economist Mariana Mazzucato has made this point again and again. "From the Internet to biotech and even shale gas," she has noted, "the U.S. State has been the key driver of innovation-led growth—willing to invest in the most uncertain phase of the innovation cycle and let business hop on for the easier ride down the way." She's provided high-profile examples, like Apple: "Every technology that makes the iPhone smart and not stupid owes its funding to both basic and applied research funded by the State." Of Elon Musk's collection of innovative entities, she points out that Tesla received a federally guaranteed loan of $465 million and that "Tesla, SolarCity, and SpaceX have also benefited from direct investments in radical technology by the U.S. Department of Energy, in the case of battery technologies and solar panels, and by NASA, in the case of rocket technologies." Mazzucato reminds us, "The conventional view of a boring, lethargic State versus a dynamic private sector is as wrong as it is widespread . . . In countries that owe their growth to innovation—and in regions within those countries, like Silicon Valley—the State has historically served not just as an administrator and regulator of the wealth creation process, but a key actor in it, and often a more daring one, willing to take the risks that business won't."[10] Over and over, and in the productive service of fostering economic growth, governments have invested in risky stuff.

The idea that governments *can't* pursue possibility will prove the hardest idea to displace. This argument is not one of philosophy but of capacity, and it's often born from experience, much of it hard-earned. Steve Blank is one of those who knows of what he speaks. An entrepreneur and a famed writer and teacher about entrepreneurship (who called Eric Ries "the best student I ever had"), Blank has voraciously and generously taken his approaches into government. He taught lean techniques for solving public problems in classes he created and distributed—Hacking for Defense and Hacking for Diplomacy. He's even served as a public official himself.[11] But in November 2019, Blank wrote an article titled "Why the Government Isn't a Bigger Version of a Startup" and called much of the innovation activities governments were engaging in "innovation theater."[12] He worried that the United States was falling farther and farther behind its adversaries when it came to defense innovation in particular, and that all the movement toward "agile"—all the hackathons, all the design-thinking classes—weren't adding up to much. He argued for a much more comprehensive approach that would reintegrate "military, academia, and private enterprise," and for a vastly more extensive mobilization of talent and technology. I agree that all these startup activities haven't gotten us where we need to be.

But Blank went even further, possibly undermining his own argument. "The government isn't a bigger version of a startup and can't act like a startup does," he wrote, and then enumerated what he described as eighteen "salient" differences between startups and governments. "Startups can do anything," Blank began. "They can break the law and apologize later (as Uber, Airbnb, and Tesla did), but a government official taking the same type of risks can go to jail." This is one of those statements that sounds shrewd on its surface, but weakens when you dig into it. First of all, whenever and wherever Uber was playing the "forgiveness" game, some public official was looking the other way, too. It took people on both sides to allow these companies to unfold for a while. A reason that the CEOs of these types of companies didn't "go to jail" is because some public official decided not to arrest them and press charges. (Uber's Travis Kalanick was in fact charged by Korean authorities for breaking public-transport laws in that country.)[13] Public officials have more flexibility than Blank lets on. They bend and even break rules all the time. And when they do so in ways that harm the public or betray the public trust, they go to jail (sometimes). But often their infractions go unnoticed or unpunished, because the officials know how to hack the bureaucracy, too. Plus, startups have less flexibility than Blank suggests. I feel silly having to write that "startups can do anything" isn't true. It may have been a mentality in Silicon Valley for a while and in some corners still, but it's not (I am glad to say) a fact. Josephine (aka "Uber for home cooking") was an Oakland-based startup in California that had tried to pair home cooks with hungry neighbors, but ultimately shut down. Eventually, it turns out, "health inspectors came knocking."[14] For every Uber, there are dozens more stories like Josephine's.

Blank also draws a hard line on risk-taking. He writes, "In a startup cluster (Silicon Valley, Beijing, Tel Aviv) a failed entrepreneur is known as 'experienced.' In a government agency, they're likely known as being out of a job."[15] Again, he knows what of he speaks, and I know what he's getting at. I wouldn't suggest that attitudes toward risk are identical in startups and in government, or I wouldn't have written this book. But the divides aren't as stark as they are often made out to be. Nor are they as unbridgeable. On the one hand, failure isn't the prize it's always made out to be in startupland. Three colleagues of mine and an economist at the Federal Reserve Bank of New York have found evidence of what they call "performance persistence in entrepreneurship."[16] They show that "entrepreneurs with a track record of success are much more likely to succeed than first-time entrepreneurs and those who have previously failed." On the other hand, failure isn't always the doomsday it is made out to be in the public sector. Yes, some failures will derail promotions or get you dragged into the hot seat at a televised hearing or punished at the polls (we'll come to more on that in a moment). But my bet would be (and I don't have data for this, yet) that if we looked at the evidence, more failures in government go unpunished than do.

Blank's list goes on and on, and I don't mean to be overly critical of it and certainly not of him. He's drawing these distinctions after decades spent leading and helping startups, and basing them on a depth of experience helping the US Department of Defense and many other large bureaucracies. He's describing what many people with similar experience have seen. And he's saying it all to ward off naivete. Government isn't just a bigger version of a startup, and if we dance into the work of solving real public problems thinking glibly that it is—that the incentives and accountability and culture and systems are the same—we are likely to fail to make things better and will just as likely make things worse. I think those things, too. The question for us now isn't whether government is or isn't a bigger version of a startup. It's not. The question is, on balance, can government act more like one?

Hot-Stove Government

Actually, that's not quite the question. Because governments don't do anything. The humans in them do. And while it's well and good (and by now, I think, correct) to believe that governments should be risk neutral and that governments should take on riskier projects more than they do, what about the humans in them? Humans aren't risk neutral. Humans are risk averse. And people who work in public office are risk averse foremost because they are . . . human. If we want Possibility Government, we'll need the people that work in government to take it up. And that will be difficult.

James March wrote an article with behavioral scientist Jerker Denrell about what they called "the hot stove effect," describing one reason why people avoid too much exploration.[17] They'd named the paper in reference to Mark Twain, who had warned of "the cat that sits down on a hot stove-lid. She will never sit down on a hot stove-lid again—and that is well; but also she will never sit down on a cold one any more." What March and Denrell worried was that people inside organizations would overlearn the lessons of past mistakes.

We have hot-stove government. Public officials, elected and otherwise, have been electorally burned or seen people burned when they tried something new. Even if punishment is not the dominant out-come of mistake-making, it's enough to warrant notice. A spate of studies show that public officials are more likely to get blamed when things go awry than praised for their successes. Among the studies: one that showed that "dissatisfied voters are more likely to turn out to vote than satisfied voters and to switch their vote among parties"; one that "uncovered little evidence of any electoral payoffs for the local authorities who handled the issue well, finding only punish-ments for those who failed dramatically"; one that found "incumbent politicians tended to be punished by voters for exceptionally poor performance on [key performance] indicators, but were not corre-spondingly rewarded for exceptionally good performance."[18]

So, if two or three of those stove burners are currently scalding, it's not hard to observe what's set them on high. A tough-on-failure electorate. Opposition research. Gotcha media. Hair-trigger Twit-ter. (I should note that however difficult these things make govern-ing, we should desire the accountability they bring. Twain also said that "there is no distinctly native American criminal class except Congress," and though that seems overly harsh, it's long been true that we need an investigative press and other public watchdogs to sniff out public corruption and ineptitude.) We, the humans, have been burned on occasion trying new things in government, and that's made us loath to try it again. Is there anything we can do to change that?

A National Commission for More Bad Ideas and Failed Programs?

In the 1990s, in the wake of David E. Osborne and Ted Gaebler's book *Reinventing Government*, the new president and vice president put its ideas at the center of their work. Is something similar what we need now? President Possibility? The entrepreneurial revolution never fully came to fruition in government. Should we just lean in harder? We need more bad ideas to get good ones. We need more experimenting and, yes, even more failed programs to get better ones. Should we form a national commission on that? Is that what it would take to get the humans in governments on board?

As much as I like the notion (and the title!), I think not. I think there are all sorts of substantive actions we could all take, without waiting on our national leaders. There is a rebalancing that needs to take place in our government that we can all help bring about. Leaders at all levels of government and the public can work together to shift the circumstances under which the humans in governments (us, our friends and neighbors) now labor fearfully, so that instead they will feel permitted and even encouraged to pursue new ideas.

The point is not to shout from our nation's capital or that of any others, "Everyone, innovate!" That will never work. We don't even want everyone innovating. What we've come across as Possibility and Probability in the governments we've met, James March long before described as exploration and exploitation. There are two kinds of activities that an organization can engage in, he observed. One of them is exploitation: using what is already known, possibly improving on it, doing it more efficiently. The other activity is exploration: examining new possibilities, experimenting with things that are not known but might become known."[19] It's near impossible, March said, to specify the optimum balance between the two, to find the right mix of exploitation and exploration. We don't want to race universally and uniformly into explore mode, but we'll want to shift governments so more people in them can move in that direction. In lieu of setting up a commission for bad ideas and failed programs, there are some things Possibility Leaders can do.

Organize for "ambidexterity"

Mike Tushman and Charles O'Reilly, two scholars of organizations and innovation, wrote of the Roman god Janus, who "had two sets of eyes—one pair focusing on what lay behind, the other on what lay ahead," and recommended that managers and executives look to the past and future, too. Government leaders need to perform the same "mental balancing act."[20] They should also organize their administrations to do the same. And Tushman and O'Reilly's work suggests that this does not mean creating a whole bunch of cross-functional "innovation teams," marrying up entrepreneurs and the more establishment types. Separate units have proved more successful. These kinds of ambidextrous organizations require "ambidextrous leaders" at the top. In our setting, this means someone in charge needs to be able to have a meeting at 9:00 about whether the department of public works is hitting its weekly key performance indicators on trash pickup and another meeting at 9:30 to see the prototypes of the trash-picking-up drones. Most people in the organization will be better suited to one kind of task (exploitation/probability) or another (exploration/possibility). It's a mistake to create one big group of people with both mandates. (Tushman and O'Reilly put it this way: "The structure of ambidextrous organizations allows cross-fertilization among units while preventing cross-contamination.") Instead, create organizationally separate units; make sure they are connected enough through points of integration, some asset sharing, and a common overarching identity; and place leaders at the top (or be the leader yourself!) who can manage the tensions between the two groups.

I'd go a step further in government. Make extra sure the "probability" functions are working darn well. Get that trash picked up on time. Doing well on the existing stuff grants the organization permission to work on the new stuff. Don't fall into the trap of chasing the future and forgetting the present. Moreover, if you are the trash-drone-exploring public-works engineers, don't forget to thank and respect and admire your colleagues who are getting the current job done. They are the ones earning you permission to explore the possible.

And by all means, tell the press and the public what you are doing. Point to the possibility units and say, "Watch this. You'll see some failure here. We promise to keep it modest, and we promise to learn from it." Being up front about the possibility agenda and why it's necessary will buy you more space than being surreptitious will. My former City of Boston colleague Nigel Jacob liked to call our Mayor's Office of New Urban Mechanics a "failure aggregator." Creating organizational space for possibility makes it safer for people in the administration to pursue it.

Lean on existing and new talent

We will need to recruit trisector entrepreneurs, like the kinds we met in chapter 6, into government. You can support and participate in internship programs like Coding it Forward and adopt term-limited programs like the Presidential Innovation Fellows. There are some essentials to making these work well. Foremost involves the types of people that are invited in. Todd Park, who had been instrumental in forming these programs under President Obama, told me he thought the main criteria were "a good head and good heart." What he meant was this new talent needs to be smart and also empathic. I agree. You need people who don't come in and condescend about the way things are and dream wistfully and ignorantly about the way they could be. Real public entrepreneurs understand that the reason problems exist in government is not because the people in government are lazy or stupid or unimaginative. Rather, they face the challenge of trying new things in a system not presently, or mostly, designed for such efforts. So it's key to bring in people who carry themselves curiously and humbly about problem solving.

In addition, any possibility strategy must involve drawing existing public employees out of the woodwork. Within your organization there are people just waiting to join these efforts, waiting for an indication that it's OK to think and try new things. In bringing in outsiders, don't forget to bring out insiders, too.

Some new talent and even new positions are called for. A handful of current and former leaders have been calling for product managers in government.[21] There's been a spate of new roles in government over the years (chief innovation officers, chief digital officers, chief data officers, etc.), and I'm hesitant to make the case for even more new titles. But product managers serve an important function in the private sector in bridging the perspectives of designers, engineers, marketers, and customers, and in helping get products from inception to fruition. Roles like this in the public sector would help make sure that many more new services made it through the development pipeline and that when they did, they delivered on their intended benefits. The proposed US Digital Service Academy, envisioned in the spirit of the nation's military service academies but for techie-types who would serve in civilian government roles, could train people for positions like these, as well as for more technical roles, in large numbers.[22]

Budget and buy for possibility

Most public budgets, budget processes, and procurement systems make pursuing new things harder than it should be. Possibility leaders can work to create funding streams for trying new things. Again, the clear message to the public and the press should be that these are relatively modest amounts of money that will be spent, in stages, in service of learning, and that such outlays are necessary because the status quo is not good enough. And then the people in charge of these expenditures must be tasked with monitoring three things instead of "performance" per se, which is what they are used to monitoring: (1) When experiments are generating negative signals, funding should be cut off or allocated toward changing something about what was tried originally. (2) When experiments are generating positive signals, more funding should be put into them, and successful new programs should be scaled. (3) Experiments should be part of a portfolio of experiments (ideally, uncorrelated), so that a few big "wins" can cover for many minor losses.

This is a dramatic reversal from how much of government is funded these days. Poor programs don't have their funding eliminated. Good programs don't get scaled. Nowhere is this more true than in the beloved government "pilot program." Some commissioner or mayor or governor stands up and heralds a new pilot program to help kids graduate college, or to eat better at school, or to be more financially stable. But after the press attention fades and the early days of the program are underway, these programs are rarely ended, altered, or grown, accordingly. If pilots are "tests," they should be described as such and budgeted that way. Money should be released in stages, and some serious capital should be reserved in case successes along the way warrant more investment.

Get to work and make new stories

There is a tendency to think we can engineer a shift toward possibility by talking about it. And for sure some amount of talking about it—of saying the status quo is what's dangerous, of declaring permission for trying something new, of promising political cover for those who do—will be required. But remember, the anxious humans in our governments already have three very powerful stories in their heads, and those stories won't be easily displaced by your talking. The first story they have in their heads is that *change can't happen*. They've heard it all before. Been there, done that. They've been through a dozen reform efforts. They've watched seasoned consultants and precocious newbies come and go. And still, what they have observed is that not much has changed. The second story they walk around with is that *change is not allowed*. They believe it's against the rules, that there's a policy against this or against that. And even if the barriers are what Jen Pahlka calls blue rules (the kinds that are told around the watercooler and that can be upended) and not red ones (the kinds that are real and are not to be broken), nervous public officials will steer clear. The third story they have is that *change will hurt me*: There goes my expertise. There goes my overtime. Or possibly there goes my job. You will not be able to convince these people to abandon these stories with all your talk about possibility. They will only, ultimately, replace these stories with new stories. One of the virtues of the methods we came across in chapter 3 is that the time to output something, anything, is relatively short. And public workers can see for themselves: Something did change. No one got in trouble. Not even me.

Engage the public and be candid with them about what this will take

The humans inside government can't change unless the humans outside do. Talk to them about how to participate in possibility and how to vote for it. Be candid about what's required to change. Recall the newly elected Mayor Melvin Carter, who said to his neighbors, "Don't clap if you're not going to help." Former mayor Mike Bloomberg said, "Show me a politician who hasn't failed, and I will show you a failure." They both were being honest about what this will all take.

There is evidence that by raising expectations inside organizations you can encourage people to try new, riskier things.[23] It's perhaps a lesson for us all. Let's raise the bar so that we can, possibly, get over it.

You Can Start Something New

It was five years after the Boston Marathon bombings, after "you can't start something new." Five years after we raised and distributed almost $60 million in seventy-five days.[24] It was after I had been to Mexico to see crowdsourced bus maps and gone to Amsterdam to see experiments with home sharing and visited the Republic of Georgia to see the blockchain protecting property from the Russians and planned a trip to China to see dockless bikeshare and to contemplate a future of sensors all over the place. Five years of exploring public entrepreneurship around the globe.

And then I went to the start line of the Boston Marathon so I could run my way back to the finish, the first time since the bombs had gone off. And there, behind the rope that separated those of us silly enough to race and those generous enough to support us, was a woman holding a handmade sign: "You are already running better than our government."

It was meant as encouragement, but for me, it was a riddle. Yes, we live in challenging times. Faith in government is at historic lows. Trust in our fellow citizens is dismal. The biggest problems remain untackled. But hadn't she seen any of what I had seen? Didn't she know there were places—pockets—of government that were working in new ways? Had she never heard of Gabriella Gómez-Mont and

James Geurts and so many others helping them? I hadn't even started running, and I was already faster than government. It wasn't all status quo all the time. Did she not know about any of that? And of what's to come? Didn't she know about possibility?

You do now. We have problems. Giant ones. But there are also countless opportunities to create, to question, to invent. I don't want you on the sidelines. I want you to help time. In a public role or private one. We all should.

We get the government we invent.

NOTES

Introduction

1. Organisation for Economic Co-operation and Development, "Trust in Government," http://www.oecd.org/gov/trust-in-government.htm, accessed February 2020.

2. Associated Press, "Putin: Leader in Artificial Intelligence Will Rule the World," September 4, 2017.

3. Deloitte, "Competing for Talent in the Public Sector: How States Can Win Hearts and Minds in a Tight Talent Market," 2017.

4. Kim Parker, Nikki Graf, and Ruth Igielnik, "Generation Z Looks a Lot Like Millennials on Key Social and Political Issues," Pew Research Center, January 17, 2019.

5. I first heard a similar phrase from Deval Patrick, then the governor of Massachusetts, who would frequently encourage people to "turn toward each other, rather than against one another."

6. Paul Gompers et al., "Performance Persistence in Entrepreneurship and Venture Capital," *Journal of Financial Economics* 96, no. 1 (2010): 18. Note that the authors' measure of success is whether a startup eventually goes public.

7. Online Etymology Dictionary, https://www.etymonline.com/word/constitution, accessed February 2020.

8. Peter F. Drucker, *Innovation and Entrepreneurship* (New York: Taylor & Francis, 2012), 170.

9. Elinor Ostrom, "Public Entrepreneurship: A Case Study in Ground Water Basin Management" (PhD diss., Indiana University, 1965).

10. Elinor Ostrom, "Beyond Markets and States: Polycentric Governance of Complex Economic Systems," Prize Lecture, December 8, 2009.

11. David Osborne and Ted Gaebler, *Reinventing Government: How the Entrepreneurial Spirit Is Transforming the Public Sector* (New York: Plume, 1993): xv.

12. Ronald Wilson Reagan, "Speech of the Former President at the 1992 Republican Convention," American History: From Revolution to Reconstruction and Beyond, University of Groningen, http://www.let.rug.nl/usa/presidents/ronald-wilson-reagan/speech-of-the-former-president-at-the-1992-republican-convention.php.

13. Tanya Somanader, "Choosing Hope: President Obama's Address to the United Nations," September 24, 2014, https://obamawhitehouse.archives.gov/blog/2014/09/24/choosing-hope-president-obama-s-address-united-nations.

14. R. Natarajan (ed.), *Proceedings of the International Conference on Transformations in Engineering Education: ICTIEE 2014* (New Delhi: Springer, 2015): 30.

15. Dan Satherley, "'This Stardust Won't Settle'—Jacinda Ardern," *Newshub*, September 8, 2017.

16. David Valliere, *Entrepreneurial Thinking: Think Different!* (Cheltenham: Edward Elgar Publishing, 2019), 2.

17. The term "platform thinking" was introduced in Michael A. Cusumano, Annabelle Gawer, and David B. Yoffie, in *The Business of Platforms: Strategy in the Age of Digital Competition, Innovation, and Power* (New York: Harper Business, 2019), chap. 1.

18. J. Edward Kellough, "The Reinventing Government Movement: A Review and Critique," *Public Administration Quarterly* 22, no. 1 (1998): 6.

19. Martin Campbell-Kelly and William Aspray, *Computer: A History of the Information Machine* (New York: Basic Books, 1996), 274.

20. Åke Grönlund and Thomas A. Horan, "Introducing e-Gov: History, Definitions, and Issues," *Communications of the Association for Information Systems* 15 (2004): 713.

21. Barack Obama, "Remarks to the Democratic National Convention," *New York Times*, July 27, 2004.

22. Brian McGrory, "Do You Hear Me Now?" *Boston Globe*, July 26, 2005.

23. Yochai Benkler, *The Wealth of Networks: How Social Production Transforms Markets and Freedom* (New Haven, CT: Yale University Press, 2006), 69.

24. Karim R. Lakhani, Robert D. Austin, and Yumi Yi, "Data.gov," Case 610-075 (Boston: Harvard Business School, 2010).

25. Jenna Wortham, "New York City Names Winners of Apps Contest," *New York Times*, February 4, 2010. Disclosure: I am Harvard Business School's adviser to the Bloomberg Harvard City Leadership Initiative, a collaboration among Harvard Kennedy School, Harvard Business School, and Bloomberg Philanthropies, and I have received compensation for my participation in its programs.

26. "2 Millionth Issue Submitted and Direct Messaging Announced," SeeClickFix, October 30, 2015.

27. Jennifer Pahlka, "Coding a Better Government," TED, February 2012, https://www.ted.com/talks/jennifer_pahlka_coding_a_better_government.

28. Dave Evans, "The Internet of Things: How the Next Evolution of the Internet Is Changing Everything." Cisco Internet Business Solutions Group (April 2011): 3.

29. The Latin phrase "Mater artium necessitas" translates literally as "The mother of invention is necessity."

30. Melvin Carter III, video call conversation with author, June 25, 2020.

31. Martin Luther King Jr., "The Other America," a speech given at Grosse Pointe High School, March 14, 1968, https://www.gphistorical.org/mlk/mlkspeech/mlk-gp-speech.pdf.

Chapter 1

1. I learned the phrase "problems as opportunities," the title of this chapter, from William Sahlman, who has written and spoken about it in the context of entrepreneurship in many venues. Portions of this chapter are adapted from Herman Leonard, Mitchell Weiss, Jin Hyun Paik, and Kerry Herman, "SOFWERX: Innovation at U.S. Special Operations Command," Case 819-004 (Boston: Harvard Business School, 2018). Unless otherwise noted, all quotes come from this case and subsequent interviews with James Geurts by the author on July 22, 2019.

2. Sean O'Kane, "Yes, the Jet-Powered Hoverboard Is Real, and Yes, the Creator Has Crashed It," *The Verge*, April 15, 2016.

3. Special Operations Forces Industry Conference (SOFIC), "Speakers: Tambrein Bates," https://www.sofic.org/vsofic/speakers/tambrein-bates.

4. O'Kane, "Yes, the Jet-Powered Hoverboard Is Real."

5. US Department of Defense, "DoD Releases Fiscal Year 2020 Budget Proposal," March 12, 2019, https://www.defense.gov/Newsroom/Releases/Release/Article/1782623/dod-releases-fiscal-year-2020-budget-proposal/.

6. Phil Goldstein, "The 5 Most Amazing Technologies DARPA Helped Invent—Besides the Internet," *FedTech*, April 29, 2016, https://fedtechmagazine.com/article/2016/04/5-most-amazing-technologies-darpa-helped-invent-besides-internet.

7. SOFWERX, "Pirates Exercise," August 30, 2016, https://www.sofwerx.org/discover/pirates-exercise/.

8. Carol L. Fleisher, director, *Navy SEALs—Their Untold Story*, PBS, 2014.

9. "Naval Combat Demolition Units," SpecWarNet, http://www.specwarnet.net/americas/NCDU.htm.

10. "Naval Combat Demolition Units," SpecWarNet, http://www.specwarnet.net/americas/NCDU.htm.

11. Gardiner Harris, "A Bin Laden Hunter on Four Legs," *New York Times*, May 4, 2011.

12. James Geurts, "SOF AT&L," unclassified PowerPoint presentation, https://www.ndia.org/-/media/sites/ndia/divisions/solic/reports-and-activities/2015-ndia-solic-presentation-geurts.ashx?la=en.

13. Amy Edmonson, "Building a Psychologically Safe Workspace," TEDxHGSE, May 4, 2014, https://youtu.be/LhoLuui9gX8.

14. Ibid.

15. Lisa Schmidthuber, David Antons, and Dennis Hilgers, "On the Bumpy Road towards Open Government: The Not-Invented-Here Syndrome as a Major Pothole," *Academy of Management Proceedings* 2015, no. 1: 14794.

16. Jonathan Rauch, *Demosclerosis: The Silent Killer of American Government* (New York: Three Rivers Press, 1995).

17. Howard H. Stevenson, "A Perspective on Entrepreneurship," Case 384-131 (Boston: Harvard Business School, 1983, revised 2006).

18. Ibid.

19. Ibid.

20. Tim Brown, *Change by Design: How Design Thinking Transforms Organizations and Inspires Innovation* (New York: HarperCollins, 2009), 67.

21. Stevenson, "A Perspective on Entrepreneurship."

22. Dana Liebelson, "Where Did the Money Donated to Columbine, Aurora, and Virginia Tech Mass-Shooting Victims Go?" *Mother Jones*, April 8, 2013; Mitchell Weiss, "Lessons from Boston's Experiment with the One Fund," *Harvard Business Review*, January 22, 2016.

23. James Geurts, "SOF AT&L," unclassified PowerPoint presentation.

24. Jet-Powered Flyboard Steals the Show at Bastille Day Celebrations," Guardian News, July 14, 2019, https://www.youtube.com/watch?v=JvEMQalsHWs.

25. Emmanuel Macron, @EmmanuelMacron via Twitter, July 14, 2019, https://twitter.com/emmanuelmacron/status/1150408570929917957?lang=en.

26. Franky Zapata, telephone conversation with author, August 28, 2019.

27. United States Senate Committee on Armed Services, "Nominations—Behler-Winslow-Modly-Geurts," November 7, 2017, https://www.armed-services.senate.gov/hearings/17-11-07-nominations_--behler---winslow---modly---geurts.

28. Megan Eckstein, "NavalX Innovation Support Office Opening 5 Regional 'Tech Bridge' Hubs," *USNI News*, September 3, 2019, https://news.usni.org/2019/09/03/navalx-innovation-support-office-opening-5-regional-tech-bridge-hubs.

29. James G. McGann, "2019 Global Go to Think Tank Index Report," Think Tanks and Civil Societies Program, University of Pennsylvania, January 27, 2020.

Chapter 2

1. Portions of this discussion are adapted from Mitchell Weiss and Sarah McAra, "Propel," Case 818-008 (Boston: Harvard Business School, 2017). All quotes come from this case unless otherwise noted.

2. Beth Simone Noveck, *Wiki Government: How Technology Can Make Government Better, Democracy Stronger, and Citizens More Powerful* (Washington, DC: Brookings Institution Press, 2009).

3. Melvin Carter III, telephone conversation with author, September 9, 2019.

4. Jessie Van Berkel, "St. Paul Mayor-Elect Melvin Carter Asks Community to Help Select Department Directors," *Star Tribune*, December 2, 2017.

5. Melvin Carter III, "Mayoral Inauguration of Melvin Carter," St. Paul, MN, January 5, 2018.

6. Melvin Carter III, telephone conversation with author, September 9, 2019.

7. Propel, https://www.joinpropel.com.

8. "Supplemental Nutrition Assistance Program—Access and Participation Rates for 2002–2015," New York City Human Resources Administration Program Facts and Reports, https://www1.nyc.gov/assets/hra/downloads/pdf/facts/snap/2002.2015NYCSNAPParticipation.pdf; Maeve Duggan and Aaron Smith, "Cell Internet Use 2013," Pew Research Center, September 16, 2013.

9. Chris Kuang, "Building a User-Centered Social Safety Net: A Conversation with Propel's Jimmy Chen," *Coding It Forward* (blog), https://blog.codingitforward.com/building-a-user-centered-social-safety-net-320433ba28ad, accessed February 2020.

10. Tom Kelley, *The Art of Innovation* (New York: Currency, 2001), 8.

11. Tom Kelley and David Kelley, "Why Designers Need Empathy," *Slate*, November 8, 2013.

12. Ryan W. Buell and Andrew Otazo, "IDEO: Human-Centered Service Design," Case 615-022 (Boston: Harvard Business School, 2014; revised, 2016).

13. IDEO.org, *The Field Guide to Human-Centered Design*, IDEO.org, 2015, 9.

14. "About Policy Lab," https://openpolicy.blog.gov.uk/about/, accessed August 2020.

15. Vasant Chari, telephone conversation with author, September 5, 2019.

16. Cyd Harrell and Kavi Harshawat, "Civic Design: User Research Methods for Creating Better Citizen Experiences," October 3, 2014, https://youtube/ipjLBcBD21I.

17. Aliza Chasan, "'Unacceptable' Video Shows Cops Pulling Baby from Woman at Brooklyn SNAP Center," PIX11, December 9, 2018, https://pix11.com/2018/12/09/unacceptable-video-shows-cops-pulling-baby-from-woman-at-brooklyn-snap-center/.

18. Eric von Hippel, *Democratizing Innovation* (Cambridge: MIT Press, 2005), 19.

19. Ibid., 22.

20. Adam Smith, *An Inquiry into the Nature and Causes of the Wealth of Nations* (Edinburgh: Stevenson & Co., 1843), 5.

21. Kelley, *The Art of Innovation*, 24–25.

22. Andy O'Brien, interview with author, Boston, December 11, 2019.

23. Janette Sadik-Khan and Seth Solomonow, *Streetfight: Handbook for an Urban Revolution* (New York: Viking, 2016), 76.

24. Ibid., 74.

25. Melvin Carter III, telephone conversation with author, September 9, 2019.

26. James I. Charlton, *Nothing about Us without Us: Disability Oppression and Empowerment* (Berkeley: University of California Press, 2000), 3.

27. Melvin Carter III, "Mayoral Inauguration of Melvin Carter."

28. GiveDirectly, "About GiveDirectly," https://www.givedirectly.org/about/, accessed February 2020.

29. Nurith Aizenman, "How to Fix Poverty: Why Not Just Give People Money?" NPR, August 7, 2017.

30. Fresh EBT, "Fresh EBT + GiveDirectly Partnership Q&A," April 20, 2020, https://www.freshebt.com/blog/give-directly-cash-transfers/.

31. Ryan W. Buell, "IDEO: Human-Centered Service Design," Teaching Note 616-038 (Boston: Harvard Business School, 2016).

32. Kelley, *The Art of Innovation*, 56.

33. Buell, "IDEO: Human-Centered Service Design."

34. Ibid.

35. Karan Girotra, Christian Terwiesch, and Karl T. Ulrich, "Idea Generation and the Quality of the Best Idea," *Management Science* 56, no. 4 (2010): 591.

36. M. Diane Burton and Tom Nicholas, "Prizes, Patents, and the Search for Longitude," *Explorations in Economic History* 64 (2017): 21.

37. Hila Lifshitz-Assaf, Michael L. Tushman, and Karim R. Lakhani, "A Study of NASA Scientists Shows How to Overcome Barriers to Open Innovation," *Harvard Business Review*, May 29, 2018.

38. Portions of this discussion are adapted from Mitchell Weiss and Sarah Mehta, "Hacking Heroin," Case 818-010 (Boston: Harvard Business School, 2017). Unless otherwise noted, all quotes come from this case and a subsequent interview with Annie Rittgers by the author on September 10, 2019.

39. Mike DeWine, "Heroin Epidemic Is 'a Human Tragedy of Epic Proportion,'" WCPO Cincinnati, June 7, 2017, http://www.wcpo.com/news/opinion/mike-dewine-heroin-epidemic-is-a-human-tragedy-of-epic-proportion.

40. Jeanna Smialek, "The Heroin Business Is Booming in America," *Bloomberg Businessweek*, May 11, 2017, https://www.bloomberg.com/news/features/2017-05-11/the-heroin-business-is-booming-in-america.

41. Hila Lifshitz-Assaf, Sarah Lebovitz, and Lior Zalmanson, "Minimal and Adaptive Coordination: How Hackathons' Projects Accelerate Innovation without Killing It," *Academy of Management*, April 2020.

42. Ferry Grijpink, Alan Lau, and Javier Vara, "Demystifying the Hackathon," McKinsey & Company, October 1, 2015, http://www.mckinsey.com/business-functions/digital-mckinsey/our-insights/demystifying-the-hackathon.

43. Billy Mitchell, "GSA Hackathons Come with Big Returns," *Fedscoop*, September 28, 2015, https://www.fedscoop.com/gsa-hackathons-come-with-big-roi/.

44. Alison Flint, "Should Cities Use Hackathons to Solve Social Problems? Lessons from America's Datafest at Harvard," *Kennedy School Review*, February 11, 2014.

45. Lisa Abeyta, "Lessons Learned: 3 Requirements for Sustainable Civic Apps," *HuffPost*, September 16, 2014.

46. Adi Abili and Rachel Katz, "The Lady Problems Hackathon Series Is Over, Now Comes the Accelerator," *AngelHack*, March 23, 2017; Maegan Clawges, "Hackathon Experience Lasts beyond the Weekend," *Major League Hacking*, August 11, 2014.

47. Scott Moorhouse, "How to End Violence in Chicago? Start with a Hackathon," *Crain's Chicago Business*, March 2, 2017.

48. Derek Eder, Steven Vance, and Christopher Whitaker, "A Citywide Hackathon? Please. Technology Alone Can't Solve Chicago's Murder Problem," *Crain's Chicago Business*, March 6, 2017.

49. Karim R. Lakhani and Robert G. Wolf, "Why Hackers Do What They Do: Understanding Motivation and Effort in Free/Open Source Software Projects," *Perspectives on Free and Open Source Software*, edited by Joseph Feller et al. (Cambridge: MIT Press, 2005).

50. Alan MacCormack, Fiona Murray, and Erika Wagner, "Spurring Innovation through Competitions," *MIT Sloan Management Review*, September 17, 2013.

51. James G. March, *Explorations in Organizations* (Palo Alto, CA: Stanford University Press, 2008), 101.

52. Ibid., 113.

53. Ibid., 18–19.

Chapter 3

1. Portions of this chapter are adapted from Mitchell Weiss and Maria Fernanda Miguel, "LabCDMX: Experiment 50," Case 817-031 (Boston: Harvard Business School, 2016; revised 2017). All quotes come from this case unless otherwise noted.

2. Ruth Puttick, Peter Baeck, and Philip Colligan, "The Teams and Funds Making Innovation Happen in Governments around the World," NESTA and Bloomberg Philanthropies, 2014, https://media.nesta.org.uk/documents/i-teams_june_2014.pdf.

3. Xerox PARC, "PARC History," https://www.parc.com/about-parc/parc-history/; Tim Stenovec, "We Just Learned about a Bunch of Secret Projects Amazon Has Been Working On," *Business Insider*, August 27, 2015; Joshua Brunstein, "The Real Story of How Amazon Built the Echo," *Bloomberg*, April 29, 2016.

4. Tobias Weiblen and Henry W. Chesbrough, "Engaging with Startups to Enhance Corporate Innovation," *California Management Review* 57, no. 2 (2015).

5. Don Bellante and Albert N. Link, "Are Public Sector Workers More Risk Averse Than Private Sector Workers?" *ILR Review* 34, no. 3 (1981): 408.

6. Margaretha Buurman et al., "Public Sector Employees: Risk Averse and Altruistic?" *Journal of Economic Behavior & Organization* 83, no. 3 (2012): 279.

7. Eric Ries, *The Lean Startup: How Today's Entrepreneurs Use Continuous Innovation to Create Radically Successful Businesses* (New York: Crown Business, 2011).

8. Thomas Eisenmann, Eric Ries, and Sarah Dillard, "Hypothesis-Driven Entrepreneurship: The Lean Startup," Background Note 812-095 (Boston: Harvard Business School, 2011; revised, 2013).

9. Paul Gompers et al., "Performance Persistence in Entrepreneurship and Venture Capital, *Journal of Financial Economics* 96, no. 1 (2010): 18. Note that the authors' measure for success is that the startup eventually goes public.

10. Eisenmann, Ries, and Dillard, "Hypothesis-Driven Entrepreneurship."

11. Karim R. Lakhani, Robert D. Austin: Yumi Yi, "Data.gov," Case 610-075 (Boston: Harvard Business School, 2010); https://www.data.gov/metric.

12. Alexis Madrigal, "Data.gov Launches to Mixed Reviews," *Wired*, May 21, 2009.

13. Ryan W. Buell, Ethan Porter, and Michael I. Norton, "Surfacing the Submerged State: Operational Transparency Increases Trust in and Engagement with Government," Working Paper 14-034 (Boston: Harvard Business School, 2020).

Chapter 4

1. Portions of this discussion are adapted from Mitchell Weiss, Emer Moloney, and Vincent Dessain, "Airbnb in Amsterdam (A)," Case 817-013 (Boston: Harvard Business School, 2016; revised, 2017); Mitchell Weiss, Emer Moloney, and Vincent Dessain, "Airbnb in Amsterdam (B)," Case 817-014 (Boston: Harvard Business School, 2016). All quotes come from these cases unless otherwise noted.

2. Harrison Weber, "Airbnb Could Be Banned in Amsterdam: Local Authorities Are Now Hunting for Illegal Hotels," *Next Web*, February 2, 2013, https://thenextweb.com/insider/2013/02/02/airbnb-may-be-banned-from-amsterdam-local-authorities-are-now-hunting-for-illegal hotels/.

3. European Commission, "Study on the Assessment of the Regulatory Aspects Affecting the Collaborative Economy in the Tourism Accommodation Sector in the 28 Member States," 2018, https://publications.europa.eu/resource/cellar/8a7383b3-5269-11e8-be1d-01aa75ed71a1.0001.01/DOC_1.

4. Molly Turner, telephone conversation with author, June 12, 2014

5. Fred Redwood, "Old Beauty, Fresh Faces," *Financial Times*, November 15, 2014.

6. Christopher F. Schuetze, "Living Above and Below the Water's Surface in Amsterdam," *New York Times*, April 23, 2015.

7. Ybo Buruma, "Dutch Tolerance: On Drugs, Prostitution, and Euthanasia," *Crime and Justice 35*, no. 1 (2007): 73.

8. Russell Shorto, *Amsterdam: A History of the World's Most Liberal City* (New York: Knopf Doubleday, 2013).

9. Memorandum of Understanding, Gemeente Amsterdam & Airbnb, December 2014, https://www.binnenlandsbestuur.nl/Uploads/2016/2/2014-12-airbnb-ireland-amsterdam-mou.pdf.

10. "Amsterdam and Airbnb Sign Agreement on Home Sharing and Tourist Tax," https://www.airbnb.dk/press/news/amsterdam-and-airbnb-sign-agreement-on-home-sharing-and-tourist-tax, December 18, 2014.

11. Portions of this section are adapted from Mitchell Weiss and Brittany Urick, "Testing Autonomy in Pittsburgh (A)," Case 819-059 (Boston: Harvard Business School, 2018; revised, 2019). All quotes come from this case unless otherwise noted.

12. William Peduto, @billpeduto via Twitter, September 14, 2016.

13. Taylor Soper, "Inside Uber's Self-Driving Tech Center in Pittsburgh, a Glimpse of the Possible Future of Transportation," *GeekWire*, February 6, 2018. See also "Uber Signs On as First Tenant for $1 Billion Development in Hazelwood," WPXI-TV Pittsburgh, https://www.wpxi.com/news/local/uber-signs-first-tenant-1-billion-development-haze/165684457/.

14. Daniel Moore, "Uber Fined Record $11.4 Million by State Public Utility Board," *Pittsburgh Post-Gazette,* April 21, 2016.

15. Cecilia Kang, "No Driver? Bring It On: How Pittsburgh Became Uber's Testing Ground," *New York Times*, September 10, 2016, https://www.nytimes.com/2016/09/11/technology/no-driver-bring-it-on-how-pittsburgh-became-ubers-testing-ground.html.

16. Troy Griggs and Daisuke Wakabayashi, "How a Self-Driving Uber Killed a Pedestrian in Arizona," *New York Times*, March 21, 2018.

17. William Peduto, @billpeduto via Twitter, May 23, 2018.

18. Aaron Aupperlee, "PennDOT Cancels Meeting on New Testing Guidelines with Self-Driving Car Companies," *Pittsburgh Tribune-Review*, May 29, 2018, https://archive.triblive.com/local/pittsburgh-allegheny/penndot-cancels-meeting-on-new-testing-guidelines-with-self-driving-car-companies/.

19. Daisuke Wakabayashi and Kate Conger, "Uber's Self-Driving Cars Are Set to Return in a Downsized Test," *New York Times*, December 5, 2018.

20. Amir Efrati, "How an Uber Whistleblower Tried to Stop Self-Driving Car Disaster," *The Information*, December 10, 2018. See also Courtney Linder, "Report: Self-Driving Uber Swerved onto Pittsburgh Sidewalk Just Days Before Fatal Crash," *Pittsburgh Post-Gazette*, December 11, 2018.

21. Courtney Linder, "Following Uber Sidewalk Incident, Pittsburgh Drafting Better Reporting Rules for Self-Driving Cars," *Pittsburgh Post-Gazette*, December 18, 2018.

22. Pittsburgh, Pennsylvania, Department of Mobility and Infrastructure, "Pittsburgh Principles for Autonomous Vehicles," https://pittsburghpa.gov/domi/autonomous-vehicles.

23. Ashley Murray, "Mayor Peduto, Self-Driving Car Companies Announce 'Pittsburgh Principles,'" *Pittsburgh Post-Gazette*, March 4, 2019.

24. Nathan Bomey, "U.S. Vehicle Deaths Topped 40,000 in 2017, National Safety Council Estimates," *USA Today*, February 15, 2018.

25. National Highway Traffic Safety Administration, US Department of Transportation, "Critical Reasons for Crashes Investigated in the National Motor Vehicle Crash Causation Survey," February 2015.

26. Association for Safe International Road Travel, "Road Safety Facts: Annual Global Road Crash Statistics," https://www.asirt.org/safe-travel/road-safety-facts/.

27. Nidhi Kalra and David G. Groves, "The Enemy of Good: Estimating the Cost of Waiting for Nearly Perfect Automated Vehicles," Rand Corporation, 2017, https://www.rand.org/pubs/research_reports/RR2150.html.

28. Heather Somerville and David Shepardson, "Uber Car's 'Safety' Driver Streamed TV Show before Fatal Crash: Police," Reuters, June 22, 2018.

29. Lara Silva, "Airbnb Use Is Down in Amsterdam Due to Strict Rent Policies," *DutchReview*, May 2, 2019.

30. Anna Paganini, "Amsterdam to Impose Stricter Daily Limit on Airbnb Rentals," *NL Times*, January 10, 2018.

31. Molly Turner, interview with author, September 22, 2017.

32. John Meagher, "Strict New Dutch Rules on Airbnb a Blueprint to Follow for Our Cities," *Irish Independent*, January 3, 2019.

33. Charles F. Manski, "Adaptive Partial Drug Approval: A Health Policy Proposal," *Economists' Voice* 6, no. 4 (2009).

34. Snigdha Prakash and Vikki Valentine, "Timeline: The Rise and Fall of Vioxx," NPR, November 10, 2007, https://www.npr.org/2007/11/10/5470430/timeline-the-rise-and-fall-of-vioxx.

35. Manski, "Adaptive Partial Drug Approval."

36. City of Boston, "Autonomous Vehicles: Boston's Approach," https://www.boston
.gov/departments/new-urban-mechanics/autonomous-vehicles-bostons-approach
#documents.

37. City of Boston, "The Purpose of Boston's Autonomous Vehicle Testing Program,"
https://www.boston.gov/sites/default/files/file/document_files/2017/09/nutonomy_av
_testing_application_part_iii_test_plan_3.pdf.

38. nuTonomy, "Quarterly AV Testing Report: 2nd Quarter 2019," https://www.boston
.gov/sites/default/files/file/document_files/2019/08/nutonomy_report_q2_2019_0.pdf.

39. Optimus Ride, "Q1 2019 Progress Report: Autonomous Vehicle Testing City of
Boston," https://www.boston.gov/sites/default/files/file/document_files/2019/06/optimus
ride-_quarterly_report_-_q1_2019.pdf.

40. City & County of San Francisco, "Final Report of the Emerging Technology Open
Working Group," https://emergingtech.sfgov.org/sites/default/files/2019-01/ET_Report
_0119Single_0.pdf.

41. Viviana A. Zelizer, "Human Values and the Market: The Case for Life Insurance
and Death in 19th-Century America," *American Journal of Sociology* 84, no. 3 (November
1978): 598; David Moss and Eugene Kintgen, "The Armstrong Investigation," Case 708-034
(Boston: Harvard Business School, 2009); David Moss and Cole Bolton, "Wall Street's First
Panic (A)," Case 708-002 (Boston: Harvard Business School, 2009).

42. Alison Griswold and Mike Murphy, "Uber's Self-Driving Cars Have Come to
Pittsburgh, but That Doesn't Mean the Driverless Era Is Here," *Quartz*, September 14, 2016.

Chapter 5

1. Portions of this discussion are adapted from Mitchell Weiss and Alissa Davies, "Waze
Connected Citizens Program," Case 817-035 (Boston: Harvard Business School, 2017). Unless
otherwise noted, all quotes come from this case and subsequent interviews with Paige
Fitzgerald by the author on November 1, 2017 and April 4, 2019.

2. Tom Vanderbilt, "Waze: The App That Changed Driving," *Men's Journal*, February 8,
2016, https://www.mensjournal.com/gear/waze-the-app-that-changed-driving-20160208/.

3. J. Clement, "Number of Full-Time Alphabet Employees from 2007 to 2019," Statista,
February 5, 2020, https://www.statista.com/statistics/273744/number-of-full-time-google
-employees/.

4. *Platform thinking* is a phrase coined by David B. Yoffie and Michael A. Cusumano
in *Strategy Rules: Five Timeless Lesson from Bill Gates, Andy Grove, and Steve Jobs* (New York:
HarperBusiness, 2015), 98–100.

5. Andrew McAfee and Erik Brynjolfsson, *The Second Machine Age: Work, Progress, and
Prosperity in a Time of Brilliant Technologies* (New York: W. W. Norton, 2014), 59.

6. Tzahi Hoffman and Shmulik Shelach, "The Waze Millionaires," *Globes*, June 10, 2013.

7. Waze, "Driver Satisfaction Index 2016," https://inbox-static.waze.com/driverindex
.pdf.

8. Vanderbilt, "Waze."

9. Alexei Oreskovic and Alistair Barr, "Google Finalizing $1.3 Billion Deal for Mapping
Company Waze: Source," Reuters, June 9, 2013; and Ingrid Lunden, "Google Bought Waze
for $1.1B, Giving a Social Data Boost to Its Mapping Business," *TechCrunch*, June 11, 2013.

10. Cusumano, Gawer, and Yoffie, *The Business of Platforms*, 13.

11. Ibid., 18.

12. Ibid., 20.

13. McAfee and Brynjolfsson, *The Second Machine Age*, 60.

14. Ibid., 16.

15. Tim O'Reilly, "Government as a Platform," *Innovations: Technology, Governance, Globalization* 6, no. 1 (2011): 15–16.

16. Ibid., 16.

17. Ibid., 15. O'Reilly credits Donald Kettl for the phrase "vending machine government."

18. Ibid.

19. Tarun Khanna and Anjali Raina, "Aadhaar: India's 'Unique Identification' System," Case 712-412 (Boston: Harvard Business School, 2012).

20. Felix Richter, "How Facebook Grew from 0 to 2.3 Billion Users in 15 Years," World Economic Forum and Statista, February 5, 2019, https://www.weforum.org/agenda/2019/02/how-facebook-grew-from-0-to-2-3-billion-users-in-15-years/.

21. Office of the Registrar General, India, "Census of India 2011: Language," 2011, https://censusindia.gov.in/2011Census/C-16_25062018_NEW.pdf.

22. Khanna and Raina, "Aadhaar."

23. Ibid.

24. Ibid.

25. Cusumano, Gawer, and Yoffie, *The Business of Platforms*, 71–72.

26. Geoffrey G. Parker, Marshall W. Van Alstyne, and Sangeet Paul Choudary, *Platform Revolution: How Networked Markets Are Transforming the Economy and How to Make Them Work for You* (New York: W. W. Norton, 2016), 79–99.

27. Ibid., 83.

28. Ibid., 93.

29. Ibid., 79–99.

30. Khanna and Raina, "Aadhaar."

31. Ibid.

32. Unique Identification Authority of India, "Welcome to Aadhaar Dashboard," https://uidai.gov.in/aadhaar_dashboard/.

33. Brilliant Maps, "The 4037 Cities in the World with Over 100,000 People," https://brilliantmaps.com/4037-100000-person-cities/.

34. Patrick Downes, "Boston Marathon Tribute: Survivor Patrick Downes Says 'Thank You,'" April 16, 2014, https://www.youtube.com/watch?v=pBc0yg6EluQ.

35. Tim O'Reilly, "Government as a Platform," *Innovations: Technology, Governance, Globalization* 6, no. 1 (2011): 15–16.

36. Cusumano, Gawer, and Yoffie, *The Business of Platforms*, 22.

37. Portions of this discussion are adapted from Mitchell Weiss, "ofo," Case 819-063 (Boston: Harvard Business School, 2018; revised, 2019). All quotes come from this case unless otherwise noted.

38. Cusumano, Gawer, and Yoffie, *The Business of Platforms*, 108.

39. Ibid., 175.

40. Anthony Tao, "In Hangzhou, This Field Is Where 20,000 Confiscated Bikes Have Gone to Die," Radii, June 28, 2017, https://radiichina.com/in-hangzhou-this-field-is-where-20000-confiscated-bikes-have-gone-to-die/.

41. Alan Taylor, "The Bike-Share Oversupply in China: Huge Piles of Abandoned and Broken Bicycles," *The Atlantic*, March 22, 2018.

42. Raymond Zhong and Carolyn Zhang, "Ofo, Pioneer of China's Bike-Sharing Boom, Is in a Crisis," *New York Times*, December 20, 2018.

43. Manveena Suri, "Aadhaar: India Supreme Court Upholds Controversial Biometric Database," CNN, September 26, 2018.

44. David Zipper, "Cities Can See Where You're Taking That Scooter," *Slate*, April 2, 2019.

45. Kate Conger, "Uber Wants to Sell You Train Tickets. And Be Your Bus Service, Too," *New York Times*, August 7, 2019.

46. Mike Isaac, "Which Tech Company Is Uber Most Like? Its Answer May Surprise You," *New York Times*, April 28, 2019.

47. Drew Harwell, "Amazon Met with ICE Officials over Facial-Recognition System That Could Identify Immigrants," *Washington Post*, October 23, 2018.

48. Amazon Web Services, "The Trusted Cloud for Government," https://aws.amazon .com/government-education/government/?nc2=h_m2.

49. Gai Berkovich, interview with author, Tel Aviv, Israel, December 19, 2016.

Chapter 6

1. Matthew Lira, telephone conversation with author, April 27, 2018.

2. Juliet Eilperin and Darla Cameron, "How Trump Is Rolling Back Obama's Legacy," *Washington Post*, March 24, 2017, updated January 20, 2018.

3. Parts of this discussion are adapted from Mitchell Weiss, Nick Sinai, and Michael Norris, "U.S. Digital Service," Case 817-032 (Boston: Harvard Business School, 2016; revised, 2018) All quotes come from this case unless otherwise noted.

4. Craig Bannister, "Obama: Using Obamacare Website as Easy as Buying 'a TV on Amazon,'" *CNSNews*, October 1, 2013.

5. Frank Thorp, "Only 6 Able to Sign Up on HealthCare.gov's First Day, Documents Show," *NBC News*, October 31, 2013.

6. Steven Brill, "Obama's Trauma Team," *Time*, March 10, 2014.

7. Ibid.

8. Jon Gertner, "Inside Obama's Stealth Startup," *Fast Company*, June 15, 2015.

9. Mikey Dickerson, "The U.S. Digital Service: An Improbable Public Interest Start Up," Medium, https://medium.com/the-u-s-digital- service/an-improbable-public-interest-start -up-6f9a54712411#.klxptkuox.

10. Steven Levy, "The Tiny Team Taking on a Massive Reform of Government IT," *Wired*, July 30, 2015.

11. Kamala D. Harris, "Digital Service Act of 2019," Office of Senator Kamala Harris, https://www.harris.senate.gov/imo/media/doc/Digital%20Services%20Act%20one %20pager.pdf.

12. Cara Giaimo, "Innovator in Chief," *MIT Technology Review*, October 24, 2019.

13. Code For All, "Our Members," https://codeforall.org/members.

14. "Welcoming Our Newest Cohort of Civic Digital Fellows," email from Chris Kuang, June 10, 2019.

15. New America, "Fifteen New Universities and Colleges Join New America's Public Interest Technology University Network," February 24, 2020, https://www.newamerica .org/public-interest-technology/press-releases/fifteen-new-universities-and-colleges-join -new-americas-public-interest-technology-university-network/.

16. Biobot, "We Are Global Leaders in Wastewater Epidemiology," https://www.biobot .io/about_us.php.

17. Terace Garnier, "NC Town Battles Opioid Epidemic by Using Robots to Test People's Poop," Fox News, July 12, 2018.

18. Disclosure: I have received compensation for a speaking engagement from ShotSpotter in the past.

19. Mitchell Weiss and Sarah McAra, "ShotSpotter," Case 817-034 (Boston: Harvard Business Review, 2016).

20. CNNtech, "15 Questions with Ron Bouganim," https://money.cnn.com/interactive/technology/15-questions-with-ron-bouganim/index.html.

21. Mitchell Weiss and Phoebe Peronto, "Urban Us," Case 818-115 (Boston: Harvard Business School, 2018).

22. Cat Zakrzewski, "Regulatory Support for Startups Comes into Vogue," *Wall Street Journal*, June 21, 2018.

23. Government Technology, "GovTech 100 Investors List," https://www.govtech.com/100/investors/.

24. Parts of this discussion are adapted from Mitchell Weiss and A. J. Steinlage, "Shield AI," Case 819-062 (Boston: Harvard Business School, 2018). All quotes come from this case unless otherwise noted.

25. John T. Gourville, "Eager Sellers and Stony Buyers: Understanding the Psychology of New-Product Adoption," *Harvard Business Review*, June 2006.

26. Amanda Albright, "The Fall of the Muni Startup That Wanted to Upend Wall Street," *Bloomberg*, October 16, 2019.

27. Shoshana Zuboff, *The Age of Surveillance Capitalism: The Fight for a Human Future at the New Frontier of Power* (New York: PublicAffairs, 2019).

28. Ash Carter, "The Morality of Defending America: A Letter to a Young Googler," *Boston Globe*, June 6, 2019.

29. Rosalie Chan, "Read the Internal Letter Sent by a Group of Amazon Employees Asking the Company to Take a Stand Against Ice," *Business Insider*, July 11, 2019.

30. "Dear Jeff," via SCRIBD, https://www.scribd.com/document/382334740/Dear-Jeff.

31. Karen Weise and Natasha Singer, "Amazon Pauses Police Use of Its Facial Recognition Software," June 10, 2020.

32. Amazon, "We Are Implementing a One-Year Moratorium on Police Use of Rekognition," *dayone* (blog), June 10, 2020, https://blog.aboutamazon.com/policy/we-are-implementing-a-one-year-moratorium-on-police-use-of-rekognition.

33. Dom Phillips, "How Directions on the Waze App Led to Death in Brazil's Favelas," The *Washington Post*, October 5, 2015.

34. Nick Lovegrove and Matthew Thomas, "Triple-Strength Leadership," *Harvard Business Review*, September 2013.

35. Ibid.

36. Ibid.

37. Mitchell Weiss and Matthew Segneri, "Public Entrepreneurs? Picking a Path," Case 818-005 (Boston: Harvard Business School, 2017; revised, 2019).

Chapter 7

1. Portions of this chapter are adapted from Mitchell Weiss and Maddy Halyard, "Voatz," Case 819-123 (Boston: Harvard Business School, 2019). All quotes come from this case unless otherwise noted.

2. "Fight Night," *Billions*, Showtime, May 5, 2019.

3. Emma Wright, "Founder's Spotlight: Nimit Sawhney of Voatz," Cambridge Innovation Center, January 14, 2018, https://cic.com/podcasts/founders-spotlight/voatz.

4. "Heavy Voting and Violence Mark Indian Elections," *Washington Post*, December 25, 1984.

5. Bradley Tusk, *The Fixer: My Adventures Saving Startups from Death by Politics* (New York: Portfolio/Penguin, 2018).

6. Fitz Tepper, "Uber Launches 'De Blasio's Uber' Feature in NYC with 25-Minute Wait Times," *TechCrunch*, July 16, 2015.

7. Matt Flegenheimer, "De Blasio Administration Dropping Plan for Uber Cap, for Now," *New York Times*, July 22, 2015.

8. Evan Halper, "The Vote-by-Phone Tech Trend Is Scaring the Life out of Security Experts," *Los Angeles Times*, May 16, 2019.

9. Kevin Beaumont, @GossiTheDog via Twitter, August 6, 2018, https://twitter.com/GossiTheDog/status/1026603800365330432.

10. Yascha Mounk, *The People vs. Democracy: Why Our Freedom Is in Danger & How to Save It* (Cambridge: Harvard University Press, 2018), 100.

11. Ibid.

12. Ibid, 107.

13. Ibid., 5.

14. Ibid., 109.

15. Ibid., 78.

16. Steven Levitsky and Daniel Ziblatt, *How Democracies Die* (New York: Crown, 2018), 168.

17. Mounk, *People vs. Democracy*, 100.

18. Ibid., 111.

19. James Miller, *Can Democracy Work? A Short History of a Radical Idea, from Ancient Athens to Our World* (New York: Farrar, Straus and Giroux, 2018), 237.

20. Veronica Stracqualursi, "US Intelligence Chief: 'The Warning Lights Are Blinking Red Again' on Cyberattacks," CNN, July 14, 2018, https://www.cnn.com/2018/07/14/politics/director-of-national-intelligence-dan-coats-cyberattacks-russia/index.html.

21. Robert S. Mueller III, "Report on the Investigation into Russian Interference in the 2016 Presidential Election: Volume I of II," US Department of Justice, March 2019, https://www.justice.gov/storage/report.pdf.

22. Rebecca Ballhaus and Dustin Volz, "U.S. Intelligence Officials Warn of 'Pervasive' Russian Efforts to Disrupt 2018 Elections," *Wall Street Journal*, August 3, 2018.

23. Maya Kosoff, "'A Horrifically Bad Idea': Smartphone Voting Is Coming, Just in Time for the Midterms," *Vanity Fair*, August 7, 2018.

24. Ibid.

25. Gabriella Mulligan, "Has the Time Now Come for Internet Voting?" *BBC News*, May 30, 2017.

26. Claire M. Smith, *Convenience Voting and Technology: The Case of Military and Overseas Voters* (London: Palgrave Macmillan, 2014), 90.

27. IDEO.org, *The Field Guide to Human-Centered Design* (IDEO, 2015).

28. Miller, *Can Democracy Work?*, 12.

29. Ibid., 21.

30. Max Roser, "Democracy," Our World in Data, https://ourworldindata.org/democracy, accessed February 2020.

31. David A. Moss, *Democracy: A Case Study* (Cambridge: Harvard University Press, 2017), 1.

32. Nafeesa Syeed, "Is Blockchain Technology the Future of Voting?" *Bloomberg*, August 10, 2018.

33. Moss, *Democracy*, 683.

34. Larry Schwartztol, interview with author, Boston, March 21, 2019.

35. Justin Florence, interview with author, Boston, March 21, 2019.

36. Ian Bassin, telephone conversation with author, June 20, 2019.

37. Schwartztol, interview with author.

38. Bassin, telephone conversation with author.

39. Miller, *Can Democracy Work?*, 236.

40. Disclosure: I am a member of the board of directors of the Case Method Institute.

41. Harvard Business School, Case Method Project, "Bringing Case Method Teaching to High Schools & Colleges: U.S. History, Government, Civics & Democracy," https://www.hbs.edu/case-method-project/Pages/default.aspx.

42. Moss, *Democracy*, 14.

43. Alan Khazei, "The Rise of the Democracy Entrepreneurs," *Boston Globe*, November 12, 2018.

44. New Profit, "Announcing New Civic Lab to Support Democracy Entrepreneurs," *Amplify* (blog), March 14, 2019, https://blog.newprofit.org/amplify/announcing-new-civic-lab-to-support-democracy-entrepreneurs.

45. The People, https://thepeople.org.

46. Echoing Green, "Darrell Scott," https://fellows.echoinggreen.org/fellow/darrell-scott/.

47. PushBlack, https://pushblack.org.

48. Yordanos Eyoel, telephone conversation with author, June 19, 2020.

49. Yordanos Eyoel, "Why Voting Isn't Enough," TEDxBeaconStreet, January 8, 2020, https://www.youtube.com/watch?v=Wi7HFSCjKs8.

50. "175,000 People Were on Hand for Women's March for America in Boston," WCVB, January 21, 2017, https://www.wcvb.com/article/womens-march-for-america-will-impact-traffic-and-parking-in-boston/8614813.

Chapter 8

1. Portions of this chapter are adapted from Mitchell Weiss and Sarah Mehta, "TraceTogether," Case 820-111 (Boston: Harvard Business School, 2020). All quotes come from this case unless otherwise noted.

2. Daniel Funke, "In Context: What Donald Trump Said about Disinfectant, Sun and Coronavirus," *PolitiFact*, April 24, 2020.

3. Lysol, "Improper Use of Disinfectants," https://www.lysol.com.

4. Alexi C. Cardona, "After Trump's Remarks, Floridians Ask Poison Control if Drinking Disinfectant Is Safe," *Miami New Times*, April 28, 2020.

5. James G. March, *Explorations in Organizations* (Palo Alto, CA: Stanford University Press, 2008), 101.

6. Singapore Ministry of Health, "Confirmed Imported Case of Novel Coronavirus Infection in Singapore; Multi-Ministry Taskforce Ramps Up Precautionary Measures," January 23, 2020, https://www.moh.gov.sg/news-highlights/details/confirmed-imported-case-of-novel-coronavirus-infection-in-singapore-multi-ministry-taskforce-ramps-up-precautionary-measures.

7. Lawrence O. Gostin, *Public Health Law: Power, Duty, Restraint* (Berkeley: University of California Press, 2008).

8. Krista C. Swanson et al., "Contact Tracing Performance during the Ebola Epidemic in Liberia, 2014–2015." *PLoS Neglected Tropical Diseases* 12, no. 9 (2018), https://www.ncbi.nlm .nih.gov/pmc/articles/PMC6152989/.

9. Luca Ferretti et al., "Quantifying SARS-CoV-2 Transmission Suggests Epidemic Control with Digital Contact Tracing," *Science* 368, no. 6491 (2020).

10. Sam Jo Yeo, "A Guide to Singapore's Covid-19 Contact-Tracing System," *Straits Times*, March 28, 2020.

11. Katayoun Farrahi, Rémi Emonet, and Manuel Cebrian, "Epidemic Contact Tracing via Communication Traces," *PLoS One 9*, no. 5 (2014).

12. Society for Science & the Public, "Development of a Rapid, Accurate, and Private Contact Tracing System Utilizing Smartphone Proximities," 2015, https://abstracts .societyforscience.org/Home/FullAbstract?Category=Any%20Category&AllAbstracts= True&FairCountry=Any%20Country&FairState=Any%20State&ProjectId=12701.

13. Rohan Suri, video call with author, May 22, 2020.

14. David Pierson, "Singapore Says Its Coronavirus App Helps the Public. Critics Say It's Government Surveillance," *Los Angeles Times*, March 25, 2020.

15. "New Report Reveals Singapore Has the Highest Smartphone Penetration in the Region," *Rebl* (blog), March 20, 2019, https://rebl.sg/new-report-reveals-singapore-has-the -highest-smartphone-penetration-in-the-region/.

16. Pierson, "Coronavirus App."

17. Karishma Vaswani, "Coronavirus: The Detectives Racing to Contain the Virus in Singapore," *BBC News*, March 19, 2020.

18. Pierson, "Coronavirus App."

19. Lee Hsien Loong, "PM Lee Hsien Loong on the COVID-19 Situation in Singapore on 8 February 2020," Prime Minister's Office Singapore, https://www.pmo.gov.sg/Newsroom/ PM-Lee-Hsien-Loong-on-the-Novel-Coronavirus-nCoV-Situation-in-Singapore-on-8 -February-2020.

20. OpenTrace, "Trial Methodologies," April 10, 2020, https://github.com/opentrace -community/opentrace-calibration/blob/master/Trial%20Methodologies.md.

21. Vivan Balakrishnan, Facebook, https://www.facebook.com/Vivian.Balakrishnan .Sg/posts/10156631322166207, March 22, 2020.

22. BlueTrace Protocol, "TraceTogether—an Overview," https://bluetrace.io/policy.

23. Singapore Ministry of Health, "Circuit Breaker to Minimise Further Spread of Covid-19," April 3, 2020, https://www.moh.gov.sg/news-highlights/details/circuit-breaker -to-minimise-further-spread-of-covid-19.

24. Andrew Roth et al., "Growth in Surveillance May Be Hard to Scale Back after Pandemic, Experts Say," *The Guardian*, April 14, 2020.

25. Ashkan Soltani, Ryan Calo, and Carl Bergstrom, "Contact-Tracing Apps Are Not a Solution to the COVID-19 Crisis," Brookings Tech Stream, April 27, 2020, https://www .brookings.edu/techstream/inaccurate-and-insecure-why-contact-tracing-apps-could-be-a -disaster/.

26. Will Douglas Heaven, "A New App Would Say if You've Crossed Paths with Someone Who Is Infected," *MIT Technology Review*, March 17, 2020.

27. Kelly Servick, "Cellphone Tracking Could Help Stem the Spread of Coronavirus. Is Privacy the Price?" *Science*, March 22, 2020; Arjun Kharpal, "Use of Surveillance to Fight

Coronavirus Raises Concerns about Government Power after Pandemic Ends," *CNBC*, March 26, 2020.

28. Ibid.

29. "Countries Are Using Apps and Data Networks to Keep Tabs on the Pandemic: And Also, in the Process, Their Citizens," *Economist*, March 26, 2020.

30. Natasha Singer and Choe Sang-Hun, "As Coronavirus Surveillance Escalates, Personal Privacy Plummets," *New York Times*, March 23, 2020.

31. Jason Bay et al., "BlueTrace: A Privacy-Preserving Protocol for Community-Driven Contact Tracing across Borders," Government Technology Agency, Singapore, https://bluetrace.io/static/bluetrace_whitepaper-938063656596c104632def383eb33b3c.pdf.

32. "Singapore Aims to Keep Coronavirus Contact Tracing App Voluntary, Considers Other Devices," *Bloomberg News*, May 23, 2020.

33. Soltani, Calo, and Bergstrom, "Contact-Tracing Apps Are Not a Solution."

34. Ibid.

35. Daniel Korski, "NHS Covid App Didn't Pass the Test but It Still Points Way to the Future," *Evening Standard*, June 22, 2020.

36. "COVID19 Press Conference: Utah Public/Private Partnership," March 20, 2020, https://www.youtube.com/watch?v=chedMU777bU; Andrew Joseph, "Utah Went All-in on an Unproven Covid-19 Treatment, Then Scrambled to Course-Correct," *STAT*, May 18, 2020.

37. Paul Leblanc, "Georgia Governor to Reopen Some Businesses as Early as Friday as Other States Signal Similar Plans," CNN, April 20, 2020; Christopher Brito, "Las Vegas Mayor Offers Up City as 'Control Group' for Reopening Amid Pandemic," *CBS News*, April 23, 2020.

38. Wherever I used the word *delusion*, I do *not* mean it in a clinical sense. *Delusional* is a label I avoid, as it is one only psychological professionals should use, and it should not be used as a pejorative. I mean the word simply in its colloquial sense, along the lines of Merriam-Webster's "something that is falsely believed."

39. Eric Paley, "The Probable, the Possible, the Delusional," *TechCrunch*, February 13, 2016.

40. Molly Turner, email to author, June 12, 2020.

41. Yordanos Eyoel specifically noted Bryan Stevenson's notion of proximity, what he calls "getting closer to the people who are suffering." See Leandra Fernandez, "Empathy and Social Justice: The Power of Proximity in Improvement Science," Carnegie Foundation for the Advancement of Teaching, April 21, 2016, https://www.carnegiefoundation.org/blog/empathy-and-social-justice-the-power-of-proximity-in-improvement-science/.

42. James Geurts, telephone conversation with author, June 22, 2020.

43. Eric Paley, telephone conversation with author, June 19, 2020.

44. Rosabeth Moss Kanter originated this framework for change management. She also has a helpful list of characteristics that make pilot projects easiest to sell in her unpublished document for her workshops, "Change Toolkit Sampler," June 2017, 12.

45. Geurts, telephone conversation with author.

46. Annie Rittgers, email to author, June 22, 2020.

47. Daniel A. Levinthal and James G. March, "The Myopia of Learning," *Strategic Management Journal* 14, no. 52 (1993): 95; Rosabeth Moss Kanter, "Change Is Hardest in the Middle," *Harvard Business Review*, August 12, 2009.

48. Moss Kanter, "Change Is Hardest in the Middle."

Chapter 9

1. Rob Reich, *Just Giving: Why Philanthropy Is Failing Democracy and How It Can Do Better* (Princeton, NJ: Princeton University Press, 2018), 141.

2. Alison Powell, Willa Seldon, and Nidhi Sahni, "Reimagining Institutional Philanthropy," The Bridgespan Group, April 19, 2019, https://www.bridgespan.org/insights/library/big-bets/unleashing-big-bets-for-social-change/reimagining-institutional-philanthropy.

3. Bill Gates, "What I'm Thinking about This New Year's Eve," *GatesNotes* (blog), December 30, 2019, https://www.gatesnotes.com/About-Bill-Gates/Year-in-Review-2019.

4. Reich, *Just Giving*, 152.

5. Ibid, 167.

6. Ibid., 164.

7. David A. Moss, *When All Else Fails: Government as the Ultimate Risk Manager* (Cambridge: Harvard University Press, 2002), 28.

8. Reich, *Just Giving*.

9. CalPERS, "Investment & Pension Funding: Facts at a Glance for Fiscal Year 2018–19," https://www.calpers.ca.gov/docs/forms-publications/facts-investment-pension-funding.pdf#page=3.

10. Mariana Mazzucato, *The Entrepreneurial State: Debunking Public vs. Private Sector Myths* (New York: PublicAffairs, 2015).

11. Steve Blank, "About Steve," https://steveblank.com/about/accessed February 2020.

12. Steve Blank, "Why the Government Isn't a Bigger Version of a Startup," *War on the Rocks*, November 11, 2019, https://warontherocks.com/2019/11/why-the-government-isnt-a-bigger-version-of-a-startup/.

13. "Uber CEO Travis Kalanick Indicted in South Korea under Transport Law," *Bloomberg News*, December 24, 2014.

14. Ainsley Harris, "Food-Sharing Startup Josephine Is Shutting Down," *Fast Company*, February 2, 2018.

15. Blank, "Why the Government Isn't a Bigger Version of a Startup."

16. Paul Gompers et al., "Performance Persistence in Entrepreneurship and Venture Capital," *Journal of Financial Economics* 96, no. 1 (2010): 18.

17. Jerker Denrell and James G. March, "Adaptation as Information Restriction: The Hot Stove Effect," *Organization Science* 12, no. 5 (2001): 523.

18. Christopher Hood, *The Blame Game: Spin, Bureaucracy, and Self-Preservation in Government* (Princeton, NJ: Princeton University Press, 2011).

19. James G. March, *Explorations in Organizations* (Palo Alto, CA: Stanford University Press, 2018), 92.

20. Charles A. O'Reilly III and Michael L. Tushman, "The Ambidextrous Organization," *Harvard Business Review*, April 2004. See also Charles A. O'Reilly III and Michael L. Tushman, *Lead and Disrupt: How to Solve the Innovators Dilemma* (Palo Alto, CA: Stanford University Press, 2016).

21. Chris Johnston and Kelly O'Connor, "The Importance of Product Management in Government," US Digital Service, August 23, 2018, https://medium.com/the-u-s-digital-service/the-importance-of-product-management-in-government-b59933d01874.

22. National Security Commission on Artificial Intelligence, "Second Quarter Recommendations, Quarterly Series, No. 2," July 2020, http://files2.dlapiper.com/DLA _Piper_Web_Images_US_2/pdfs/NSCAI%20Q2%20Memo_20200722.pdf.

23. March, *Explorations in Organizations*.

24. Among those funds were nearly $1 million from "the century-old foundation." While we disagreed at the very outset, that foundation's collaboration throughout was unequivocally generous. See the Boston Foundation, "Boston Foundation Donors Rally to Provide for the One Fund Boston," https://www.tbf.org/news-and-insights/press-releases/ 2013/june/boston-foundation-donors-contribute-to-one-fund.

INDEX

INDEX

ACKNOWLEDGMENTS

The late Mayor Thomas Menino often said, "The status quo is moving backwards." He loved that my son's initials, N. E. W., spelled "new," something I hadn't focused on until the mayor pointed it out. Tom Menino was an urban mechanic through and through and never would have thought of himself as a "public entrepreneur," because he would have said it sounded too fancy. But he was one for the ages. Moreover, he let me and so many others be public entrepreneurs. I remain immensely grateful for his mentorship and his friendship.

David Moss, a professor of mine at Harvard Business School when we first met, wrote an essential book on government risk management, but his influence on me extends way beyond that. David taught me to aim bigger, think harder, and argue more bravely. A book like this one isn't the only way to thank a life-changing teacher, but I hope he'll find it a fitting one.

Harvard Business School seems like an unusual perch from which to write a book on government, but it has been the perfect place for me. Nitin Nohria asked me what I planned to do after my time in government, and this—all of this—is it. He has been a steadfast supporter, guide, and friend along the way. Frances Frei welcomed me back to the school in all the most amazing and "Frances" ways possible. Anita Elberse gave me a running start.

Jan Rivkin invited me to help put together the Young American Leaders Program at the school, and thus started a collaboration that has meant so much to me, both professionally and personally. I have learned so much from Jan about what great teaching is. I have met more than five hundred amazing cross-sector leaders through the program and shared and honed some of the stories in this book with them. I am indebted to the team at YALP, led by the indefatigable Manjari Raman. My involvement at YALP also deepened my relationships with two other colleagues: Karen Mills and Rosabeth Moss Kanter. Karen spent countless hours in my office, sharing some of her own experiences in government, assuaging my author anxieties, and providing chocolate-covered cherries for stamina. Rosabeth has been a friend throughout. She read the manuscript and gave me invaluable comments during a socially distanced porch visit.

The Entrepreneurial Management Unit at HBS welcomed a public-oriented interloper with open arms. I am grateful to my two unit heads, Josh Lerner and Bill Kerr, both of whom demonstrated, in their own scholarship and in their encouragement of mine, what it means to think deeply about entrepreneurship and its public value. Tom Eisenmann has been a consummate adviser, and it was a special joy to undertake book journeys contemporaneously, swapping proposals and chapters along the way. I've mentioned Tom's ideas and Bill Sahlman's earlier in the book, but my citations don't do justice to their influence on me. That Bill, one of the school's and the field's luminaries, would listen to me go on and on about some new case and share in my enthusiasm was a gift, and one he gave early and often. Lynda Applegate and Bob White, too, were frequent boosters. Tom Nicholas, Ramana Nanda, and Scott Kominers enlightened my thinking over lunches and coffees and often pointed a would-be academic in the direction of just the right paper or book. Joining HBS's first-year course, The Entrepreneurial Manager, has been a great joy. Joe Fuller and Shikhar Ghosh were course heads when I first came on board, and both have become dear friends and mentors. Joe's comments on the manuscript were incredibly helpful and not nearly as saucy as I had expected. Later, Paul Gompers welcomed my voice and my cases into The Entrepreneurial Manager. If it weren't for Paul, I doubt I would have been in Israel to ask Waze's leadership, "How many cities will you be in?" Now I have the responsibility of leading the course, and all of my teaching-group colleagues have added volumes to what I know about entrepreneurship. Many of them participated in a seminar on the book and helped me refine my ideas, particularly on the question of "possibility or delusion?" Jeff Bussgang has been a constant and welcome connection to the real world of entrepreneurship. He's also one of the first people I broached the idea of this book to, the one who said "Get started now," and the person who hosted the first book club reading of a draft version.

Emma Tavolieri provided faculty support to me while I was writing this book, but also so much more. She conceived of and crafted novel ways in which I could share the ideas in this book. Emma also administered the Public Entrepreneurship course without any glitches and made students feel supported and eminently prepared. Adria Brown and Lara Zimmerman helped me nurture Public Entrepreneurship in its earlier days, and their imprints still remain.

The Social Enterprise Initiative (SEI) at HBS played such an important role in my shift into public service and then to writing about it that it's difficult to know where to start with my thanks. Dutch Leonard and Kash Rangan have cultivated an essential home for work on the leadership of social enterprises at the school and made me feel welcome there. As just one example, Kash organized a seminar for me to share the ideas in this book with the SEI community, and Dutch offered opening comments and questions. (Dutch also generously and opportunely introduced me to James Geurts and to the idea of our SOFWERX case in the very first place.) I'm grateful to everyone who participated. Sarah Appleby, Margot Dushin, Laura Moon, and others on the SEI team during the last two decades of my engagement there have made it so easy. Matthew Segneri, who directed SEI for much of the time I worked on this book, always looked for ways to make public innovation a core part of SEI's work. He was an expert collaborator on our case on trisector entrepreneurship and is a wonderful trisector entrepreneur himself. The late John McArthur was dean of HBS when SEI came to be, and he took me under his wing when I later joined the faculty there. Richard Menschel, from the beginning of my engagement with SEI as a student, to my practice of public leadership in my career, to my return to the school, has always provided generous encouragement, humor, curiosity, and a healthy dose of skepticism. I therefore felt especially fortunate that I was the Richard L. Menschel faculty fellow while writing this book. He and Ronay are marvelous friends.

The Bloomberg Harvard City Leadership Initiative (BHCLI) was birthed to help city leaders be bolder, more innovative, and more effective, and my lucky involvement with this organization has elevated my own thinking on these fronts. The BHCLI was also the reason I met some of the public leaders mentioned in this book, including Mayor Bill Peduto of Pittsburgh, or why I saw others I already knew in illuminating new contexts, like Saint Paul's Mayor Melvin Carter. I am grateful to Mike Bloomberg for his extreme generosity in the service of better public leadership. I have always felt energized in the presence of Patti Harris, CEO of Bloomberg Philanthropies. Mike and Patti have made their foundation a great lever for possibility. I have watched admiringly as Jim Anderson, Katie Appel Duda, Josh Skolnick, Stephanie Wade, and so many others in their orbit identified, convened, and supported public leaders in surprising, delightful, and, ultimately, transformative ways. Jim belongs in the pantheon of people humbly championing Possibility Government in word and deed, often behind the scenes. I was in New York, prepping to be with the mayors whom Mike Bloomberg and his team had convened, when I came up with the term "Possibility Government." I had been searching for a phrase that would encapsulate all that these leaders were doing in order to try new things, and why it was all so difficult and yet still worthy. Jim was the first person I told. At Harvard, Jorrit de Jong has been our most able leader in partnership with the Bloomberg team, and I am grateful that he welcomed my strain of work into the program from its earliest days. I thank him and Rawi Abdelal for putting me in front of so many mayors and their senior leaders. Dave Margalit and the entire BHCLI team, including Mahlet Aklu and Bulbul Kaul, are brilliant entrepreneurs themselves, creating an amazing suite of programs from nothing in a few short years, and I am thankful to them for their advice and support. BHCLI also brought me back to Steve Goldsmith, who was such a help while I was in government and has become a friend.

Many of the stories in this book originated as HBS cases, and many of them I wrote in collaboration with the amazing people at HBS's Case Research and Writing Group and its Global Research Centers. I am indebted to the leadership teams of both these groups, and to all the individuals I was lucky enough to work with, including Kerry Herman on "SOFWERX" and "TraceTogether"; Sarah Mehta on "Hacking Heroin" and "TraceTogether"; Adina Wong on TraceTogether"; Fernanda Miguel on "LabCDMX"; Sarah McAra on "Propel" and "ShotSpotter"; Michael Norris on "US Digital Service"; Emer Maloney and Vincent Dessain on "Airbnb in Amsterdam"; Jingsheng Huang, Essie Alamsyah, and Christopher Kralik on "ofo"; Elena Corsi on "Bitfury"; and Christine Snively on "Bigbelly."

The school's supporters have made my research and writing possible through their generosity. I am grateful to Leslie Perlow, Senior Associate Dean for Research, and to Cynthia Montgomery, my research director, for all they have enabled me to see and do. Alex

Caracuzzo and the team at Baker Research Services dug into many corners of history to help me support the stories in the book. The Rock Center for Entrepreneurship has also been very supportive, and I thank Jodi Gernon and her team. The school's Digital Initiative has been wonderful to include me, and I am grateful to David Homa and everyone there. I thank the teams at HBS's Executive Education and HBS Online programs for putting me in rooms (physically and virtually) with hundreds of global leaders. I want to make special mention of Pam Hallagan, who found many opportunities to insert public entrepreneurship into the school's executive programs. Brian Kenny and so many talented people in communications and marketing at HBS have generously spread the word about public entrepreneurship beyond the school.

I've also benefited from the work of two talented research assistants, Matt Higgins and Mariana Oseguera Rodriguez. Mariana tracked down answers to my esoteric questions for the book and offered helpful comments on the manuscript, all while helping me build out the curricular materials for the Public Entrepreneurship course.

So many HBS colleagues have improved how I think about entrepreneurship, leadership, book writing, or all of the above. Among them are Alison Wood Brooks, Ryan Buell, Shawn Cole, Tom DeLong, Amy Edmondson, Willis Emmons, David Fubini, Jan Hammond, Rob Huckman, Leslie John, Tarun Khanna (who also introduced me to Nandan Nilekani), Karim Lakhani, Mike Luca, Alan MacCormack, John Macomber, Joshua Margolis, Tony Mayo, Warren McFarlan, Youngme Moon, Kristin Mugford, Tsedal Neeley, Michael Norton, Earl Sasser, Len Schlesinger, Mike Toffel, and Matt Weinzierl. Arthur Segel has been a champion of mine for the last fifteen years. Michael Tushman has been a wonderful mentor and, in yet another example of his generosity, provided very helpful comments on the manuscript.

Colleagues from other Harvard schools have been enthusiastic co-conspirators on this topic, especially Nick Sinai (a coauthor on "US Digital Service") and David Eaves at Harvard Kennedy School. Ed Glaeser took me seriously from my earliest days in government to the first days I was contemplating this book, and I thank him for that. Ash Carter and Frank Doyle graciously invited me into their Boston Tech Hub faculty working group. I've benefited from my interactions with Susan Crawford, Monica Higgins, Howard Koh, David Parkes, Julie Wilson, and many others in our Harvard community. Two Harvard presidents, Drew Faust and Larry Bacow, showed generous curiosity about my work whenever we met, as did the university's provost, Alan Garber—and it was all fuel for me.

My most effusive thanks I reserve for my students. When I created the Public Entrepreneurship course in 2015, it was the new, unlikely thing. And I told the MBA students who took a chance on it that the course's coming to be would depend on them. We'd build it together. They responded with care and rigor, and every class since then has done the same. The course has therefore been coproduced by amazing young leaders, and I have been so enriched in their presence. I also had the great pleasure of getting to know many of them individually and trading questions and ideas. Many became collaborators along the way, including Alissa Davies on "Waze," Maddy Halyard on "Voatz," Phoebe Peronto on "Urban Us," Kristin Rhodes on "Hacking Heroin," A. J. Steinlage on "Shield AI," and Brittany Urick on "Testing Autonomy in Pittsburgh." Bhumika Agarwalla, Omosefe Aiyevbomwan, Moriya Blumenfeld, Kyra D'Onofrio, Gavriel Goidel, Jiyoon Han, Matt McCalpin, David Reiff, Iris Rhee, Will Stemberg, and Rohan Vora all helped with a rush of research on COVID-driven innovation. Some students became case protagonists along the way, including Ellen DaSilva, Adam Gunter, Sasha Pang, Annie Rittgers, Yael Schiff, Henry Tsai, and Brandon Tseng. Others became energetic interlocutors during and after their time at HBS, among them Chelsea Banks, Danny Clark, Amina Edwards, Asaf Gilboa, Justine Hong, Andrew Kahn, Michael Martin, Sarika Mendu, Rebecca Milian, Giuseppe Morgana, Apoorva Pasricha, Matt Piltch, Eduardo Russian, Kiernan Schmitt, Ned Shell, and Billy Tabrizi. Kiernan helped me shape the proposal for this book and encouraged me to try to carry the sort of "serious hopefulness" that distinguished the course (and its students) into the book.

Several people in the wider community of public entrepreneurship made early appearances in my class and/or exchanged ideas along the way, helping give flight to this work. They include Zac Bookman, Ron Bouganim, Jennifer Bradley, Dan Doctoroff, Jeremy Goldberg, Dustin Haisler, Jay Nath, Beth Noveck, Jen Pahlka, Shireen Santosham, and David Spielfogel.

The idea of the book only began to feel real when Jim Levine agreed to take on this project. He offered sage guidance and reassurance all along the way, even as a global pandemic upended so many other projects he was at work on at the same time. And Jim brought me back together with Jeff Kehoe at Harvard Business Review Press. Jeff had edited my very first piece for HBR in March 2014, and words on these pages trace back to those I'd put in my first article with him. I am grateful for Jeff's continued confidence in me. I'd also like to thank production editor Anne Starr, as well as other members of the outstanding team: Julie Devoll, Erika Heilman, Felicia Sinusas, Lindsey Dietrich, Alexandra Kephart, and everyone on the commercial team. Special thanks to Stephani Finks, who gave the book jacket its superhero look, and to so many others at the Press. In 2019 they felt a book like this would prove timely "given the skeptical view of government's ability to solve problems." Twelve months would prove that skepticism warranted in so many areas, and I can only hope I have fulfilled their expectations in offering something to remedy that. I'd also like to thank Kerri Kolen, Phyllis Strong, and Jayson White, all of whom provided advice on the proposal I sent to Jim. Alec Ross's super *The Industries of the Future* loomed large for me in style and tone as I wrote, and I am thankful to Alec for his encouragement and advice.

I am especially appreciative of three anonymous reviewers who provided feedback on the manuscript. Because of them, the book offers more practical suggestions than it did originally—and more on the moment we are living through than it otherwise would have.

The people in this book who let me tell their stories gave me a priceless gift. I promised no praise, only to put leaders in their shoes, and I am grateful they let me. Thank you to James Geurts, Tambrein Bates, and all those who hosted us for a visit to SOFWERX; Jimmy Chen and the team at Propel; Mayor Melvin Carter in Saint Paul; Annie Rittgers, Colleen Reynolds, Emily Geiger, and all those who worked on Hacking Heroin; Gabriella Gómez-Mont and the team that welcomed us to LabCDMX; Molly Turner, who was at Airbnb and is now a fantastic teacher/practitioner of possibility in urban settings; Nanette Schippers, Laila Frank, Albert Eefting, and others in Amsterdam; Mayor Bill Peduto in Pittsburgh and his team, including his chief of staff, Dan Gilman; Di-Ann Eisnor, Paige Fitzgerald, Gai Berkovich, and all those who met with us at Waze in Tel Aviv and Mountain View; Nandan Nilekani and Sanjay Purohit, who updated me on societal platforms in India; Dai Wei and the founders at ofo; Haley Van Dyck, Mikey Dickerson, Todd Park, and all those who introduced me to the United States Digital Service; Nimit Sawhney and the team at Voatz; Bradley Tusk and Sheila Nix at Tusk Philanthropies; Secretary of State Mac Warner, Mike Queen, Donald Kersey,

Chuck Flannery, and others in West Virginia; Justin Florence, Ian Bassin, and Larry Schwartztol at Protect Democracy; Yordanos Eyoel at Civic Lab and New Profit; Chee Khern Ng, Ping Soon Kok, Jason Bay, Joel Kek, and many others at GovTech Singapore and in the Singapore government; and Vernie Oliveiro and Whee Jim Yeo at Civil Service College Singapore. Other stories I've told through cases and classes didn't wind themselves as deeply into this book, but certainly were in my head, and I want to thank those whom I haven't yet named, but who helped me learn: Shaun Abrahamson, Stonly Baptiste, Ben Berkowitz, Scott Burns, Ralph Clark, Scott Crouch, Damaune Journey, Jack Kutner, Dave Mitchell, Joe Morrisroe, Rachel Pipan, Matt Polega, Andrew Reiter, Jill Shah, Jamie Smith, Ryan Tseng, Thea Tsulukiani, Valery Vavilov, and Ross Wilson.

As much as Tom Menino teased about our new ideas being lonely, new-idea makers and chasers proliferated at Boston's City Hall. It was an honor to be in public service alongside so many of them, more names than I can mention here. I remain fondly and especially thankful to Meredith Weenick, who first hired me to work for the mayor and was the most able public manager of people and resources I've ever known; and to Martha Pierce, who spread her utter devotion and wacky humor generously to lift up so many in the city, including me. Dot Joyce and Michael Kineavy showed this naïve Harvard kid the real work of politics. We went through a lot together and emerged an odd, happy trio. Annette Gales, Michael Galvin, and Peggy Gannon took care of us all in their own unique ways. Nigel Jacob and Chris Osgood gave life to New Urban Mechanics, and with them Patricia Boyle-McKenna, Kris Carter, Bill Oates, and so many others. John Auerbach, Barbara Berke, Ed Davis, John Dunlap, Andrew Feinberg, Barbara Ferrer, Nicole Fichera, Rene Fielding, Seth Gitel, Eliza Greenberg, Daphne Griffin, Sam Hammar, Justin Holmes, Jim Hunt, Dan Koh, Katharine Lusk, Nick Martin, Joanne Massaro, Virginia Mayer,

Matt Mayrl, Reed Passafaro, Amy Ryan, Chloe Ryan, Kairos Shen, Jake Sullivan, Jim Tierney, Tom Tinlin, and Sarah Zaphiris were just a few of the many other sources of fresh thinking and good times at City Hall. "Go see Angela" was the best advice I got upon taking the job as Tom Menino's chief of staff. Angela Menino was much more than the First Lady of Boston, and she remains a source of insight and purpose for me.

I never planned to tell the story of what we did in the wake of the Boston Marathon attacks. But Patrick Downes and Jessica Kensky told me one year later, "You have to show people that government can do new things," and so I've tried. Patrick and Jess have become treasured and encouraging friends. That they let our family love theirs, including their dog, Rescue, has meant so much in our lives. I also thank the Richard family for giving me the opportunity to run the marathon again; many thoughts in this book first took root in my head during training runs, wearing Martin's number eight on my back. Even a partial telling of how One Fund Boston came to be is also a story about the many people who brought it to life. I want to thank Susan Abbott, Paul Connolly, Jack Connors, Tom Crohan, Ken Feinberg, Rebecca Frisch, Jim Gallagher, Nick Lopez, Mike Sheehan, and Barbara Thorpe, among many others. I really got to know Governor Deval Patrick that week in April 2013 and in the years since. I admire his leadership and am grateful for his unique wisdom and support. He never fails to single me out in a room as someone who did new things in government, and his gesture never fails to make me want to do more.

I dedicate this book to my parents, Albert and Susan Weiss. They taught me to think and to care, and then they gave me everything so that I could. My siblings, Laura and Josh, have been my most vocal supporters throughout my life, and that has meant the world to me. So much of who I am is because of who the five of us were and are.

Sherrie, Natalie, Karen, Eugene, Brian, and Amy—all have come later into my life and made my work feel important and urgent. Sarah Pang helped me get my first taste of public service. I think my late grandparents would have been proud of this book; my grandfather might have written a short poem on possibility and certainly would have shared a stored-up joke on the topic. Too many friends and family to name, in Chicago, Boston, Miami, and beyond, have made me feel that I should try to contribute something important, and that I could. I am thankful to all of them.

The question, "Do we make each other better off?" lurks at the center of platforms. The same is true in marriage, and my wife, Lori, warmly, patiently, unreservedly, unabatingly, and unequivocally makes me better off. She expressed the perfect amount of curiosity on the progress of the manuscript and took on massively more of our parental responsibilities, both before and during a pandemic, than could ever be expected or fully acknowledged. I like to joke that between the two of us, we average half a PhD; Lori was the first published author in the family and works every day on the most important challenges: human ones. I treasure the day I found possibility at her doorstep and every day since. Our children, Hannah and Noah, are already dreamers and young inventors; there is no end to the pleasure I get from hearing them say, "My hypothesis is . . . ." The two of them gamely suffered my distractions, even as I wrote a book on "entreprenerdship." I thank Hannah for adding these most important words into the book: "Save the world," and Noah for his: "Save people and make better stuff to survive."

ABOUT THE AUTHOR

MITCHELL WEISS is a professor of management practice in the Entrepreneurial Management Unit at Harvard Business School, where he is also the Richard L. Menschel Faculty Fellow. Weiss is an award-winning teacher and the creator of the school's popular course, Public Entrepreneurship, which focuses on public leaders and private entrepreneurs inventing a difference in the world. He helped build the Young American Leaders Program and is an adviser to the Bloomberg Harvard City Leadership Initiative. Prior to joining Harvard Business School, Weiss was chief of staff and a partner to Boston's Mayor Thomas Menino. In 2010 he cofounded the Mayor's Office of New Urban Mechanics. In April 2013 he guided the mayor's office response to the attacks on the Boston Marathon and played a key role in starting One Fund Boston.